Advance Praise for
Ila's War

"[A] compelling story with vivid sketches . . . The world of a rural Kansas family in the 1920s and 1930s and a woman in the service of her country during wartime are vividly presented in Cindy Entriken's story of her great aunt Ila Armsbury's life through her letters and other original sources, including oral accounts."

—**Dr. Ramon Powers,** Executive Director, retired, Kansas State Historical Society

"This is a dramatic story, heartbreaking yet inspirational, of family life in Kansas in the 1920s. It's told by a remarkable new writer who turns her family history into an emotional and absorbing adventure. For the reader, the pain of betrayal will leave a dent in your chest, but also a deep love for the family in your heart. It's smoothly written and well researched. A great read."

—**Marlin Fitzwater,** Native Kansan and Press Secretary to Presidents Reagan and Bush

Copyright © 2020, Cindy Entriken, *Ila's War*

All rights reserved. No part of this publication may be reproduced, in whole or in part, or stored in a retrieval system, or transmitted in any form or by any means — electronic, mechanical, photocopying, recording, or other — without written permission from the author.

ISBN: 978-1-7342890-0-8 (paperback)
ISBN: 978-1-7342890-1-5 (epub)
ISBN: 978-1-7342890-2-2 (hardback)

Disclaimer:
Ila's War is a WWII memoir as told through the eyes of Ila Armsbury and recorded by me. Wherever possible, I've used Ila's letters, her tape-recording, personal interviews, and records from the United States National Archives to describe the events and convesations in the book. Apart from the actual people, events, and locales that figure in the story, I've taken narrative and artistic license to interpret situations and dialogue alluded to in Ila's tape, letters, and family interviews.

Ila's War

Cindy Entriken

CONTENTS

Foreword 9
Family Tree 13
Preface 15
Acknowledgements 19
Guide to People in Ila's War 25
Ila's War 31
One 33
Two 44
Three 55
Four 61
Five 78
Six 88
Seven 91
Eight 102
Nine 108
Ten 118
Eleven 122
Twelve 125
Thirteen 135
Fourteen 140
Fifteen 147
Sixteen 154
Seventeen 158
Eighteen 168

Nineteen	*176*
Twenty	*184*
Twenty-One	*191*
Twenty-Two	*202*
Twenty-Three	*207*
Twenty-Four	*213*
Twenty-Five	*216*
Twenty-Six	*219*
Twenty-Seven	*223*
Twenty-Eight	*228*
Twenty-Nine	*232*
Thirty	*239*
Thirty-One	*242*
Thirty-Two	*249*
Thirty-Three	*253*
Thirty-Four	*256*
Thirty-Five	*263*
Thirty-Six	*266*
Thirty-Seven	*275*
Thirty-Eight	*280*
Thirty-Nine	*285*
Afterward	*289*
Ila	*289*
E.B.	*292*
Photo Gallery	*301*
Endnotes	*313*
Sources	*331*
Index	*341*

Foreword

Diaries of pioneers who settled the American West during the 1800s leave Twenty-First-Century readers with a sense of awe at the determination and courage required for day-to-day life. Before electricity, indoor plumbing or cars, men, women, and their young children endured summer droughts, survived inhospitable winters and weathered financial booms and busts. Living in the isolation of the sparsely populated prairie could strain or strengthen familial relationships depending on individual personalities and behaviors.

The Kansas Territory became a state in 1861, although by 1870, only 500 residents populated the 1,300 square miles of Lincoln County, Kansas. Then followed four decades of sustained growth and by 1910 the county's population exceeded 10,000. New residents, many not speaking English, came by railroads and wagon trains from the East Coast, Scotland, Germany, and Scandinavia to claim land offered by the Homestead Act, to purchase relatively cheap farms or to join immigrant relatives. The area's turn-of-the-century prosperity, briefly interrupted by World War One, returned in the 1920s, enabling farmers and merchants to afford automobiles and the accompanying freedom to travel in a few hours distances that previously required days.

In 1920, five-year old Ila Armsbury, daughter of Ira and

FOREWARD

Florence, was among the fifteen hundred residents of Waldo, the county seat. While some of the extended Armsbury family were comfortably well-off, Ila's childhood was one of poverty, moving from community to community with her parents and sisters. Grandparents provided assistance in the most desperate days, but to Ila such a life was normal. A casual observer would see the Armsburys as no more or less remarkable than their neighbors.

Coming of age after World War I, Ila and her classmates, wealthy or poor, were the first generation of the new century. The decade of the "roaring 20s" offered heady optimism for social mobility and professional achievement. Then came September 1929. With the shock of the stock market crash and a world-wide depression compounded by bank failures, droughts and land foreclosures, the dreams of Ila and her generation were challenged as severely as the 1880s had tested the will of the pioneers to sustain their homesteads.

But then times were different. Just as American industry was revolutionized by technology, a rising female voice would mark a watershed in America's social and political history. Daughters and granddaughters of women, who are justly honored for sacrifices made raising families and breaking Kansas sod alongside their husbands, were graduating in record numbers from high school and attending college. They were recognizing life possibilities beyond the once expected pattern of "he earns a living while she cooks, cleans and takes care of children."

Ila's story is both unique and representative. In one sense she was a survivor—of an impoverished, dysfunctional family of confining social expectations in adolescence, of financial desperation as a young adult, of physical exhaustion as a war-time nurse, and of the deception of an alcoholic lover. From another perspective, Ila is every woman who craves independence, who finds the world arrayed against her or who seeks to balance love for family with a personal passion to excel.

ILA'S WAR

As a teenager, Ila determined she would make her own destiny, not have it imposed by parents or society. In that she succeeded, but beyond her family and a circle of friends in Lincoln, Kansas City, and eventually California, she was not well-known. Ila, like thousands of other women of her time who chose to shape their own history, never became a celebrity. Yet they are among the heroes of their age. Their stories deserve telling and hearing.

In reading *Ila's War*, those who live in the thousands of small Midwestern towns and surrounding farms will recognize threads of their great-grandparents' history in the cafes, churches and social life of present-day communities. Those whose parents and grandparents lived in towns like Lincoln, Lucas, and Waldo will recall hearing stories similar to Ila's about neighbors, weather, families and main street businesses that wove the tapestry of pre-World War II rural America. Those whose experience of Central Kansas is a few minutes of flying over the wheat fields and pastures will sense that in Ila's story, despite its unfamiliar time or geography, the best of American individualism and community is celebrated.

> Robert Wallace, former Lincoln County Resident
> Director (Retired), Office of Technical Service
> Central Intelligence Agency

Family Tree

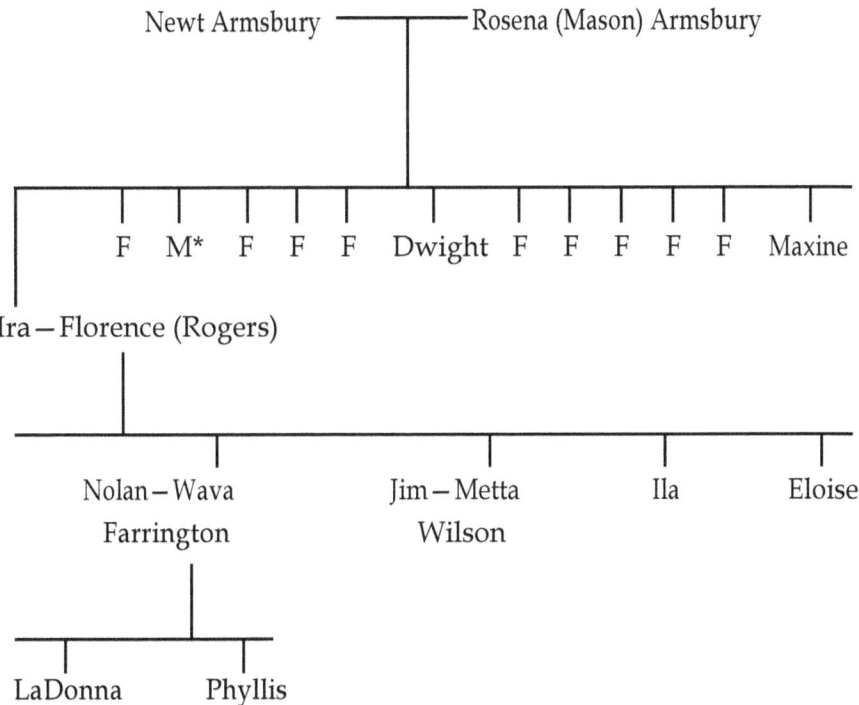

F = Female
M = Male

*Died in Infancy

Preface

In the spring of 1991, Wava Farrington, my 82-year-old grandmother, decided it was time to start sorting through her accumulated treasures to distribute them to family and friends. Grammy had lived in Lincoln, Kansas, in the same house for 50 years, and as someone who'd grown up in stifling poverty, she'd saved everything. Her house was big, and every drawer, closet, and shelf was packed. We agreed that we wouldn't have time for her to tell me the history of every item. She was simply going to look at each article and identify the prospective recipient. My job was to put each piece in a paper grocery sack labeled with the person's name.

The first sign that things weren't going well came with the twelve posters of Jesus' disciples. "Now, Cindy," she said, hauling them out, yellowed, brittle, and peeling. "Remember these? I used them when I taught Sunday School. I thought you might like to have them," she said as she handed me the faded poster of Simon Peter.

Over the years my grandmother, like so many elderly women, had shrunk in height so that I was finally taller than she. Her face was unlined—she gave up smoking when I was 10 "to set a good example for you, Cindy." Her head was wreathed in soft white curls and she had beautiful blue eyes that either sparkled or glared depending on whether you were on her good or bad side. But I was still her granddaughter

PREFACE

and had been raised to refrain from talking back to my elders. I had no use for torn, faded posters and I was sorely tempted to say, "Grammy, it's not like they were personally autographed by the twelve disciples," but I knew a comment like that would spell the end of any more sorting and distribution. When I suggested we toss them, Grammy gasped and looked at me with horror, her lips pursed in a thin, frowning line. "Why, I'll do no such thing," she said. "Someone else in the family will want them," and she snatched the poster from my hands.

Despair settled over me like a cloud.

Replacing the posters on the closet shelf, she reached for a hat. "When I was wearing this," she said as she perched the tattered blue felt hat on her curly, white hair, "I thought I was really something!" I had to stifle a laugh as she placed her right hand on her hip and sashayed across the bedroom floor to the mirror above the dresser, like a model on a catwalk. There were two other hats sitting on the shelf and I was afraid that she'd model all of them, so I reminded her that we had a lot of work and couldn't spend time on each item. I didn't want her to put the hat back on the shelf, so I offered to take all three.

We made faster progress on her gas and electric receipts from the 1930s. She agreed, reluctantly, to let them go. The waste basket slowly began to fill. A stack of old papers bound with string seemed a promising candidate for the trash, until she blew off the dust, saying, "These are the letters your great Auntie Ila wrote to Mother and Daddy during the war."

I'm rarely speechless, but the discovery of the letters was one of those times. I stared at my grandmother, struggling to find words to describe my surprise. My heart beat faster, and in my excitement, I could feel my face flush. I wanted those letters. I knew from my own correspondence with Ila that she was candid, outspoken and a great storyteller. I hoped her correspondence from the war would be just as salty and unvarnished.

ILA'S WAR

"Grammy, can I have those letters?"

According to Grammy, no one had laid claim to them, so after a moment's consideration, she said, "I don't see why not. They haven't been read since we got 'em, and I'm sure no one even remembers them."

The letters, over 450 pages, are hand-written and typed missives dating from 1934, when Auntie Ila entered nursing school until 1946 when she resigned from the U. S. Army. In December of 1940, she'd enlisted for a year but after the bombing of Pearl Harbor Congress changed the enlistment requirement of all military personnel to "the duration plus six months."

Years later as I read the letters, I began remembering family stories I'd heard while growing up. About that same time, I got a letter from Auntie Ila telling me about an incident between the Ku Klux Klan and her father—my great grandfather. I realized that Ila had lived through some extraordinary historical events including the arrest and trial of her father, Klan activities in Lincoln, the Jamaica Ginger scandal, and World War II. I was sure a story was buried among her letters, but I'd have to dig to find it.

In October 2000, Ila stayed with me for two weeks. I hadn't seen her for years and didn't know what to expect. Like my grandmother, Ila had shrunk in height, but she was still slim as ever. Her hair was now gray, and her breathing was sometimes labored due to Chronic Obstructive Pulmonary Disease (COPD), but she was still feisty and opinionated. Her expressive face made it impossible for her to hide her feelings. A big smile on her lips and in her eyes conveyed happiness or joy. But when narrowed, her glaring eyes were a warning that she was mad, and you'd better look out because she was preparing to tell you exactly what you'd done wrong.

I told her about the letters and that I wanted to write a book about her life. Her eyes lit up and she laughed. "Imagine that. Those old

PREFACE

letters…" After a moment's reflection, she offered to send me a copy of a tape recording she'd made about her life if I "was serious about writing a book."

When I started writing *Ila's War*, I intended to celebrate the life of my great aunt whom I admired for her intelligence, humor, and outspoken honesty. But as older relatives died, I began to look at this book as a way to transmit my family's history to my daughter who is constantly busy with her family and career, and to my grandsons who are currently too young to appreciate the story. I hope you, my readers, will enjoy it, and that my daughter and my grandsons will, too.

Acknowledgements

I can think of no words adequate to acknowledge the contribution of my great aunt, Metta. Starting in the fall of 2008, I went to Grand Junction, Colorado, every three months to visit Auntie Metta, age 97. Prior to each visit she prepared a list of tasks for us including shopping for new clothes for her, eating out, and going for drives, plus work she wanted me to do around the apartment. Like cleaning out the refrigerator or the kitchen pantry. And during each visit we talked about family history, especially Metta and Ila's lives. Auntie Metta added a depth of sensory detail that I couldn't find anywhere else. Metta died in November 2012, at the age of 101—still sharp, funny, and loving. Her encouragement meant the world to me, and I miss her greatly.

To obtain copies of Ila's military records, reports of the 155th Station Hospital, the U. S. Typhus Commission, the 107th Medical Battalion, the final report of Guadalcanal operations of the 1st Marine Division, and the Third Medical Laboratory I hired Kevin Morrow, an independent researcher from Arlington, Virginia, with experience in locating materials at the National Archives. Norm Richards, another researcher, obtained copies of E. B. Settle's military records for me from the National Archives in St. Louis, Missouri. Thanks to both for their hours of work on my behalf.

ACKNOWLEDGEMENTS

I planned to go to Australia in March 2009, to visit the Camp Cable area and do research about the war. But the best laid plans of mice and men and women...

On January 19, 2009, while enjoying an afternoon walk through the neighborhood with my husband, I fell, broke my left arm, and sustained a severe back injury. X-rays revealed that the break was not clean and that I would need surgery to reset the bones. As a result, the orthopedic surgeon forcefully told me that I could not travel, and the Australian trip was cancelled.

Thankfully, I found the fabulous website www.ozatwar.com by Peter Dunn. This website contains everything you'd ever want to know about WWII and Australia, and Peter answered all my questions quickly and completely. I also hired a researcher in Australia, Denis McCarthy, who provided background information and photographs of the Camp Cable area.

Another excellent website I used is the WW2 US Medical Research Centre co-created by Alain Batens in Belgium and Ben Major in England. Between them Alain and Ben own the largest private collection of WWII U.S. medical memorabilia in the world and they were incredibly generous in sharing their knowledge. My husband and I had the pleasure of meeting Ben and touring D-Day sites with him, his dad, and two friends during D-Day activities in June 2014. I can never repay the debt I owe to Peter, Alain, and Ben for all their help and patience.

Ms. Julia Church of the National Archives of Australia (NAA) was an invaluable resource in helping me access documents through the NAA website. She also assisted me in preparing a list of places to visit for my planned trip and sent me sincere condolences when I was forced to cancel it.

The Rock Port, Missouri, public library was a fantastic resource for me in learning about E. B. Settle's life and family before and after the war. I owe special thanks to Darlene Schmidt, Genealogy; Karen Culjat, Technology Specialist; Janice Rosenbohm, Director; Bob Simpson, cataloger; and Diane Boatman, a library volunteer.

I also owe thanks to the staff of the Lincoln, Kansas *Sentinel-Republican* for use of their offices and microfiche equipment as well as staff and volunteers of the Lincoln, Kansas, Carnegie Library.

Several current and former residents of Lincoln, Kansas, also deserve recognition for their help in providing details about events in Lincoln during the mid-20s and early 30s. I owe particular thanks to Ms. Susan Marshall who directed me to David Healy and his mother, Edna Healy. Mrs. Healy described seeing the Hundertmark's laundry, including sheets used in KKK parades, drying on the clothesline. Ernie Liggett added more details about KKK activities in Lincoln during the mid-1920s, and about the sale of Jamaica Ginger from the back door of the Rexall Drug Store. Barbara Gourley confirmed that her grandfather was one of the men crippled by Jamaica Ginger. Also, thank you to Ms. Mickey Suelter, who told me about her cousin, Jack Donley, after he survived being thrown through the plate glass window of my great grandfather's restaurant.

Employees of the district courts for Lincoln and Russell Counties in Kansas; Atchison County, Missouri; and Mills County, Iowa, were extremely helpful in providing me with copies of old court records.

Robert Wallace, retired director of the Office of Technical Service of the CIA, author of several books about the CIA and spycraft, and a former Lincoln County resident graciously read early drafts of the book and offered excellent feedback and encouragement. Thank you, Bob, for your generosity and kindness.

James Campbell, author of *The Ghost Mountain Boys: Their Epic March and the Terrifying Battle for New Guinea—The Forgotten War of the South Pacific,* answered my questions and filled in some blanks

ACKNOWLEDGEMENTS

about the 32nd Infantry Division—The Red Arrow Men—and their time at Camp Cable.

Prior to undertaking this project, the only writing I had done was for graduate coursework or for my work as a licensed master's level social worker. I thought to myself, "I've done lots of writing. How hard can it be?" I quickly learned just how hard it is to write a book vs. a policy analysis or legislative testimony. Undoubtedly, I'd still be struggling with this book had it not been for meeting Dan Baum, an excellent writer, and his spouse, Margaret Knox, a wonderful editor. Margaret and Dan, at different times during the development of the book, worked with me as editors, teachers, mentors, friends, and cheerleaders. I will never be able to thank them sufficiently for everything they did to help me complete this book. Thanks also to Brian de Silva who took up the reigns of editorial assistance when Dan had to bow out.

Another individual to whom I owe thanks is Ms. Pat Blake, a writer and friend from Wichita. She read one of the final drafts, from beginning to end, and gave feedback which helped enliven some of the scenes.

The amazingly talented staff of Cassandra Bryan Design, Cb{d}, created the original stunning home page for my blog, **cindyentriken.com**, and demonstrated immeasurable patience as they taught me how to use the software to create my blog entries. Cb{d} also gets credit for the gorgeous photo of Ila, which inspired the book cover for *Ila's War*. And when the software supporting the blog needed updating, Ms. Angela Ford of Angela J. Ford Marketing collaborated with Ms. Bryan to make the necessary upgrades.

To understand topics discussed in Ila's letters, I compared dates among her military and medical records, those of Dr. Settle, and reports from the 155th Station Hospital. All these sources combined provided me with a fuller picture of events that happened so long ago. But there are some instances that I simply had to use my imagination and best guess as to the circumstances. Those instances include: 1) the exact details of Ila's and E. B.'s first meeting; 2) what transpired at the apartment E. B. rented for himself and Ila; 3) Ira's trial for which I could find no court records although the facts were told to me by several family members; 4) the location and date of Ila and Emmitt's last argument; 5) how Florence first learned that Ira was seeing another woman; and 6) specific dialogue which appears throughout the book.

I wrote this book in the first-person voice from Ila's perspective to convey the honesty and intimacy that exists in her letters and the tape recording she made about her life. Wherever possible I used direct quotes from Ila's materials, military records or interviews from other family members and friends. Because the book is written from Ila's perspective, I did not write about things that she did not know.

In spite of the letters, tape recording, interviews with family members, and stories told to me by my grandmother, I discovered lots of gaps when I began writing *Ila's War*. Sadly, by the time I realized I needed more information or explanation the people who could have filled in the blanks were dead. So, knowing what I did about the times and my family, I adopted the historical fiction technique of dialogue and used appropriate language of the era.

I have one more person to thank—my long-suffering spouse, Jim Hammer. We both lost count of the number of drafts he read, the number of times I said, "Jim, what do you think about ..."

He's also endured my ill humor when I couldn't figure out what was wrong with the section I just wrote, or how to write the next section. He's heard me cry in frustration, yell in anger, and whisper in despair. But he has encouraged me throughout the entire 12 years it took me to write this book. Thank you, my Sweetheart.

Guide to People in *Ila's War*

Ira Armsbury "Daddy"—Ila's father. First of thirteen children born to Newt and Rosena Armsbury.

Ila Armsbury—the narrator

Florence (Rogers) Armsbury "Mother"—Ila's mother.

Wava (Armsbury) Farrington— the first of four daughters born to Ira and Florence Armsbury; Ila's oldest sibling.

Metta—Ila's second oldest sibling.

Grandpa Newt Armsbury—Ira's father and Ila's grandfather.

Rosena Armsbury—Ira's mother, Ila's grandmother. Although her name was Rosena, everyone in the family pronounced it Rosenie.

Reverend Noah Rogers—Florence's father, Ila's grandfather. Died before Ila was born. A fire-and-brimstone minister according to all the family stories.

Minda—married to Rev. Noah, mother of Florence, and Ila's grandmother. Also died before Ila was born. Her given name was Arminda but everyone in the family called her Minda.

Nazier Mason—Rosena's father, Ila's grandfather. French Canadian, and a Civil War veteran. Fought for the Union.

Dwight Armsbury—Ira's younger brother and son of Newt and Rosena Armsbury. Ira's only brother. Enlisted in the Army for WWI but

GUIDE TO PEOPLE IN ILA'S WAR

the war ended before he was called up.

Emory C. Farrington—Nolan Farrington's father.

Mrs. Mary E. Wilkerson—the woman with whom Ira had a three-year affair.

Maxine—the youngest of 13 children born to Newt and Rosena Armsbury. Maxine was only a few months older than Ila.

Mrs. Hughes—the woman who employed Florence before and after Florence left Ira.

Uncle Walter—Walter Mason was one of Rosena's brothers. He owned Mason's Florist in Rocky Ford, Colorado.

Oat and Lottie—Lottie was one of Florence's older sisters, and Oat Trexler was her husband. They owned a grocery store in Hill City, Kansas.

S. P. Dinsmoor—a resident of Lucas, Kansas. He built his version of The Garden of Eden and his home from cement. The Garden of Eden is on the National Register of Historic Places. For a small visitor's fee, you can tour the building and the grounds.

Eloise Armsbury—Ila's younger sister.

Porky Zink—owner of Zink's Grocery in Lincoln, Kansas, and a member of St. Patrick's Catholic Church. Porky hosted the party where Ira and several other Lincoln men were poisoned by adulterated Jamaica Ginger.

Herman Knoch—owner of a bakery in Lincoln, member of a protestant church and of the Lincoln, Kansas, branch of the KKK.

Nolan Farrington—Married Wava and became Ila's brother-in-law.

Mr. Hundertmark—George August Hundertmark was the head of the Ku Klux Klan organization in Lincoln, Kansas, during the 1920s. He owned the Hundertmark Store.

Jack Donley—the teenage son of a local farmer, a member of St.Patrick's Catholic Church in Lincoln, and one of Wava's Lincoln High School classmates. Jack worked part time for Ira in the restaurant.

James Mitchell—Lincoln's only African American resident. He settled in Lincoln in the 1880s.

Judge Joslin—a probate judge and well-respected man in Lincoln. Judge Joslin was one of several community leaders who encouraged Ila to go to college.

Miss Rose—a nursing student, one year ahead of Ila at the University of Kansas School of Nursing.

Miss Lewick—an instructor at the University of Kansas School of Nursing.

LaDonna—Ila's niece and the oldest of two girls born to Nolan and Wava Farrington.

Phyllis—Ila's niece and the youngest of two girls born to Nolan and Wava Farrington.

Marguerite Coffman— one of Ila's classmates at the University of Kansas School of Nursing. They became lifelong friends during their school years and maintained their friendship up until Marguerite's death in 2000.

Miss Ella M. Miller—a U.S. Army nurse stationed at Fort Leavenworth.

Emmett Bird (E. B.) Settle—a doctor in the U. S. Army stationed at Fort Leavenworth.

Craig—a real person, the one who told Ila that E. B. was in Australia. Ila wrote about Craig in a letter home to her parents, but she never mentioned his last name.

Mary Francis—a nurse and one of Ila's best friends while she was with the 155th Station Hospital in Australia.

Jim Wilson—Metta's first husband. During WWII he died of endocarditis because penicillin was not available for civilians.

Karl Menninger—one of the psychiatrists working at Winter General Hospital, the VA hospital in Topeka, Kansas, where Ila was hospitalized after she returned from Australia. Dr. Menninger treated Ila and later hired her to work with him. She also became a fourth playing bridge with Dr. Menninger, his wife and whomever else they could find.

GUIDE TO PEOPLE IN ILA'S WAR

Major Howard J. Lee—one of the officers and a doctor appointed as a medical witness for Ila's hearing before the Army Nurses Retiring Board.

"We can't choose where we come from,
but we can choose where we go from there."

—Stephen Chbosky, *The Perks of Being a Wallflower*

Ila's War

ONE

My dad was a scoundrel. Ask anybody who knew him, and they'll tell you the same thing: "That ole Ira Armsbury was a sonofabitch."

But when you're a kid, you don't see your parents' flaws—at least I didn't. I thought my dad was the tallest, handsomest, strongest, funniest man in the whole world. His naturally curly black hair was parted in the middle and you could see the hint of a dimple in his chin which deepened when he smiled. At six feet with broad, muscular shoulders and long legs, he was incredibly handsome, even when he was much older. His good looks got him into bushels of trouble with the ladies. He always had a ready joke, a hearty laugh, and a pocketful of peppermint candies—small red and white striped cushions of sweetness—for every kid he encountered.

Daddy was frequently gone overnight, sometimes for days at a time. By the age of four, almost five, I was used to his absences. They were all I'd ever known. But my mother, Florence, and my two older sisters, Wava and Metta, could remember a time when Daddy was home in the evenings, so around bedtime, when it was obvious that Daddy wasn't coming home for the night, they'd cry. I couldn't understand why.

Life in our house wasn't much better when Daddy was there because Mother looked and acted angry.

CHAPTER ONE

"Evening, girls," Daddy said one night as he sauntered through the back door into the kitchen where we had just finished supper.

"Whacha eating, Mother?" Daddy asked, as he took off his hat and hung it on a peg by the door. "Sure smells good and I'm hungry, too."

Mother shot up out of her chair, threw her napkin on the table, turned on her heel and stalked out of the room without saying a word.

"Mother? Mother? Girls, what's wrong with your mother? She had a bad day?"

Before any of us could answer Mother hollered into the kitchen from the living room. "Girls, you've had enough to eat. Get ready for bed this minute and no lollygagging around."

We girls had no way to please both our parents at the same time. If Daddy talked to us or asked us a question and we tried to answer, Mother would get mad at us.

"Hi, Daddy," I called one summer evening as he entered the house. "I …"

"Ila, hush up. Leave your dad alone. You're just putting off getting ready for bed. Now git!"

If we didn't answer, Daddy would get angry.

"Girls, I said, what's wrong? One of you better answer me if you know what's good for you."

We girls knew that Daddy wouldn't punish us for not responding. He only whipped us for big transgressions like lying or stealing—things we'd never do anyway. But Mother always kept a switch handy and was quick to use it for minor infractions like talking back, getting a dress dirty after she'd told us not to go outside—piddling things. So, our safest course of action was to obey Mother, leave the kitchen lickety-split and leave her and Daddy alone.

The fact is that Mother and Daddy's problems existed long before they ever married—because of their differences. Daddy's folks were well-off for rural Kansans in the early 1900s. Grandpa Newt Armsbury owned a ranch and a hardware store in Luray, where he and Grandma Rosenie and their kids lived. In his youth, Grandpa was a cowboy who drank, gambled, and fought, but he gave up hard living when he married Grandma Rosenie in 1886, all except for the drinking, which he continued until Daddy was almost 18.

Daddy was the oldest of 13 children, and one of only two boys in the household. Grandma Rosenie, a teacher when she was young, wanted all her children to complete high school. But with so many mouths to feed, Grandpa Newt expected Daddy to quit school after eighth grade and go to work. Daddy didn't mind because he didn't like school anyway. Grandpa worked Daddy like chattel and when Daddy didn't meet Grandpa's expectations, especially when Grandpa had been drinking, he beat Daddy with a bull whip. The upshot was that Daddy and Grandpa Newt never got along once Daddy was grown.

Grandma and Grandpa, who attended Sunday services at the Cheyenne United Brethren Church, had a solemn but forgiving view of religion. They stressed responsibility to family and hard work so you could have a nice home and all its comforts. If you followed the Ten Commandments, did your best, and repented your sins, you'd go to heaven.

Unfortunately, Daddy's views about hard work and responsibility were different from his folks'. He worked hard when it suited him, especially if he had in mind an immediate reward for himself—like new clothes or money for a dance. While we girls never doubted that Daddy loved us, each of us eventually learned that he was irresponsible and put his own comforts and desires ahead of ours.

As for repentance, Daddy relied on his charm and winning smile, coupled with an apology, always sincere when it was offered, as a surefire way to be forgiven in this life and the next. The routine was always the

CHAPTER ONE

same—I watched it play out over and over during my early years as I silently ate my oatmeal at the breakfast table.

"Mother, I'm awful sorry I woke you when I came in last night." Daddy'd look chagrined as he offered her a sad smile, mumbling his apology.

But Mother never accepted them no matter how heartfelt they seemed. Sometimes she'd refuse to respond or even look at him. Other times she'd glare and quote scripture.

"The Bible says, 'Who hath woe? Who hath sorrow? Who hath contentions? Who hath complaining? Who hath wounds without cause? Who hath redness of eyes? They that tarry long at the wine; They that go to 'seek out' mixed wine.'"

Mother's store of biblical scripture was prodigious. Given enough time, she could find a scripture for any occasion, from sour milk—"Hast thou not poured me out as mild, and curdled me like cheese?" Job 10:10—to butterflies—"Therefore if any man be in Christ, he is a new creature; old things are passed away; behold, all things are become new." II Corinthians, 5:17.

Daddy always had a ready comeback. "Remember, Mother. Jesus turned water into wine at the wedding at Cana in Galilee."

And Mother's response was just as predictable. "It wasn't wine, it was grape juice." They'd bicker for a bit before they reached the inevitable conclusion to their argument.

"Mother," Daddy'd say, looking serious, with tears in his eyes, "I really am sorry. I'll try to do better next time." He'd offer her a sweet smile and after a moment, Mother would nod her head once without smiling and the conversation would end.

As for instruction about sex, Grandpa Newt and Grandma Rosenie didn't tell Daddy anything. They believed the farm animals were the best teachers and Daddy could figure things out for himself. He did.

Mother's family was dramatically different. Her father, the Reverend Noah Rogers—Mother called him Rev. Noah—was a fire-and-brimstone preacher whose religious training of Mother—I'd call it brainwashing—scarred her for life and spelled disaster for her marriage. Grandma Minda, her mother and Rev. Noah's wife, agreed with his religious strictures.

"Florence, the marital act, as ordained by God, is an act with two sides. Just as in our world where we are confronted with the eternal conflict between God and Satan, the marital act can be good and Godly or sinful and degrading," Rev. Noah preached.

"In that everlasting battle between good and evil, God wants you, God *needs* you to procreate, to go forth and populate this earth with Christians who will follow His word. It is your responsibility as a follower of God to procreate. That is the good side of the marital act."

"But to participate in that act for pleasure is a sin of the most heinous kind. For pleasure takes your eyes and heart and mind away from God. Pleasure is the seducement of the devil. To induce you into his lair he offers you pleasure now but you face eternal damnation and torment later."

"Make no mistake. It is your duty to God to procreate, but to desire pleasure is sinful and no punishment is too harsh."

Grandma Minda's teachings weren't any better.

Pain, Florence. Pain that roots into your bowels and belly. And the filth of a man, touching your body. When you get older, Florence, you will discover that filth also flows from your own body. It will happen every month. You'll be sick with pain and blood that will worsen as you grow. Marital relations, always painful and disgusting, are even worse during your sick time. But you must submit, as the Bible says, when your husband demands it. That is a wife's duty and burden to carry throughout life because your husband is always, *always* the head of

CHAPTER ONE

the household."

It's no wonder Mother abhorred sex and tried to teach us girls the same. Thankfully, we had friends and magazines—magazines prohibited by Mother and all the more appealing to us girls—which taught us the real facts about sex and its role in a fulfilling and happy marriage.

Rev. Noah dominated his family. He taught the Old Testament view of God as judge, jury, and executioner presiding over a world that was one big cesspool of sin. Earthly rewards were false and led to a life of torment in hell. The purpose of life was suffering to purify the Christian soul and store up treasures in heaven.

Rev. Noah didn't become a minister until 1891, after eight of his ten children were born. But even prior to his ordination he thought of himself—if not the right-hand of God, then one of God's fingers—as blessed with the ability to interpret God's will. His interpretation extended not only to his children and his flock, but his marriage to Grandma Minda. After each of their first three children died before the age of one, Rev. Noah decided that their deaths were a punishment—that God had not wanted Noah and Minda to marry—and that it was God's will that the babies die. So, Rev. Noah and Minda separated for almost a year.

But in the end, they couldn't stay away from each other, and Rev. Noah decided that he'd misinterpreted God's intent. He and Minda reunited and practiced what Rev. Noah preached—procreation. They had seven more children, with Mother the next to youngest. The older children escaped much of Rev. Noah's toxic teachings, but not Mother.

As the minister of a tiny, rural congregation, Rev. Noah was paid very little and frequently in kind—a chicken or two, some home-canned fruits and vegetables, and little in the way of cold, hard cash. He couldn't even purchase a house for the family. They lived in a rented home furnished with hand-me-downs from the congregation—mis-matched and wobbly wooden chairs with their scarred dining room table, old wood or iron beds with lumpy, sagging mattresses, and other pieces of furniture or crockery that should have been thrown out. Rev. Noah's constant rejoinder, should anyone complain about the lack of funds, was that "God will provide."

Because of Rev. Noah's complete domination and mind control, Mother never learned to think for herself or make decisions. No decision was too small for Rev. Noah or Grandma Minda to make and force onto Mother:

-What dress Mother wore.

-How she spent her time.

-Activities that were approved—Bible reading and prayer.

-And activities that were not—playing outside, skipping rope, drawing a picture — all activities that were of this world and therefore bad because they weren't focused on God's will as spelled out in the inerrant Bible or by Rev. Noah.

Whenever Mother did something that displeased Rev. Noah, and by extension God, Rev. Noah would respond with cold, disapproving glares and silence which could last for days. As a result, Mother was terrified of abandonment.

Unlike Daddy, Mother learned responsibility at a young age. While making the rounds to his members' homes one March day of 1899, Rev. Noah's spring buggy tipped over on him and he fractured his leg. His convalescence was slow and painful but by the end of September, 1899, Rev. Noah seemed to have healed enough to begin a new ministry. Then without warning late on the night of November fifth, Rev. Noah died—probably from a blood clot—leaving the family penniless and Grandma Minda with five children ranging in age from 17 down to one. Grandma Minda stayed home with the baby, who turned one year old on the day Rev. Noah died, but the four older children were forced to go to work to support the family.

CHAPTER ONE

Mother was just ten years old. She dropped out of grammar school and went to work as a farm girl helping local families with housekeeping and laundry. Her two older brothers worked for local farmers, and her older sister found a job as a cook.

But Mother's family had no reprieve from tragedy. Just four months later, in March 1900, the baby died of smallpox. Those two deaths dealt a mortal blow to Minda, who became seriously depressed and confused.

Over the next six years, Grandma Minda's health declined; she couldn't keep food down, lost weight, and was fatigued all the time. She died on Saturday morning, April 21, 1906. Everyone assumed she died of a broken heart, but I suspect she had a slow-growing cancer.

They buried Grandma Minda at the Cheyenne Cemetery the next day. Mother was suddenly alone, an orphan at 16 with no skills, no education, and no home. She moved to San Diego to live with her older brother and his wife, and found a job working at a nearby hospital. But Mother was homesick. She missed Daddy, her older sister, who she was closest to, and Lucas, Kansas, which was worlds away from San Diego.

Mother and Daddy had courted before Mother left Kansas. Both families attended the Cheyenne United Brethren Church, so it was natural that Mother and Daddy met at church functions or saw each other in town where they talked with each other while surrounded by friends or family. They engaged in activities arranged by others, but they did not talk openly about sex or religious beliefs, hold hands, sit or walk alone, and they certainly never kissed or hugged. Perhaps if Mother and Daddy'd had time alone, or if they could have attended social events like dances or card parties, Mother might have seen Daddy drinking, and might have realized that Daddy wasn't the man for her. But they were never alone together; that just wasn't done in those days.

Daddy was miserable without Mother—he hadn't wanted her to

go—so he wrote Mother long letters, pleading with her to come back and marry him.

> *Dearest Florence—I got your letter about your job. Those are long and hard hours working in that hospital and I worry about you around those sick folks who might make you sick, too. I wish you'd come home where you know folks who love you and would take care of you and I would be the first one to say I'll take care of you and you'll never have to work so hard again. You know how I feel, because I've told you in all my letters that I want you to come home and marry me.*
>
> *Please, Florence, think about it and say you will marry me and leave that job behind. I miss you something terrible and I hope you miss me, too.*
>
> *Your Faithful Friend, Ira Armsbury*

She finally agreed and came back to Kansas after 18 months in California. They were married in November of 1907.

I've looked at my folks' black and white wedding picture a million times over the years, and each time I'm struck by the same thing—Mother's beauty on her wedding day. Her long, dark brown, naturally curly hair is parted on one side, pulled back into a neat bun, and she's wearing a white carnation at the part. Her two-piece wedding dress—a peplum jacket and gently gathered, floor-length skirt—appears to be ivory cotton with white rick rack around her tiny waist, the lapels, arms holes, cuffs, and jacket. She's wearing a snow white, high neck cotton blouse with a lacy button-front under her jacket, and a round, painted locket on her left lapel.

But it's Mother's oval face that I'm drawn to—beautiful lips with a perfect cupid's bow and a hint of a smile and clear eyes looking into

CHAPTER ONE

the camera lens with no fear or regret. I can't say that about any other photo of Mother that I've ever seen. In the old photos that followed—photos that documented her 50 years of married life—there are no smiles, just a grim look of resignation. The photos of her last years of life show an old woman with snow white hair and stern, thin lips. I don't think she ever intended or expected a camera to record her deep disappointment and dissatisfaction with marriage, but it is there for all the world to see.

The wedding picture shows Daddy wearing a dark suit, white shirt, and tie. His naturally curly black hair is parted in the middle, and you can just see his dimple. He looks the epitome of a mature, strong young man ready to take on the responsibility of marriage, wife, and family. Just goes to show you how looks can be deceiving.

The first sign of trouble in my folks' marriage was the wedding night. Mother's apprehension coupled with the horrific indoctrination she'd endured guaranteed that any martial relations would be a disaster. Daddy was a normal, healthy young man who wanted to have sex with his wife. He learned quickly that their sex life would never be fun or exciting. Mother "submitted" but she ordered him away from her as soon as he was done.

Their first battle over alcohol occurred after they had been married three months. Mother and Daddy were invited to a neighbor's home for a party, and Mother saw Daddy drink alcohol for the first time. Years later, she told us girls that seeing him drink was when she lost all respect for him and decided that she couldn't trust him ever again. Yet Mother deferred to Daddy in all things, which was like letting a five-year-old make decisions.

Now you might be thinking, "with all these differences, why in the world did Florence and Ira ever marry?" They'd grown up together, lived in the same rural Kansas area, attended the same one-room schoolhouse during the same time period, knew each other's families, and attended the same country church. Because of their shared history, everyone they knew expected them to marry.

Besides that, Daddy loved Mother and thought that he could change her by showing her the love and laughter of life—that not everything was sin, pain, suffering and doom. He was also very lonely and Mother's willingness to defer to him in every area made Daddy feel strong and competent.

As for Mother, her fear of abandonment and the world with all its sinful temptations, and her ingrained habit of doing what others expected, propelled her into marriage. Depending on how you look at it, you might say that for Mother, Daddy was a known quantity—just not as well-known as she thought.

When I think back on my childhood and when my sisters and I talk about our early lives, we always agree on one thing: it was a tragedy that Mother and Daddy married. They spent their entire wedded life locked in constant battle while my sisters and I tried to stay out of the line of fire.

TWO

Daddy was a terrible businessman mostly because he was more interested in having fun with his buddies—drinking or carousing—than in working. At Grandma Rosenie's insistence, Grandpa Newt loaned Daddy money to open a hardware store and later a creamery among other businesses. Daddy's businesses failed, because he'd either run out of money to pay the bills or he'd get caught with someone else's wife. But the arrival of the "horseless" carriage changed all that.

Daddy was good with his hands. He liked to tinker, could take anything apart and put it back together, and sometimes could even make things work better than they had when they were new. When cars and trucks began to appear, the opportunity to repair them thrilled Daddy and he discovered he was good at it. So, after moving us around central Kansas eleven times in nine years, Daddy settled our family in Waldo, Kansas, a tiny town in Russell County, where he opened Ira's Garage next door to the cream station.

Mother was sick of all the moving and thought that buying a house would keep Daddy in one spot, so she insisted that he borrow $600.00 from the bank and they became homeowners of a tiny wood-sided house in Waldo. It had a small living room, kitchen, and two bedrooms. Metta and Wava shared the front bedroom, which was a smidge smaller than the back one Mother, Daddy, and I shared. I slept on a tiny cot at the end of their regular-size bed.

Mother was proud of her new home despite its humble appearance. We didn't have running water or indoor plumbing, so we used a privy—a one-holer—as a toilet. It sat near the back fence, several yards from the kitchen door. Our one convenience was a hand pump in the kitchen.

Right outside the kitchen door was Mother's garden. She grew a bounty of fruits and vegetables like lettuce, tomatoes, strawberries, watermelon, corn, and green beans, which she put up throughout the summer and early fall. She also raised chickens for eggs and for sumptuous Sunday dinners. With all this domesticity, our family settled into community life.

Part of that community life was the annual Decoration Day observance in the years following World War One. It was a huge event in 1920 rural Kansas, the year I turned five. We gathered at the Delhi (pronounced Del High) Cemetery for a church service and picnic to honor the area's veterans both living and deceased. The celebration drew families from the entire area including Lincoln, Lucas, Luray, Waldo, Hunter, Tipton, and Covert. It was common to see 200 or more people gathered in the churchyard, all enjoying the incredible food and community that marked the event.

Like most rural Kansas cemeteries, Delhi had a large frame church and lots of sweet-smelling cedar trees that provided shade on hot afternoons and shelter for meadowlarks, whose high-pitched trills wafted through the air on the Kansas breezes. The burial plots were covered in prairie grass that undulated like waves of green or brown sea depending on the season. The beautiful grounds were peaceful, and it was common practice throughout the year for families to pack a lunch and go to the cemetery for a picnic when the weather was good.

Our family attended the Decoration Day celebration every year because Daddy's grandpa, Nazier Mason, a respected farmer in the area,

CHAPTER TWO

was a Civil War veteran who'd served with the 4th Illinois Cavalry. There weren't many Civil War veterans still alive by 1920, so folks always gave Grandpa Mason a big hand when he appeared at the cemetery wearing his Civil War uniform which still fit his trim figure.

And this year was especially important to Daddy because his only brother, Uncle Dwight, who had served briefly in WWI, would be present. Uncle Dwight registered for the draft in September of 1918 and joined the Army on October 1, but the armistice was signed on November 11, 1918, which quickly ended Uncle Dwight's military career a month later. Daddy was, nevertheless, very patriotic and inordinately proud of Uncle Dwight for his willingness to serve his country, especially since Daddy had signed up during the first registration period in June 1917 but couldn't join the military because he was already married with three children.

Mother was up before dawn on Decoration Day. The smell of her fried chicken woke me, and my mouth started watering even though I knew it would be hours before I could bite into one of the crisp, juicy chicken pieces I loved so much.

As I walked into the kitchen, I heard voices outside. Looking through the window in the back door, I saw Daddy sitting on a short brown wooden stool, cranking the handle of our White Mountain ice cream freezer as Mother poured rock salt onto the ice surrounding the silver metal canister that held the world's best homemade vanilla ice cream.

"Mother, pour that salt slow so it gets spread out even on the ice."

"Ira, I know how to do this. I've been doing it for years."

I walked outside and over to them, watching Daddy turn the crank.

"Ilie, you're just in time. I got a job for ya." He put a burlap sack on top of the freezer can and said, "Sit." Making homemade ice cream was a ritual in our family—one that all us girls loved. Usually, we took turns sitting on the sack on top of the ice cream maker but Wava and Metta were in the house, so the task fell to me.

* * *

This is as good a time as any to tell you about us girls. Wava was 11 in May of 1920, born in 1908, and seven years older than I. She had a round face—like Mother's—blue eyes, a tiny dimple in her chin, and dark brown hair which was cut to just above her shoulders with a wisp of bangs.

She was a voracious reader who loved English, literature, history and social studies. She could spell anything. Her handwriting was beautiful, and she could design and make a stunning dress just by seeing a picture in a magazine. Math, however, was the bane of her existence.

Wava felt humiliated by our poverty and envied her friends who had nicer clothes and fancier houses. She was timid as a child and stayed close to Mother, which resulted in Wava acting the way Mother did when Daddy got into one of his many scrapes. If Mother cried, Wava cried. If Mother denied or lied about something that Daddy did, Wava did, too.

Mother and Wava did differ in how they showed anger. Mother'd stop talking—just glare or mope, and act like a martyr whereas Wava would blurt out the first thing that came to her—comments that were frequently caustic and hurtful. Mother's humiliation was magnified in Wava, which might explain why Wava made some of the poor decisions she did when she was older, like marrying at the age of 15.

Metta, born in 1911, was four years older than I. She had beautiful naturally curly blonde hair that spiraled down her back, a face not as round as Wava's, and warm brown eyes.

CHAPTER TWO

Metta, like Wava, loved school, excelled in reading, writing, and social studies and was an accomplished seamstress, too. She was also a talented artist. In her later years Metta painted wonderful oils and watercolors, which she gave to all the family. I have one she did in 1981, entitled "Peach Shack," a watercolor showing the old shack that Mother and Daddy used to store fresh-picked peaches in the summer.

Metta and Wava's demeanors could not have been more different, and although Metta was three years younger than Wava, many folks assumed Metta was the oldest because she acted more mature—no whining when things didn't go her way and always willing to help Mother with chores as opposed to Wava, who preferred to play "house."

Metta's response to anger was slow. Even so, you knew when she was mad because her eyes could burn a figurative hole through your chest. But Metta was cautious about what she said, maintaining a quiet and thoughtful manner, not wanting to hurt anyone's feelings.

Then there was me. I was four. I've always thought I looked more like Daddy than Mother, my face was thinner, and my nose and lips were a carbon copy of his. My hair was bobbed—short—medium brown, and straight as straw, which was okay with me because I didn't have time to mess with it. I was too busy playing football or baseball, climbing trees, throwing rocks into nearby creeks or farm ponds, playing tag, and getting into trouble. I preferred wearing britches, but Mother insisted on dresses because "britches on a girl are ungodly, Ila." I was outspoken as a child, which means I was in trouble frequently because I couldn't keep my mouth shut. If I didn't like something—or I disagreed with you—I felt compelled to tell you the error of your ways. My friends and Metta didn't mind so much; they'd just ignore me. But Wava would tell on me. Not surprisingly adults, especially Mother, did not appreciate my comments. Mother washed my mouth out with her homemade lye soap more times than I care to count.

ILA'S WAR

* * *

It didn't take long before Daddy said, "It's done. That crank won't budge and my arm's 'bout to fall off." He slowly stood and stretched before squatting down again and tipping the wooden barrel to one side, allowing the salt water to drain out.

"Ilie, pick up that stack of old newspapers and follow me as soon as I put more ice in here so's the ice cream'll stay cold."

Daddy picked up the freezer, carried it to our car which was parked by the east side of the house, and set the freezer on the floor of the back seat. Next, he took my papers and layered them on top. Grandma Rosenie's heavy wool quilt, the one filled with wool sheared from her own sheep, was laying on the back seat, and Daddy used it to cover the freezer and the papers. Standing back, he looked at his work, nodded his head and said, "That oughta do the trick. Keep the ice cream froze, 'til we're ready for it."

Turning to me he said, "Ilie, go help your mother and get your sisters so we can leave. We'll be gone before you know it."

A big wicker basket was sitting by the back door when I walked into the kitchen. Mother pointed towards it. "Ila, you get Wava and take that out to the car." Quart jars of Mother's home-canned watermelon pickles, chow-chow (a pickled relish made with summer vegetables fresh from the garden), and corn relish, plus a two-layer chocolate cake filled the basket. We were going to eat well today.

It was about a 20-minute drive from our house to the Delhi Cemetery. The churchyard was full of horse-drawn farm wagons by the time we arrived. If Daddy had been a farmer, we probably would have owned a horse and wagon, too. Because he owned Ira's Garage, the only car and truck repair shop in the area, he thought it was important to drive one of the new vehicles and show that he could keep it running when so many other folks had trouble with theirs.

CHAPTER TWO

We couldn't have asked for a more beautiful day to drive to the cemetery. No hedge rows or tree lines broke my view of the gently undulating landscape where limestone fence posts, the silent sentries of north-central Kansas, and fields of ripening, deep green wheat, or dark chocolate velvet soil—plowed and ready for planting—rushed up to greet blue Kansas skies. In those days, farmers plowed and planted every available inch of cropland. Of course, the dirty thirties taught us all a lesson about soil conservation but that was years away as Daddy motored the 22 miles to Delhi Cemetery, down the dirt auto trail known as The Blue Line. Nowadays we take US 281 and K-18 to get to the cemetery.

The day was comfortably cool for Kansas at the end of May, a steady but gentle breeze moved cotton-ball type clouds across the sky as Daddy parked the car on the freshly mown grass near the church. Mother expected Daddy to accompany us to church but as she opened the car door Daddy said, "You go ahead, Mother. I'll just help set up out here." He turned and started walking towards a stack of hay bales and boards that were scattered on the ground. Mother glared at Daddy for a moment, before she tugged on her white gloves and walked briskly toward the church. Metta, Wava, and I trailed behind.

The front double doors of the church were propped wide open and the milky white-paned windows that ran the length of each side of the church were open to let in the breeze and the occasional bee or fly. The front pews on both sides were already full so we sat towards the back.

It was the usual type of service you saw in a small country church in 1920. The minister stood to welcome us, gave a brief prayer, and led us in a hymn while the little pump organ at the front accompanied the congregation. Prayers, scripture readings, and a sermon followed. I was squirming by that time because all I could think about was the delicious food and playing outside. Finally, the word I'd been waiting for… "Amen."

The churchyard had been transformed in the short time we were inside. Tables made of boards resting on hay bales had been erected in the shade on the east side of the church, and a few women were already laying out platters of fried chicken, bowls of potato salad, baskets of bread and biscuits while others were rounding up their children or spreading blankets on the ground under the big cedar trees. Several ice cream freezers, many covered with newspapers, were sitting in the deep shade provided by the church building.

The picnic was followed by a rest period, designed to help us digest the huge meals we'd eaten. Some folks sat quietly on their blankets, visiting with friends and neighbors, while others took cat naps. After a brief rest, older boys and men played baseball, younger children played tag or hide-and-seek, while the women sat in small groups visiting, some doing knitting, crochet, or embroidery as they talked.

Around 4:00 P.M., folks started meandering toward the church for the next event, the afternoon's entertainment, which consisted of a few musical performances by attendees, and sometimes a skit or two, and a group sing-along. Mother was always reluctant to attend or to let us girls watch because she said music that made you want to dance was one of Satan's tools. But Mother surprised us this year by allowing us to stay—a decision she later regretted. We all trooped into the church and sat down in a pew about halfway from the back.

A man I didn't know stood at the front, holding a piece of paper. After brief introductions and a hearty welcome, the program began. One performer sang a solo while another accompanied him on the pump organ. The audience gave rounds of applause after each selection. My eyebrows shot up when the MC stood and said, "Now, Ira Armsbury's going to serenade us all with his harmonica. Irie, what you gonna play?"

Daddy hadn't said a word to us. We girls grinned at each other as he stood and walked toward the front. Mother didn't look happy, but

CHAPTER TWO

there was nothing she could do except sit, a weak and puny smile on her thin, clenched lips.

Daddy answered as he stepped up onto the platform. "Well, seems fitting to me that we mark this Decoration Day with some patriotic music, 'specially since so many of the folks here round had loved ones that fought in the war." Heads nodded, and you could hear murmurs of "that's right" or "my boy was one."

"Wish I coulda gone, too, but the government thought I was too old, I guess, so I stayed behind. But every day I said a prayer for our country and all our brave boys who went over there." Daddy paused for a moment, then he said, "How 'bout I play that? 'Over There?' You can sing along if you want."

Daddy removed his Hohner harmonica box from his front shirt pocket, carefully opened the box and pulled out the small silver harmonica. He looked at it for a moment, wiped an invisible spot off of it with his shirt front, and put the harmonica to his mouth. That harmonica was only four inches long but when Daddy filled his lungs with air and blew, you could hear him all the way to Christmas.

It was easy to see why some women acted giddy around my dad, since he looked so handsome up on the stage, his beautiful and intense blue eyes twinkling as he played.

So, Daddy belted out that great patriotic song amid the sound of some folks singing, some clapping, and some stomping their feet. Afterwards he got a standing ovation and beamed all the way back to his seat.

After the program ended and the applause had died down, I stayed seated and watched as small groups of men and women gathered to visit one last time before collecting their families and leaving. Daddy was shaking hands with several men as he stood by our pew, but it was Mother whose behavior I was most interested in.

A lady I didn't know had steered Mother towards the front of the church, up by the simple railed alter where no one else stood. She and Mother were huddled together, the unknown lady speaking rapidly and gesturing while Mother stood stock-still, her face rapidly losing color. I wondered what was going on, but I was too tired to get up and walk over to Mother to ask. Besides, I was comfortable where I sat.

My head had started to nod when I heard Daddy call, "Come on, Ilie. It's time to go." I stood and walked down the aisle toward the exit, Daddy a couple of feet behind me. I guess I wasn't fully awake because just as I started down the front steps of the church I stumbled, and Daddy caught my shoulder to keep me from hitting the ground.

"Think I better just hold onto you 'til we get to the car. You look like you're ready for bed if you ask me," Daddy teased as we walked toward the car.

Wava, Metta and I were already in the back seat and Daddy was just opening the front, driver's side door to get in when we heard someone calling him.

"Ira. Ira Armsbury. Come on over here you old son-of-a-gun."

We watched as Daddy made his way back towards the church where another man was smiling and waving as Daddy approached. The other man clapped Daddy on the back as they visited. Finally, they went to their respective cars.

None of us girls knew who the man was, and it was years before I learned the story. During the flu epidemic of 1917—18, when so many folks were sick and dying, my dad drove the hearse when the other man—the county coroner—was too tired to drive it. And when Daddy was tired, he just climbed in the back and took a nap.

Daddy had just settled himself behind the steering wheel when I saw Mother walking towards the car. She was moving fast, her face grim, her eyes glaring. She walked around to the passenger side of the car, got in, and closed the door.

CHAPTER TWO

The drive home was quiet, no conversation. The others may have been thinking about all we'd seen and done earlier but I was napping and just wanted to go to bed.

Daddy was parking the car by the side of the house when Mother turned around and looked over the back of the seat at us girls. "I'm real tired and don't feel good, so I'm going to bed. You girls take in the leftovers and put the food away, and get to bed, too." Daddy had barely stopped the car when Mother jumped out, slammed the car door, and stalked into the house.

"Daddy, what's the matter with Mother?" Metta asked.

"Don't worry, honey. It's been a long day and she was up early. Just pooped, I 'spect. I'll get the food and put it away, and you girls run along, get to bed. I'll be there in a minute."

The last I saw of Daddy that night he was sitting in his favorite chair, an old, upholstered rocker, covered in a faded nubby tan fabric with dark walnut arms that ended in perfectly carved lions' paws. As I headed into the bedroom I shared with Mother and Daddy, I said, "Night, Daddy. See you in the morning."

Boy was I wrong.

THREE

I'd been asleep for what seemed like hours when something startled me awake. Nothing for a minute, until I heard a thump—a shoe hitting the floor.

"Ira?"

"Yeah."

There was a pause then I heard Mother, her voice harsh as she spoke in a distinct whisper, "The Bible says, 'Marriage is honorable in all, and the bed undefiled: but whoremongers and adulterers God will judge."

Daddy sounded confused and tired as he whispered, "What?" I heard the rustling of bedding before Mother spoke again.

"He that committeth fornication sinneth against his own body." Mother's words flew through the air like poisoned darts aimed at their target—my dad—and while I had no idea what those words meant, the way Mother said them I knew it couldn't be good.

"Florence, it's been a long day. I'm tired. You're tired. Go to sleep."

"Ira, I know. I know about you and…and…that fornicatress." Mother paused, drew in a deep breath, and continued. Her voice changed. I could hear little hiccups—like she was trying not to cry. "I figured you were seeing someone. If anyone asked me about it, and believe me some did, I denied it, but I can't no more, not after today when someone told me about you and that woman, Mary Wilkerson. The Bible says, 'Now

CHAPTER THREE

the body is not for fornication, but for the Lord; and the Lord for the body.' You've sinned against the Lord and me. You and that dirty old woman in that dirty old cream station. The same one where you bought the cream for our ice cream."

There was a long pause and a big sigh. "Florence…" then Daddy's voice dropped so low I couldn't hear any more. I waited but it wasn't long before my eyelids became too heavy for me to keep open and I drifted back to sleep hearing only faint mumblings and a shushing sound.

The next morning Daddy was gone when I wandered into the kitchen. Wava and Metta were already sitting at the table eating cold cereal. They looked up at me but when I smiled and gave them a half-hearted wave, Metta quickly looked back down at her bowl, and Wava shook her head at me and put her left forefinger to her lips, shushing me although I hadn't said anything yet.

Mother was standing in front of the white cast iron sink furiously pumping water into a big white enamel bucket. Usually, she pumped the water with smooth graceful movements, but this morning her arm seemed to be detached from her body—flying up and down. There was a violent metallic sound each time her arm came down and the handle hit the side of the pump.

I sat down at the table, filled my bowl with cereal and milk and started eating. I was oblivious to the tension, so I was surprised at the way Mother jumped down my throat after I asked her a simple question.

"Mother, are you mad at Daddy?"

"Ila," Mother's voice was as cold as the spring water flowing into the bucket. "Eat your breakfast and go outside… all three of you. I don't want to see a one of you in the house today and I mean it." We looked at each other and I started to say something but Metta shook her head at me, so I thought better of it. As soon as we were outside, we started talking at once.

"What's wrong with her?" Metta asked. "Boy, is she mad."

"Ila, did you do something? You did, didn't you. You're always getting into trouble. What'd you do?" That was Wava, ready to blame Metta or me when things weren't going right.

"I didn't do anything, "I protested. "I think they had a fight last night when Daddy came to bed."

"What makes you say that? You just trying to get out of trouble? Did you do something to make Mother mad?" Wava fumed.

"No, I didn't," I huffed indignantly. "I didn't understand everything, but I heard Mother saying something about buying cream and that lady who sells it."

I mean to tell you that was one long, miserable day spent outside. Around mid-morning Mother set a pitcher of water, three glasses, and a plate with sandwiches and apples out on the back porch. So, with the provisions that Mother had provided we made it through. She let us in right around dinner time. The only thing she said to us was "Girls, go wash your hands."

The table was set for four—no one expected Daddy home that early—so we were all surprised when he walked in just after we had seated ourselves. Mother took one look at him, frowned, pushed back her chair, stood up, and marched into the living room without a word to anyone. Daddy's gaze followed her out but after a few seconds he turned his attention to us and said, "Evening, girls. How're you this fine summer night?"

We told him about our day—Mother being upset and making us stay outside. He listened carefully as he pushed his hat back on his head. "Girls, why don't you go outside and play for just a few minutes while I go in and talk with Mother."

"But Daddy," Wava whined, "I'm hungry."

"It's okay. I'll only be a few minutes." He handed us each a

CHAPTER THREE

peppermint candy from the stash he kept in his left front pants pocket, gave us a wink, and left the room.

Daddy was true to his word. We weren't outside for very long—maybe twenty minutes—when the back door opened and Daddy called, "Girls, come on in for supper."

Mother was already seated at her place when we came in. We sat, too, but Daddy remained standing by the stove. After the prayer he started filling his supper plate and headed for the back door. On his way out, he turned, grinned at us and said, "I've got some work to do on the car and need to get it done before dark, so I'll just eat outside while I work."

Over the next two weeks Daddy came home every night, usually before seven, and followed the same supper routine, fixing his plate, and taking it outside to eat as he worked on one thing or another. After the dinner dishes were done, we'd go outside and play, and Mother and Daddy would go into their bedroom and close the door. It was a big change that's for sure. Daddy came home every night. Then he and Mother closed themselves away from us in the bedroom, doing what, we didn't know.

* * *

Mother never did explain to us why she sent us outside for the day, or what she and Daddy did in the bedroom every night after supper. Not until years later, did I understand the truth—that my dad had conducted a three-year long affair with a married woman in town, Mary Wilkerson, the woman who worked at the cream receiving station. That the affair had been confirmed for Mother at the Decoration Day celebration and that she and Daddy had fought about it until Daddy finally agreed to end it.

And that Mrs. Wilkerson wouldn't take no for an answer. Over the summer months, Daddy repeatedly told Mrs. Wilkerson that he didn't want to see her anymore. He and Mother apparently thought that would end the affair, but they were wrong. Mrs. Wilkerson started showing up at Daddy's garage. She even drove past our house because one evening after supper Mother said to us, "Girls, do you know the cream station lady, Mrs. Wilkerson?"

Metta and I both shook our heads no but Wava piped up, "I do, or at least I know her son. He's in my class at school and plays with the boys. But I've seen her."

"When I was hanging the laundry on the line this morning," Mother explained, "I saw Mrs. Wilkerson, the cream station lady, drive by. This is important. If you see her go by, I want you to come in the house and tell me."

"Why, Mother?" Being the inquisitive sort, I had to ask. "You never mind why. You just do as I say," Mother huffed.

"But if it's important, shouldn't we know why, Mother? What if we see somebody else and Mrs. Wilkerson is with them, should we say something? I don't understand." That was Metta, rational as always, wanting to know the background so she'd be sure to do the right thing, whereas I was usually busy and didn't always consider what the right thing might be.

Mother was quiet for a minute, staring hard at Metta and then me. Finally, she said, "Mrs. Wilkerson has been bothering Daddy at work. You know how much we need the money Daddy earns and he can't earn any if she's bothering him. Understand?"

All three of us girls nodded. We certainly understood about money because of the nights when we went to bed hungry for lack of money to buy food.

"So, if you see Mrs. Wilkerson, you tell me," Mother concluded, and we nodded agreement once more.

We did see Mrs. Wilkerson—one day while we were outside

CHAPTER THREE

playing—as she drove by delivering cream to the neighbors. We went in, told Mother, and waited to see what she'd do. It didn't take long to find out.

Mother and Daddy decided that more drastic measures were needed because of Mrs. Wilkerson's persistence, so Daddy packed a bag and left town, not once but several times. He went to Natoma, Luray, Russell, and even Lincoln, all in an effort to get away from Mrs. Wilkerson. But no matter where he went, she found him after a few days. In the end Daddy came back home, but both he and Mother were upset. Mother believed that Daddy was encouraging Mrs. Wilkerson and nothing Daddy said could change her mind.

Now, you may be wondering what Mr. Wilkerson was doing all this time. I never knew him, don't even know what he looked like. He and Mary had four sons and a daughter who died in infancy. Days he worked farming his own land or doing carpentry to provide for the family, and nights he took care of the children when Mary was gone. I'm sure he tried to keep Mary at home, God knows, but he wasn't able to slow her down.

Everybody—at least the grown-ups—in town knew what was going on between Daddy and Mrs. Wilkerson and folks felt sorry for Mr. Wilkerson and for Mother, too. But what could anyone do? Nothing, that's what. So, while Mrs. Wilkerson followed Daddy to one or another of the surrounding towns for an overnight tryst, she always returned home—that is until the last time, which really was the last time.

FOUR

When school started in September 1920, our house was like a pressure cooker. One little mistake, and the whole place would blow. To this day, I don't know what happened. All I know is that one morning in early October, we woke up to an announcement from Mother.

"Girls, Daddy's gone. He left late last night. He's going to set up his business in a new town, and if it works out good, we'll go stay with him, so I don't want you to be upset." Of course, we were upset. We hadn't said goodbye and we worried about him. But Mother reassured us he was okay. Beyond that, she refused to answer any questions.

Two weeks later, we learned where Daddy was and what he was doing. The supper dishes were done. We girls were all sitting around the kitchen table. Wava, now twelve, had her math book open struggling through math problems. Metta, who had turned nine in July, was sitting beside Wava practicing her beautiful cursive writing, and I, grown up at five, was sitting across from them drawing a picture of a horse.

Mother set a cup of tea on the table, pulled out a chair, sat down and said, "Girls, there's a letter here from Daddy. I'll read it to you." We all stopped what we were doing, giving Mother our full attention.

"Dear Mother and my little Girls,

CHAPTER FOUR

I'm in Colorado Springs, Colorado, an up-and-coming town if ever I saw one. People come for the clean air or to get over being sick. Some even go on to Manitou Springs, a close-by town, to take the waters which are supposed to cure what ails you. I don't know about that, but once folks get here, they want to see the mountains so they're building roads to the Rockies faster than I can dance a jig. Once the road's done and all those tourists try driving up into the mountains, they'll need someone like me to fix their cars. I've found a nice little shop, a barn, that I'm using for 'Ira's Garage' so I'm working hard. I'm sleeping there at night to save money. I surely do miss you all and think about you every day."

"*Before I left, Mother and I talked about moving someplace else. Well, I haven't had a bit of trouble here, so I think this could be a mighty fine place for us to start fresh and I'd surely like for you to come see for yourselves. You just let me know when you're coming, and I'll find us a place. Please write as quick as you can.*"

Mother looked up at us as she folded the letter.

"We're not moving are we, Mother?" asked Wava, panic rising in her voice.

"No, Wava. At least not yet."

"But I don't want to move," Wava whined. "Waldo is a great town and I love my school. I love this house and the new curtains you just made for Metta's and my bedroom. We've lived in Waldo the longest of anyplace. Why do we have to move? If we moved again, it would be the tenth time."

"Wava, I don't know if we're moving or not. Daddy's just asking us to come out and see him, see the town. We might not like it. We'll just have to see." Mother explained. Her voice sounded strained, like she was trying to stay calm.

"Nooooo! I'm not leaving this school. I finally have friends here," Wava began sobbing, tears running down her face, her nose dripping, and her arms wrapped around her middle as she hugged herself and rocked back and forth in her chair. Mother, never a hugger, just sat there looking stern and grim.

"Wava, that's enough," Mother growled, but Wava continued to sob and rock. I'd never seen her so upset.

"But what about Grandpa Newt and Grandma Rosenie? Will they go, too?" I asked. I couldn't imagine moving anyplace without them and their seven youngest children, all girls—our aunts. We loved going to Grandma and Grandpa's big, two-story house in Lucas, especially to stay overnight. In good weather we slept on cots in the second story sleeping porch and when it was cold, Grandma let all us girls sleep together in a big feather bed in one of the upstairs bedrooms. We got very little sleep because of all the giggling. Spending the night, tucked into bed with my aunts—those are some of my most treasured memories.

Wava snorted. "Don't be a dummy. They don't hafta move; we're the ones who'd move."

Mother was out of patience as she said, "That's it. Not another word or I'll get the strop."

Now I was upset too and started crying. I glanced over at Metta but she hadn't moved, like she was in shock. Instead, she sat with her head bowed, her eyes staring at some invisible spot on the kitchen table. Mother glared at Wava, "Now see what you've done?" she snapped as she turned to me. "Ila, stop crying. It'll be okay."

Everyone sat in stunned silence at the table as I sniffled. After a brief moment, Mother resumed drinking her tea while Wava and Metta finished up their homework. Finally, it was time for bed. I wanted to ask

CHAPTER FOUR

Metta what she thought about Daddy's letter and about the possibility of moving, but there was no opportunity the rest of that night.

Fall afternoons in Kansas can be warm, sunny, and colorful with the turning of the leaves. The next day, after Wava and Metta arrived home from school, the three of us went out into the back yard where we raked up a pile of leaves to jump in and where we could talk without Mother overhearing.

"Metta, you didn't say anything last night after Mother read the letter. Do you want to move?" I asked.

"No," she sighed. "It makes me tired just thinking about it. Daddy wants us to come out and Mother wants to be with him, so that's what's going to happen, and I guess I'll make the best of it. That's all I can do."

"But why does she want to be with him when she cries so much when he's home?" I didn't understand.

"I've wondered that, too, Ilie," Metta answered. "The best I can figure is that she doesn't know what to do when he's not around."

"What do you mean, what to do? She's always doing stuff…laundry, cooking, looking after us."

"Yes, but that's not what I mean. He tells her what to do and she does it, even if she's unhappy about it."

"Well, I'm the one who's unhappy now and I hate this, and I don't want to move and…" Wava blurted out before Metta interrupted her.

"You were awfully hard on Mother last night." Metta pointed out. "You know she's going to do what Daddy tells her to do. She always does."

"But why? I don't understand why she does what Daddy tells her if she doesn't want to," I repeated.

Wava explained, "Don't you remember what the preacher said at church one Sunday? 'Wives, submit to your husbands.' Mother's submitting."

"What's 'submit' mean?"

"It means that the husband is the boss, Ila. So, when you grow up and get married, you better do what your husband says, or you'll be in trouble."

I couldn't let that go by. "Well, if that's the case, I just won't get married 'cause I don't want someone telling me what to do when I'm grown up and can do what I want. So there."

Wava shook her head and walked away, but Metta gave me a little smile and said, "You and me both, kid."

I want to stop here and explain something. It's not that I was a feminist in 1920 Kansas. I'm not even sure the word 'feminist' existed then. And, if it had, I surely wouldn't have understood the meaning at five.

No, what I meant then, and have carried with me through the years, is how painful it was for me to see my mother constantly crying and complaining about how unhappy she was in her marriage. Yet, despite her unhappiness with him, she continued to ignore her own desires in favor of his.

* * *

Mother wrote Daddy a letter, telling him that we were coming and to expect us by train at the end of October. She told us that our trip would take all day.

Mother and Daddy were still paying for our little house in Waldo, and Mother didn't want to sell it just yet, so she packed only our clothes, bedding, and a few toys in a couple of old wooden crates. The last day in our house, Grandpa Newt drove over, loaded the crates and us into his big car and we left Waldo. Mother's last act before entering the car was to lock the front door, leaving behind everything she and Daddy owned but didn't want to move to Colorado Springs just yet.

CHAPTER FOUR

We spent our last night in Kansas with Grandpa Newt and Grandma Rosenie in Lucas. I suppose all grandchildren love going to their grandparents' home, and we girls were no exception. You could tell, just by looking at their house, that Grandpa was a successful businessman—he'd made his money in a hardware store in Luray but by 1920 had sold the hardware store, moved the family to Lucas and owned 360 acres of prime farmland. The house was huge—a white clapboard, two-story affair, with a large, formal front parlor and an adjoining music room for receiving and entertaining guests, a smaller, more intimate back parlor for the family, a dining room, and a big eat-in kitchen on the ground floor and six bedrooms and a big bathroom with running water upstairs—the biggest house in Lucas. A far cry from the measly little unpainted four room clapboard house we lived in—with a privy out back. A deep front porch, complete with porch swing, extended across the front and around the east side of Grandma's house, offering plenty of shade in the hot summer.

With seven girls, Grandma's house was always noisy with the sound of feminine voices laughing, talking, sometimes fussing or crying. Grandpa Newt was a man of few words, so when he spoke in his deep, gravelly voice, people listened.

Grandpa met Grandma when she was teaching in a one-room school. The story was that he fell in love with her the instant he saw her. You could tell, just by watching Grandpa, that the story was true.

Whenever he looked at Grandma, his face took on a relaxed, almost soft look, and his eyes shone with adoration. And whenever Grandma walked into a room, Grandpa stopped what he was doing to look up at Grandma and smile.

At home, Grandpa usually sat back and observed and let Grandma Rosenie run the roost. She was no bigger than a minute, not even five feet tall to Grandpa's six feet plus, but when Grandma spoke, the girls and

Grandpa hopped to.

Grandma always said that Daddy was the spitting image of Grandpa Newt, just a younger version. By the time I came along, Grandpa's hair was snow white while Daddy's was still thick, wavy black, but Grandpa had the same piercing blue eyes, a long, narrow face with the strong jaw and chin and a Roman nose.

Daddy and Grandpa's personalities were similar, too. I guess that's why they didn't get along. When the whole family would go to visit Grandpa and Grandma, Daddy usually stayed outside, tinkering with our car or Grandpa's. Or he'd sit and whittle—anything to avoid spending much time with Grandpa.

We pulled up in front of Grandma's house just before dinner which, in case you don't know, was the noontime meal in rural Kansas. My aunt, Maxine, who was just a few months older than me, was sitting on the porch swing.

"Ilie, I been waiting. Dinner's almost ready but I got something to tell you. Come on." She stood up from the swing, ran across the porch, jumped off the front steps and we ran around to the back of the house towards the alley. We crouched down by the side of the garage under some spirea bushes where no one could see us.

"Ilie, Ma and Pa had a big fight last night about your Pa."

"What'd they say?"

"Pa was mad and said that it was your Pa's fault that you had to move. Ma said, 'Now, Newt, you've always been extra hard on that boy. He's moving the family to start over and do things right.'"

"And then what?"

"Pa said, 'If he'd done things right in the first place, they wouldn't have to move.' And Ma said, 'I hate to see them go. Florence just doesn't stand up to him and those girls need a place to call home and food on the table. How many times have I fed them because Ira couldn't or

CHAPTER FOUR

wouldn't?'"

"Then Pa said, 'That's what I'm tellin' ya, Rosenie. I'm going to worry about those girls.' After that, their voices got so quiet, I couldn't hear any more."

* * *

Now I need to stop here and explain something to you. Some of you may have had experiences similar to mine where one or both parents didn't do a very good job with you. They might have been physically violent—although in those days beating a child was considered discipline—or drunkards like my dad, or maybe even something worse, God forbid. But as children most of us are very protective of our folks because whatever happens in our households is all we know. We just figure it's the same everywhere. So, when Max told me what she'd heard I was mad at both my grandparents for saying bad things about my dad, and I was mad at Max for repeating them, too.

Once I was grown, however, and realized what had happened, I was angry with my grandparents but for a different reason. I used to wonder if they knew what was going on, that Mother couldn't stand up to Daddy, that we girls were suffering at times—went to bed hungry, were moved from one home and one town to another, saw Mother constantly crying and complaining about how awful her life was—because of the crises that Daddy created, why in God's name didn't they step in and help us girls more? Why didn't they protect us especially since they knew that Mother couldn't or wouldn't?

I didn't come to these realizations until I was in my thirties. Grandpa Newt was already dead, and I couldn't see any good coming from asking Grandma Rosenie those questions. I just had to shake my head and accept what had happened and that's what I did. But don't let anybody tell you that acceptance is easy because it's not.

* * *

Before I could say anything, I heard the back kitchen door open and Mother calling.

"Ila. Maxine. Dinner's ready. You need to come in and get washed up."

By the time we got to the dining room, everyone was already seated around the huge round, walnut table. As we sat down, Grandma Rosenie nodded to Mother and said, "Florence, will you say grace?"

"Lord, bless this food to the good of our bodies. Be with our absent ones. Guide, protect and comfort them, and give us all strength and comfort for our needs. Amen." A prayer I heard every meal, every day of my life while I lived at home.

The rest of the day went by too fast and before we knew it, it was time for bed.

We three girls and our seven aunts trooped upstairs to the bedroom with the feather bed, put on our night clothes and climbed into bed for our last sleepover. In order for us all to fit, we slept head to foot, with five at the head of the bed and five more at the foot. Our biggest problem was always a battle over the blankets.

"You've pulled all the blankets up so high that my shoulders aren't covered and they're cold."

"Stop shoving! I don't have all the blankets. Maxine and Ila do."

After settling comfortably in bed with the blankets evenly distributed, the older girls started telling jokes that they'd read in Captain Billy's Whiz Bang, an endlessly attractive magazine that was forbidden to us all.

"I learned a new poem," Wava bragged.

"Oh, yeah? Let's hear it."

CHAPTER FOUR

Wava cleared her throat and began.

"My parents told me not to smoke;
I don't.
Nor listen to a naughty joke;
I don't.
They told me it was wrong to wink
At handsome men, or even think
About intoxicating drink;
I don't.
To dance or flirt was very wrong
I don't.
Wild girls chase men and wine and song;
I don't.
I kiss no men, not even one—
In fact, I don't know how it's done;
You wouldn't think I have much fun—
I don't."

All the older girls started laughing but I didn't get it. Still, everyone else, except for Max and me, was laughing so we joined in.

"Wava, that's awful. If mother heard you, she'd tan your hide," commented Metta as she laughed.

"Why do you think I haven't told you before? I know she'd hate it."

Laughter and the usual gabbing continued for an hour or more, but as we settled down for the night, we became quieter and more somber.

"Wava, I wish you weren't going," declared Mayetta who was two years younger than Wava.

"I know. I don't want to go, either, but we have to. Mayetta, you have to promise that you'll write me."

"Well, of course I will, but you'll be back won't you? This isn't forever, is it?"

"No," said Metta. "I have a feeling. Daddy likes it there, and Mother doesn't like being alone, so I bet we'll stay."

Wava nodded her head as tears appeared. Before you knew it, we were all sniffling.

* * *

It's interesting that three people—in this case my two older sisters and me—can all go through the same experience yet be affected by it differently. Because of all the moves that Wava went through as a child nothing was more important to her than a house of her own where she could stay put. And when her first grandchild—a girl—was five years old, Wava paid to have a gardening shed moved to her granddaughter's yard and turned that dirty, old shed into a beautiful playhouse complete with a climbing rosebush, windows that opened and closed, and a brick patio.

Metta was affected in a different way. Education was the most important thing to her. She believed that if she went to college, she could earn the money to support herself and create stability so she wouldn't be the unwilling victim to someone else's whims.

As for me, I had mixed emotions about the whole thing. My sadness was moving away from Grandpa and Grandma and my cousins. But I was excited about our upcoming trip. I'd never been on a train before and I liked new experiences, even as a child. I hadn't experienced the loss of friends and family because of constant moving, like Wava. I was always more adventurous than she when we were kids, and more rough-and-tumble, willing to take a risk, than Metta.

CHAPTER FOUR

It became quiet after that and I drifted off to sleep, holding Max's hand.

* * *

Friday morning, October 29 arrived soon enough. Grandma Rosenie woke us up early—it was still dark. Wava, Metta, and I wore our Sunday-go-to-meeting dresses, anklets, and our Sunday Mary Janes. After all, it wasn't every day—or in my case, ever before—that you rode on a train. After getting dressed, we headed downstairs to breakfast.

Mother was dressed up, too, wearing her Sunday dress including her pale green silk collar with the tiny pink silk roses.

Everyone was quiet at the big round oak table in Grandma's kitchen. I noticed that neither Wava nor Metta were eating anything which made me feel better because I didn't feel like eating either. A lump in my throat choked me every time I tried to swallow a bit of toast or egg. Grandma Rosenie must have noticed, too, because she started urging us girls to eat.

"It's a long train ride from Ellsworth to Colorado Springs and your mother doesn't have the money to buy food when the train stops. I've packed a hamper with some sandwiches for you to take on the train, but you need to eat now. It'll be a long time 'til lunch."

"That's right. I don't want to hear no whining and complaining if you get hungry later." Mother's eyes were puffy—I couldn't tell whether she'd been crying or was just tired from too little sleep. I ate some egg and a glass of milk but that was all I could get down.

Finally, it was time to go. Grandma Rosenie said, "Leave everything on the table. The girls will clean up after us." Then she turned and walked out of the room toward the front door. By the time I got to the kitchen doorway she was standing on the front porch holding the screen door open for Mother who was putting on her worn black wool coat. The sun was just peeking over the horizon.

As I approached Mother, she handed me my winter coat. "Mother," I whined. "It's too warm for a winter coat. I'll sweat to death."

"You may be hot now, but you'll thank me when we get to Colorado Springs where it gets mighty cold. Now put it on." I grumbled, but I put my coat on. So did Wava and Metta. It was going to be a long day and we didn't want to get on Mother's bad side from the start.

Mother picked up her old brown felt hat from the oak hall tree bench and put it on, and as she walked out onto the front porch she pulled on her dark brown gloves. Thank goodness we were just kids and didn't have to wear hats and gloves, too.

Our aunts followed us out onto the front porch and down the front steps toward Grandpa's big black car which was parked by the side of the house.

"Girls," Grandma Rosenie said, "Tell everyone goodbye now, because you won't be seeing them again for a while." That was all it took for invisible clouds to open and tears to fall like heavy rains.

I cried along with everyone else, even though I was excited about riding a train, seeing new things, and having Daddy back with us where he belonged. You can do that—cry and be excited at the same time.

Grandma Rosenie and Mother stood on the porch; Mother a good six inches taller than Grandma. Grandma's left arm was around Mother's waist and Mother's right arm was around Grandma. I could tell that they were both trying hard not to cry, but I could see their eyes glistening with unshed tears. Grandpa, a scowl on his face, was standing on the top step, his hands in his pants' pockets. At the time I thought he was mad because he had to drive us to Ellsworth to the train station. Later

CHAPTER FOUR

I realized he was mad because he blamed my dad for making us move.

By this time, everyone was sobbing and hugging each other. The crying would have gone on much longer if Grandpa hadn't taken control.

"That's enough. We need to get going or they'll miss their train. Everybody in the car." By "everybody," Grandpa meant Grandma, Mother, Wava, Metta, and me. In ones and twos our aunts climbed the steps to the front porch, turned and waved as Grandpa backed the car out of the drive and headed down the dirt street toward the country road that took us to Ellsworth, Kansas, and the train station.

* * *

That goodbye, the one just before we left for the train station, was not near as hard as later goodbyes when I was older. I think that's normal. As a child you want to go out and explore the world, so leaving your family isn't that difficult. But once you're older and you've been away—that shared history, those memories and stories—home and family become more important. At the time, though, I was young, so I was ready to go before everyone else.

* * *

The town of Ellsworth was started by settlers who sought the protection of Fort Ellsworth which had been built by the U. S. Army because of ongoing trouble between settlers and the Cheyenne and other Indian tribes who lived in the area. When the railroad reached Ellsworth, it became a cow town—cowboys drove longhorns from Texas to Ellsworth where the cattle were loaded onto trains bound for eastern markets. By 1920 the cattle business had dried up, but Ellsworth still had two train depots, one for the St. Louis—San Francisco—we called it the Frisco—railroad which moved freight across country, and one for the Union Pacific, which was a passenger train.

Grandpa drove slowly through downtown Ellsworth towards the Union Pacific depot which was at the south edge of town. Like many Kansas towns of the period, the buildings on main street were made of either limestone or brick. One especially impressive building had a large round tower-type structure that jutted out from a second-story corner and extended over the sidewalk below. Arched windows surrounded the tower walls letting in natural light from every direction. I'd never seen anything like it, and I was thrilled by all the new sights. We'd already said all our good-byes, except for our final ones to Grandma and Grandpa at the train station, so I was anxious for us to get going on our trip—my first real adventure. This, I'm sure, was the beginning of my desire to travel and see the world.

Although a few of the streets in Ellsworth were brick, Main Street, which ran behind the Union Pacific depot, was sand. The street was lined with hotels and restaurants and kept busy by the travelers who needed a night of lodging or a quick meal before their trains departed. Directly across the street from the depot was a boarding house that had seen better days.

The depot was a white clapboard affair with tall, narrow windows accented by dark trim. An overhanging roof protected passengers while they stood on the platform waiting to board. Four sets of railroad tracks ran in front of the depot, a testimony to its status as a transportation hub for the surrounding area. Across the road and behind the boarding house was a big field. The crops had already turned brown and russet, the dry stalks and leaves dancing in the fall breeze. Occasionally a gust of wind, like a miniature tornado, picked up leaves and bits of grass, swirling them across the landscape.

Once we arrived at the train station, Grandpa supervised while our

CHAPTER FOUR

two crates were moved from the car to the station platform. An elegantly dressed black-suited conductor lifted our valises into the doorway of a passenger car while a man in grey overalls shoved the crates back out of sight in the baggage car. Grandma Rosenie waited just outside the depot by the door while Mother purchased our tickets. As Mother walked out the door onto the platform, Grandma gave her a covered basket full of sandwiches and fruit and a quart mason jar of water. Then Grandma and we girls walked across the platform where we waited for the conductor to holler, "All Aboard!"

I can't tell you how many train stations I've been in over my lifetime. I love train travel and the pulsing life of a busy train station. But none of them will ever be as memorable to me as that tiny train station in Ellsworth, where I boarded a train and took the first train ride of my life.

The steam locomotive with its loud hiss sounded like a giant snake ready to strike. The bell clanged constantly, and clouds of white steam shot out from the front. I was overwhelmed by the sight and sound of this monster. My first time leaving home for a new land—Colorado—and mountains which I'd never seen except in picture books. My imagination was on fire with images of what I might encounter. Were mountains so high that they touched the blue sky? Could I step from a mountainside onto a cloud and float away? I loved the story of the *Three Billy Goats Gruff*. Would I see a billy goat? I was wiggling with excitement so that Mother had to lay a hand on my shoulder and whisper, "Calm down. You're bothering the other passengers." But, in truth, I was bothering only her.

Standing on the station platform, we mouthed our goodbyes because we couldn't hear above the cacophony from the engine. Mother's left hand kept her hat on her head while she hugged Grandma and Grandpa one more time. Everybody, even Grandpa Newt, had tears in their eyes. We boarded the train and had barely found our seats when we heard the conductor yell, "All Aboard!" one last time. The whistle blew, the train lurched and chugged, and we started moving—toward Colorado and our new life.

FIVE

Having never been on a train before I looked around real careful to remember every detail when I was grown. Even though I hoped that this was just the first of many train trips, who knew if I'd ever get to ride a train again? I'd never seen anything so fancy—an arched ceiling with clerestory windows and a row of fancy electric lights that ran the length of the car down the middle of the ceiling. Mother and I sat together with Mother by the window. Wava sat across from Mother and slouched against the window frame staring at the floor with Metta across from me, her hands folded in her lap looking expectantly at Mother. I think Metta was offering silent encouragement to Mother and hoping that Mother would offer some reassurance that everything would be okay—reassurance that never came.

It was cool in our train car when we first boarded, but it warmed up once the train began to move. I was so excited that I couldn't sit still as I inspected our surroundings. Two-person seats which faced each other were upholstered in a beautiful, deep purple velvety-type material—it was soothing and kind of hypnotic to run my hand over the seat cover. The blinds and carpet were the same color as the upholstery. If I stared at the carpet long enough, when I looked up, everything and everyone in the car looked purple. At one point I leaned across the narrow aisle toward Wava—I was going to tell her she looked purple, but when we made eye contact, she glared at me and abruptly turned back to stare out her window.

Around noon, Mother retrieved the basket of sandwiches from under her seat and we ate lunch. Other passengers were doing the same thing—I smelled onion behind me and heard the crinkly sound of wax paper as sandwiches were unwrapped. Since I hadn't eaten much breakfast, I was hungry, and the ham sandwich, apple and water from Grandma Rosenie hit the spot.

After lunch, I began to feel drowsy, probably a combination of food and the pleasant warmth of our car, so I leaned against Mother and took a nap. The clickety-clack of the train wheels moving over the tracks played a soothing lullaby and sleep came easily. I was in the middle of a great dream about sailing on the ocean when Mother woke me, pulling on my arm and saying, "Get up, Ila. We need to get off here."

"Where are we? Are we there yet?" I mumbled as Mother pushed me down the aisle towards the open door and the stairs.

"Course not, Ila. We're in Limon, Colorado."

"Is Daddy here?"

"No, Ila. We're just changing trains."

I'd never heard of Limon, but I walked ahead of Mother and down the steps onto the depot platform and into the building where we waited about an hour for our train. Although the railroad was different—this time we rode the Rock Island—our passenger car was very similar. The only difference was the color of the upholstery, carpet, and blinds—brown instead of purple. Once we'd entered our train car, we returned to our former seating arrangement with Mother and me in one seat and Metta and Wava across from us in another.

From the moment we left Ellsworth, I was overcome with wonder.

CHAPTER FIVE

The train track followed the course of numerous small streams and the countryside, which appeared out the windows on both sides of the train car, was a celebration of fall colors. Tall trees with their long branches dangled over glistening, slow-moving water.

Once I realized that we had left Kansas and were in Colorado, I was disappointed that Colorado didn't look different from Kansas. The countryside was flat with few trees and lots of short bristly-looking shrubs. It was fall, and the fields looked like brown quilts with brilliantly colored and textured vegetation of red, orange, yellow and brown. Mother had said there were mountains in Colorado, and I kept a lookout for them but didn't see anything until we were closer to Colorado Springs.

I was also fascinated by our fellow passengers, people I'd never seen before and would never see again, but for a brief moment our lives were entwined. I turned around in my seat to watch a portly gentleman, sitting behind and across from us, dressed in a black suit with a bowler hat sitting beside him on the vacant seat and a watch chain peeking from a vest pocket. I caught his eye and waved, and he nodded once and gave me a wink.

Directly behind me was an elderly lady, dressed all in black from head to toe, sitting upright, rigid and cold, her hands clasped tightly in her lap. She wore a black veil, which she had pulled back to reveal her face, sad, pale, and drawn. I must have made a small sound because she looked up at me, our eyes locked so I smiled and said, "Hello." Mother swatted my behind and hissed, "Ila, stop bothering that poor woman. Turn around, sit down and behave yourself," before I could say anything more. I thought to myself, "When I grow up, I'm going to travel everywhere on the train, talk to all the passengers, hear their stories. For now, though, I had to look straight ahead and, as Mother said, "not bother" anyone.

At one point I glanced over at Wava who had maintained her grumpy demeanor throughout the trip. She was staring out the window but occasionally looked over at me and scowled. She even stuck her tongue out at me when I gave her a smile. I looked up at Mother to see if she'd noticed that Wava was being mean to me but saw that Mother, too, looked unhappy, a deep frown on her face and her brow furrowed. It puzzled me that they looked so unhappy when we were together on this great adventure and I was having such an exciting time. Metta wasn't unhappy either—she was asleep.

Our trip lasted all day because we made lots of stops along the way. We finally pulled into the Colorado Springs depot right at sunset. The sky was streaked with pink and orange, and wispy clouds that had been white now glowed gold at the top and purple at the bottom. It looked like thousands of sunsets I'd seen before, yet there was a difference I couldn't name. "Mmm" I thought to myself, "leaving home and going to new places means I can see different things that still remind me of home. Maybe I won't get homesick after all." Now, that was something I hadn't considered before.

We were all exhausted. Looking out the window, I saw Daddy standing on the platform, his hat in his left hand as he wiped his brow with a soiled white handkerchief. He looked as handsome as ever. His hair was a little mussed from where he'd just removed his hat. He'd dressed up to meet us—probably his way of letting Mother know how much he'd missed her—wearing a dark blue suit, white shirt, and a dark tie. Our eyes met and he gave me a big smile as I waved and yelled, "Daddy, Daddy, it's me. We're here." Mother gave a deep sigh as she slowly stood. She smoothed her wrinkled skirt, patted her hair back into place, and said, "We're here. Let's go, girls." Even though I was excited about seeing Daddy I noticed a decided lack of enthusiasm in Mother's voice.

Metta stood and stretched before picking up the old blue valise Grandma had given her. As she turned toward the aisle, she looked at

CHAPTER FIVE

me, gave me a rueful smile, straightened her shoulders, and said, "I'm ready." I was proud of Metta for the way she acted. She hadn't wanted to move, but she also understood that Daddy wanted us with him, and Metta refused to make a difficult situation worse by being angry. Over the years I've thought back on how Metta handled difficult situations, her stoicism, and her quiet courage. I've always tried to be like her so that I wouldn't be devastated in the face of adversity.

Wava, on the other hand, just sat there looking at the floor. "Wava. Wava, get up. Let's go. Daddy's waiting." Mother spoke softly, but there was a strain in her voice. Wava looked up with a glare but I saw Mother shake her head "no" and after a few seconds, Wava slowly stood, grabbed her valise, and moved toward the aisle, pushing Metta out of the way.

Wava led us off the train, walked towards Daddy and stopped about three feet from him, and started to sniffle. She refused to look at him and when he stepped toward her and tried to hug her, she backed away. Although she was the oldest at twelve, I thought Wava was acting like a baby, unlike me and I was only five. Metta was the most grown up of the three of us and she was only nine.

After stepping down from the passenger car, Metta walked over to stand by Wava and gave Daddy a little smile as he hugged her and said, "How's my girl? Glad to see you." He ruffled the hair on my head and gave me a wink. By this time Mother had joined us and she and Daddy looked at each other but there were no kisses or hugs, just head nodding of acknowledgement.

"Well, I'm mighty glad to see everybody. It's been real lonesome here, even though I've been busy. Got the garage set up and even had a couple of customers. All right. Yessir, it's going to be all right."

The Colorado Springs train depot was the biggest one I'd seen yet, a long, narrow two-story red brick building with red shingles. Lots of other folks followed us off the train, and it wasn't long before a huge pile of valises, trunks, and boxes were sitting on the platform. Many sported colorful travel stickers advertising exotic places like the Royal Hotel of London and the Eiffel Tower. Looking at those travel stickers, I resolved that when I was grown, I'd go see those places and more.

Daddy had no trouble loading our crates into his car, along with us, and before I knew it, we were off.

I was exhausted and fell asleep almost the second the car door closed. The next time I opened my eyes, daylight was shining through a solitary window. I was lying in bed, nestled between my two older sisters, looking up at a dingy white ceiling high overhead. Trying to figure out where we were, I rose up on my elbows and looked around. Mother and Daddy were asleep in another bed, identical to ours but separated from us by a small wooden table that had been painted brown and was now covered with chipped paint, scratches, and water rings. The room held no other furnishings except for a small three-drawer bureau against the wall at the end of the bed, and a wall-mounted porcelain sink.

I had just laid back down and started to close my eyes when I heard a rustling of covers. I looked over to see Daddy standing by his side of the bed, stretching. As he turned towards me, he smiled and raised his right index finger to his lips, motioning me to keep quiet. I nodded and smiled and waited to see what he'd do next. In just a few moments he was dressed and standing by our bed. He reached over Metta with those long, strong arms and gently lifted me straight up and out from under the covers. Pointing at my clothes, he indicated I should get dressed, too, and then we'd leave.

As I hurriedly dressed, I glanced out the window and was surprised to see that we were up high—higher than I had ever been in my life, even when I climbed the trees at Grandma's house. I stepped closer to the window for a better look, and down below I saw cars and trucks driving along the busy street and even more parked at the curb. There were more

CHAPTER FIVE

cars and trucks on that one street than I'd ever seen in Lucas at one time.

Once outside the room, I couldn't contain myself.

"Daddy, did you see all those cars and trucks? This must be the biggest city in the world. Where are we? Is this our new home?"

"Shush, Ilie. Calm down. Don't want to wake the others. Don't you remember?" He took my hand and lead me down the hall away from the door of our room, and chuckled as he explained, "This is Colorado Springs…and no, this isn't the biggest city in the whole world, just bigger than Lucas. This isn't our new home, just a place to stay for a few days while we find us a place to rent." He smiled as he guided me down a long, narrow hall toward some steps.

"This is just an old hotel here in Colorado Springs, not too expensive but not real cheap either. Don't want to live here, this ain't no place to raise kids, but it was all I could find on such short notice," he explained as we walked down the stairs into a big lobby with over-stuffed chairs, tables, and spittoons scattered around the room. "We'll find us a little house, close to my new garage, I hope. Get us settled in and start our new life." He was all smiles as he explained the plan to me.

* * *

Unfortunately, Daddy's plan didn't work out. It started out well enough—Daddy arose early every morning and drove to his garage where he worked all day and returned to the hotel at night for our evening meal and bed. During the day, Mother looked for a house and a job, talking to folks at the hotel and at surrounding businesses. We girls were left on our own, Wava and Metta weren't even enrolled in school yet. Mother, I think, had decided to take things one at a time, and the most important in her mind was finding a job and a place to live that wasn't a cheap hotel.

Mother found a job in only two days, and it was a good job, too. She was bubbling with excitement when she told us that night over supper.

"I'm going to be working for a wealthy lady, as her cook and house cleaner. She has one child—a boy with tuberculosis—living in a little house in her back garden, and she'll tend him while I take care of the house."

"That's fine," Daddy beamed at her. "You did real good and it'll help us out. I believe this is the best thing we've ever done" and he reached out to touch her hand. She started to draw her hand away, but must have thought better of it, because she stopped, and slowly moved her hand back to within Daddy's reach. He smiled at her and patted her hand, and she finally smiled back, not a big smile, but it was a beginning.

"When do you start, Mother?" Daddy asked.

"Today's Monday. I start Wednesday. Got to use tomorrow to get ready. You know," She said expansively, "It'll be good to earn some money for the family. I always feared that because of no schoolin', I wouldn't find a job. But I know how to do everything Mrs. Hughes needs doing, so that's good."

Mother turned to us girls and said, "Now, girls. Don't think that you can get a good job without an education. I want you to stay in school, so you can get jobs that earn money, more money than you can earn as a cook." Daddy nodded his agreement.

The next few days passed without incident. Daddy and Mother left for work at the same time every morning with him driving her to Mrs. Hughes' home. After work, Mother took a trolley and got back to the hotel before Daddy. She'd look tired but otherwise okay. But every evening, right about the time that Daddy was supposed to arrive, we girls would notice a change in Mother—she'd get quiet, her lips pressed tight together as she sat and fidgeted with her fingers, picking at imaginary

CHAPTER FIVE

lint on her dress or sweater. Each night Daddy arrived back at the hotel, sober, cheerful, and happy, and then Mother's face would relax, the tight, grim frown replaced by a weary smile. Over supper, Daddy'd tell us how his day had gone and ask Mother about her day. It was a big change from life in Waldo where Daddy didn't come home at night, and if he did, you could usually smell alcohol and sometimes perfume.

I should have known it couldn't last but I was young and not jaded, yet. It was the Tuesday after we'd been there almost two weeks, and Daddy didn't return for the evening. Mother became more agitated the longer she waited. Finally, she decided he wasn't coming home for the night, we ate dinner and went to bed.

After two more days and nights of Daddy being a "no-show", Mother announced on Friday morning that she was going to look for Daddy.

"But, Mother," Wava spoke softly, like she really didn't want to ask the question. "What about your job? Did you quit?"

"No. Especially not now. I'm just taking this one day off. Mrs. Hughes knows I'll be there tomorrow, and she was nice about me asking for today.

"Now, you girls stay in the room or you can go down to the lobby, but no further and don't bother anybody. You understand?"

We nodded agreement and watched silently as she put on her coat, hat and gloves and left. Our day was quiet—we stayed in the room until we became restless, then went to the lobby to watch people come and go for a while, then back to the room.

Mother returned just as the sun was setting. She looked terrible—the skin on her face—she was very light complexioned—was red and chapped from the cold and the wind coming down off the mountains—and her eyes were red and puffy. She trembled as she took off her coat, hat, and gloves and sat down on the end of the bed she shared with Daddy.

"Mother ..." she looked at me and shook her head before I could say another word, so I just stood at the end of her bed, near enough to touch her but in truth, it seemed like we were miles apart as she looked from me to Metta then Wava and then the floor. After a few moments, she cleared her throat.

"Girls, after we eat supper, we need to pack up all our things and get to bed early. We have a big day tomorrow." Long pause...

"Tomorrow, we're moving to Mrs. Hughes' house and I have a full day of work ahead of me after we get there."

"Why are we moving, Mother?" Metta wondered. "You didn't tell us this before."

"I found your father this morning." We all smiled. That meant he was okay, but then she stopped and looked at her hands which were tightly clasped and laying in her lap. When she looked up again a lone tear was sliding down her right cheek and dropped onto her dress.

"Mother," Metta whispered as she took a step toward her, "what's wrong?"

"Ahem. Ahemm. Well... um... He's at his garage... Anda, um... so's that woman—that Mary Wilkerson. That's why he hasn't been back here." More tears ran down her face as she spit out the words, her eyes blazing with anger. It wasn't until many years later that I understood you could feel rage—so strong your body trembled—and heartbreak—a physical pain in the middle of your chest so intense it hurt to inhale—at the same time.

The rest of that night so many years ago is all a blur to me now. There are just some things you don't want to remember because they're too painful. We made it through the night—that's all there is to say—and the next morning we took our clothes, left everything of Daddy's in the room, and rode the trolley to Mrs. Hughes' house, our new home.

SIX

Although Mrs. Hughes' house was smaller than Grandpa and Grandma's, it was grander and looked bigger because it was three stories tall. Mr. Hughes made lots of money and the furnishings were elegant with plush carved oriental rugs; heavy furniture with silk upholstery; fine tapestries hanging on the walls along with beautiful, original art, and shining crystal chandeliers. The butler, a tall quiet man who had a room off the kitchen, ignored us girls, which was okay with us because he never smiled and that was scary. Just one look from him would send me to find Mother so I could hide behind her full skirts.

We lived on the third floor. Mother had her own bedroom, and we three girls shared a big room that had been used for storing trunks, clothes, and furniture. The rest of the third floor was unfinished and we never ventured in there. We ate all our meals in the kitchen, and Mother was real strict about us staying out of the rest of the house.

The first weekend we were at Mrs. Hughes', we girls stayed in our room, or went to Mother's room, although she wasn't there—she was downstairs working. The only time we ventured below the third floor was for our meals.

We lived at Mrs. Hughes' house for several weeks and quickly developed a daily routine. Mother woke up before dawn to start her day, awakened us girls to get dressed and eat breakfast and got Wava and

Metta off to school. Wava and Metta left the house—by the back door naturally—at 7:30 and walked to school. Mother spent the rest of her day cooking, cleaning, doing laundry and ironing. Sometimes, if I was tired, Mother let me go back to bed to sleep a little later. I spent the rest of my time in the kitchen playing or helping her—as much help as a five-year-old can be—or up in our room. If Mother was caught up on her work and the weather was nice, we sometimes went out into the back yard where I could play while Mother sat and watched me. When the girls got home from school, they did their homework and then we played 'til suppertime.

An atmosphere of anxiety and sorrow surrounded Mother, Wava and Metta. They couldn't escape from their thoughts about Daddy and what had happened. I guess I was the lucky one. Because of my youth, my attention span was short. I was happy until I remembered that Daddy wasn't with us. Then sadness and confusion would set in because I didn't understand what had happened.

Mother believed and frequently told us that idle hands are the Devil's playground, so after supper we read books or the Bible, memorized Bible verses, wrote letters, practiced our sewing stitches, embroidered tea towels, learned to tat—anything to keep busy until bedtime.

We spent Christmas at Mrs. Hughes', just the four of us without Daddy, who didn't even call or send us a card. But Mrs. Hughes remembered us three girls, giving each of us a distinctive, tiny porcelain baby doll. Generally speaking, life was boring but predictable, something we all welcomed after so much chaos when we lived with Daddy. But the calm didn't last.

Early on Saturday morning, January 22, 1921, Daddy showed up at the back door of the Hughes' house. We girls hadn't seen him in weeks, and we were overjoyed—even Wava seemed glad to see him. The minute Mother invited Daddy in to sit at the table and have a cup of coffee while

CHAPTER SIX

she finished the breakfast dishes, we knew something out of the ordinary was happening and it didn't take long to find out what it was.

"Girls," Mother said as she dried her hands on a dish towel, "I have a letter from Grandma Rosenie saying that her brother, Walter Mason, will let us live with him in Rocky Ford, Colorado, for a while—just 'til your Daddy can get his business set up. You go upstairs and pack all your clothes and toys. Daddy's going to drive us to Rocky Ford."

"Mother," Metta asked with a puzzled expression on her face, "Is Daddy going to live with us again?"

"Mother, what about that other woman, the one who follows Daddy around? Is she moving, too?"

"Girls," Mother replied in an exasperated tone of voice, "We don't have time for questions. This is between Daddy and me. We're moving to Rocky Ford to get away from that woman and she isn't moving with us. And yes, Daddy is going to live with us. Now do as I say. Let's go."

That was it. A brief explanation with no real detail—no other discussion—just do it. But that was Mother's way. So even though we were shocked and surprised—we hadn't seen Daddy in weeks, and we thought that Mother hadn't seen him either—we did as we were told. We didn't have much, so we were packed, the car was loaded, and we were on the road by 10:00 a.m. and in Rocky Ford by 3:00 p.m.

SEVEN

I was greatly disappointed there were no mountains to see as we approached Rocky Ford. And a lot fewer trees—even fewer than we had in Lucas. But snow covered the ground, so I wasn't completely disappointed.

Once we entered the town of Rocky Ford, Daddy drove straight to Uncle Walter's house, a white clapboard bungalow set back from the curb.

"See that yard, full of snow? In the spring and summer, it's full of flowers 'cause Uncle Walter's a florist here in Rocky Ford, and he can grow flowers from rocks, if you ask me," Daddy said proudly of his uncle whom he had met when he was just a boy living with Grandpa Newt and Grandma Rosenie.

Daddy was the first one out of the car and started across the snow-covered lawn towards the house. The rest of us got out of the car and began stretching, when he stopped suddenly, turned back towards us and said, "Girls! Mother! Stay in the car." He had that I-won't-brook-no-backtalk tone of voice, so we all got back in the car and watched what he was going to do next. Mother's car door was open, so she put her right leg back out, stood up with her right hand holding the top of the passenger door and called out, "Ira, what is it?" But he didn't answer or turn back towards us—he just waved his right arm and hand

CHAPTER SEVEN

in a downward direction, so Mother sat back down in the car and complained, "Well, I never," punctuating her displeasure with a harrumph.

Daddy slowly approached the house, climbed the two front steps to the porch, and walked up to the front door where he began reading a big placard attached to the door. We were too far away to see what it said, so I hollered out, "Daddy, what's it say? Why can't we get out of the car?"

Again, the downward wave of his right arm and hand but he still didn't turn around. All of a sudden, he started bobbing his head up and down, and then something even stranger.

"Mother, he's talking to the front door. Why's he doing that?" I asked. Sometimes I just couldn't keep my mouth shut. Besides, I was curious, and you have to admit, it looked mighty strange.

"I don't know, Ila. Just be still. We'll see in a minute."

A minute passed. Then two. Then a whole bunch of minutes passed—I don't know how long we sat there before Daddy finally turned and walked across the porch, down the steps and back to the car.

Daddy was as still as a rock when he got back in the car. His eyes were big, and all the color had gone from his face—he looked like he was in shock, not knowing what to say or do. Finally, he turned towards Mother, who had been glaring at him in impatient silence, and said, "Mother, they've got the smallpox there. The whole family is quarantined. We can't stay here."

"What do you mean quarantined? How do you know?"

"That's what the sign on the front door says. 'Quarantined by order of the Board of Health. No one may enter or leave these premises until further notice.'"

"Well, who was you talking to? It looked like you was talking to the door." Mother's voice had a panicky edge to it that hadn't been there earlier.

"Uncle Walter. He was on the other side of the door. He couldn't be more sorry; he's upset that he couldn't let us know before we left the Springs, but he says there's nothing he can do 'til the quarantine ban is lifted."

"And when will that be, does he know?" demanded Mother.

"Course not. The smallpox has to run its course. They just have to wait and see. And their girl's real sick, too."

We fell silent, thinking about a cousin we'd never met, who was very ill, might even die. That we had no place to go and the clock was ticking. It was getting up toward 4:00 p.m.

Metta and I started sniffling. Wava sat in stony silence glaring at Daddy. It didn't take much to make her mad and most of the time she directed her anger towards Daddy, just like Mother did. I was real glad I wasn't him.

"I know this all sounds bad, and it is bad, but Uncle Walter has a solution, so we'll be all right. Just let me sit here a minute to collect myself and I'll explain." Daddy turned towards Mother and gave her a weak smile and patted her left hand before turning back towards the steering wheel. He stared out the windshield for a few moments, took a deep breath and said, "When he realized that we couldn't stay here, and he couldn't notify us, Uncle Walter called his pastor for help. There's a little house—vacant—over by their church and we can stay there 'til we get on our feet. It's small, just a living room, kitchen, two bedrooms, and a privy out in back. But there's a hand pump for water in the kitchen, electricity, a gas range, a fireplace, and some firewood so we won't freeze. Some of the members of the congregation have taken over a little food so we can get through the night. And tomorrow, Sunday, we'll meet the pastor and he'll help us with whatever we need. The parsonage is just on the other side of the church, so he's real close. He can even help us get some furniture, 'cause the house is unfurnished."

Well, it wasn't great, certainly not what we were expecting, but it

CHAPTER SEVEN

wasn't the worst thing either—that would have been sleeping in the car in the cold with no food, water, heat, or access to a bathroom. So, Daddy followed the directions he'd been given and in less than five minutes we were parked in front of the vacant house that was to be our new home.

We were a somber group as we trooped up the two front steps, Daddy in the lead with Mother right behind him, Metta and Wava on either side of Mother, and me bringing up the rear. We had no idea what awaited us, and the sun was getting lower in the sky. It wouldn't be long 'til it was dark.

The little stucco house looked like no one had lived there for a while. Stucco was missing in some places, exposing bricks underneath, while in other places you could see the remaining stucco, which was a faded, dirty tan color. In a couple of spots, it looked like someone had tried to replace the missing stucco with cement, but it looked worse than the spots where the bricks showed through. The house looked unloved and sorrowful the same way we all felt at that moment.

The house was just a box with a cement front porch and a small overhang, supported by two huge brown beams, for a porch roof. The front door was a heavy plain brown slab of wood in the middle of the front wall with two small windows on either side. Firewood had been stacked haphazardly on the porch beside the front door.

Daddy grabbed the front doorknob and turned. It wasn't locked—remember this was 1921 Colorado and nobody locked their doors. When he pushed the door open, a rush of cold air blew into our faces. Daddy stepped inside followed by the rest of us. The room was freezing. A stack of empty wooden boxes of different shapes and sizes and a large pile of rags were the only furnishings in the living room. A single naked light bulb hung down at an angle from a cord in the middle of the living room ceiling. A fireplace, long unused, was centered on one wall between two big windows that in the daytime let light in from the east.

Mother, Wava, Metta and I all huddled around Daddy right inside the front door, looking at the large room. The walls were covered in faded beige wallpaper with small multi-colored flowers scattered throughout. When the wallpaper was new the room must have looked bright and cheery with its pink, blue and yellow trumpet-shaped flowers, but now an atmosphere of benign neglect permeated throughout.

To our right was a small rectangular bedroom—no closet and no curtains—with two small windows that looked out onto the street in front. The old wooden floor was scarred and dusty. Even a little rag rug would have warmed up the room and made it more appealing, but we didn't have a rug. After a disheartening look at the bedroom Daddy turned back towards the kitchen and we all followed.

The kitchen, which was situated directly behind the living room, was big enough for a table and chairs—if we ever got them— and almost as bare as the living room except for an old, scarred white cast iron sink that hung off one wall, and a huge black gas stove that sat against another, but no ice box. It was surprising to see that in spite of all the neglect and age of the house a hand pump sat on the drainboard of the sink. Seeing that, Mother smiled for the first time since we'd entered the house. Another pile of rags lay on the floor by the sink. The only light for this room other than four windows was another single bulb suspended from the ceiling on a dirty cord.

The floor was covered in old red and black linoleum made to look like a braided rug. You could see someone—most likely the previous lady of the house—had stood for hours in front of the sink and the stove. The linoleum in those spots was so worn you could see where the color had faded to grey and pink. And sitting over just inside the back door were two small wooden boxes and a round tin can with the label "Campfire Marshmallows."

CHAPTER SEVEN

"Oh, boy," exclaimed Wava. "I love marshmallows, especially when they're toasted." She ran across the room and picked up the can but the expression on her face changed instantly. "This is too heavy to be marshmallows" and she shook it. "Doesn't sound like marshmallows either." She started to open it, but Mother intervened.

"Put that down, Wava. Daddy, go outside and take a look at that privy before it gets too dark to see. We'll look at this other bedroom." To the right, off the kitchen, was an empty square room, bigger than the first bedroom. After a quick look Mother said, "You girls will sleep in here 'cause this is bigger and you need the space. Daddy and I will take the front bedroom."

As Daddy re-entered the kitchen from the back yard he noted, "Well, Mother, I checked out the privy. It's just a one-holer. Hasn't been used in a long time. But it's so damn cold, don't have to worry about spiders or other bugs right now."

"I found a lantern outside right by the back door. It's full of kerosene so we can use it to see our way to the privy. Just do your business quick and get back into the house."

Mother nodded, turned to Wava, and said, "Now you can bring me the marshmallow tin and we'll see what's there." Mother pried open the top and resting inside, partially wrapped in a clean tea towel, was a big loaf of homemade white bread. It smelled fresh, too.

"Let's see what's in the boxes," said Daddy as he knelt down by them. One box had several jars of home-canned foods—quart jars of peaches, corn, green beans, tomatoes, and some type of vegetable soup plus a pint of preserves. The other had one small metal pan with a handle and several pieces of mismatched china—six cups but no saucers; a cracked platter; four soup bowls, one chipped around the edge; and five plates. The only thing that the china pieces had in common was the flowery decorations and the faded colors from heavy use and countless washings in scalding hot water and homemade lye soap. Several pieces of mismatched tableware including five forks, seven teaspoons, four butter knives and one black-handled steak knife lay at the bottom of the box under the china.

Sitting on the floor, back behind the two boxes, unnoticed 'til now was a small drip coffee pot, and a paper sack with some coffee beans. "Thank the good Lord, I can have some coffee in the morning," exclaimed Daddy as he smiled up at Mother.

"Well," noted Mother, "at least we've got something to eat for tonight and tomorrow morning. We won't starve."

Whatever Mother thought or felt about the house, she didn't indicate to us. After a few seconds she said, "Okay, girls. Why don't you bring those boxes from the living room in here? We'll use them as a table and chairs."

It took us two trips to move in enough boxes for chairs and Daddy had to move the biggest wooden box that sat in a corner of the living room. Once he had moved it into the kitchen, we girls arranged the smaller boxes around it. "I don't like this, Mother," Wava whimpered. "That big box is too short for a table and those other boxes aren't really chairs. I want to go home."

Mother looked at her for a minute, inhaled a deep breath and softly said, "We are home, Wava. These boxes are only temporary. But we have to make do for a while. It's late, we're all hungry and tired. We're going to eat a bite, and then get some sleep. Now wash up at that sink and sit down here."

Mother opened the quart jar of peaches, sliced off five big hunks of bread and passed the preserves—sand hill plum, one of my favorites.

After our meager supper—it doesn't take long to eat bread, jam, and fruit—we huddled together back in the living room while Daddy went outside, grabbed some firewood, and returned to start a fire. He

CHAPTER SEVEN

broke up one of the smaller wooden boxes to use as kindling and in a few minutes warm air began to circulate.

"Girls, it's late. We need to get some sleep."

I don't think we girls had given any thought to bedtime 'til Mother said it, but we all thought the same thing at that moment. Wava beat me to the punch asking the question.

"Where're we going to sleep?"

I turned toward Mother just as Wava asked in a panicky voice, "What are we going to do about beds? I'm tired."

Daddy looked down and didn't say a word. The tip of his right shoe worried a spot on the scarred old linoleum floor—if he'd had more time, he probably would have worn a hole clean through. Mother looked at him but realized he had nothing to offer, so she turned back towards Wava. "Those rags. We'll have to use those rags. Keep your clothes and coats on to stay warm, besides, they'll give you a little extra padding. Spread those rags out on the floor here close to the fireplace. We'll sleep right here tonight. What else can we do?" She didn't expect an answer and she didn't get one. We were too tired to argue but I can tell you it was one of the lowest points of my life—sleeping on that hard floor on a pile of rags and listening to Wava cry. I felt like crying, too, and I think Mother might even have shed a few tears.

We were all awake early the next morning, Sunday. Daddy had to help Mother get up off the floor and she moaned a couple of times as she straightened, put her hands on her hips, and stretched. Daddy moved pretty slow, too.

The fire had burned out hours before and it was so cold you could see your breath when you exhaled. After a mad dash to the outhouse, Daddy started a fire.

Mother called from the kitchen, "Ira, I need your hammer so I can make some coffee." After another dash outside Daddy walked into the kitchen with his hammer while we three girls stood in the living room with our backsides towards the fire soaking up its warmth.

"Whack-crunch! Whack-crunch! Whack-crunch!"

"I haven't had cowboy coffee in a long time, Mother. This is just what I need to warm up and perk up," exclaimed Daddy.

Breakfast was the leftovers from the previous night but satisfying for five empty stomachs. We'd just finished eating when we heard a knock at the front door.

"I'll get it," said Daddy as he walked into the living room. In a few seconds, we heard the sound of two male voices, Daddy's and someone whose voice we didn't recognize.

"Mother, Girls. This is the Rev. McIntyre from next door. He's invited us to services this morning and lunch with him and his good wife afterwards. He says church starts in just a few minutes so he has to get over there. I told him we'd be mighty glad for some new friends and a hot meal."

The church congregation—small by any standard—was welcoming to us strangers. At one point during the service the minister introduced Mother and Daddy to everyone and explained that we were new to Rocky Ford and in need of some help because of a problem with our housing. He didn't go into any more detail, just said we needed some basic stuff to furnish the little house next door while Daddy set up his garage and started working.

Over the next few days household items—a bed frame and feather mattress, some old handmade quilts, mismatched curtains, an ancient wooden table that had long ago been painted robin's egg blue, several wooden chairs, no two alike, and even food—a big sack of potatoes and onions, and two chickens—appeared on the front porch. Although we'd had a difficult start in Rocky Ford, it seemed like things might work out.

Mother and Daddy got a lot done in the few days between our

CHAPTER SEVEN

arrival in Rocky Ford and when Metta and Wava started school. Mother enrolled the girls for the spring 1921 term. Daddy met with a man from the church who offered to let Daddy set up his garage in an empty barn near downtown. Two ladies from the church brought over a huge bag of rags and at night, after the supper dishes were done, Mother sat by the fire working those rags into rugs for the floors. Because it was cold outside and we didn't know anyone, not even our quarantined cousins whom we'd never met. We played or bickered with each other, or helped Mother around the house washing the floors, walls, and windows.

Finally, the big day arrived. Mother woke Wava and Metta extra early so she could braid their hair special for their first day at the new school. We all dressed, and I watched while each girl sat on a box in the kitchen, with Mother standing behind, carefully crossing one hank of hair over another until all the hair was braided. Getting their hair braided looked painful and occasionally Metta or Wava let out an "ouch" which reaffirmed my decision to leave my hair short!

Finally, their hair braided, the girls were ready to leave when Daddy announced, "Okay. Line up. Time for shoelace inspection."

"But Daddy. I'm not going anywhere."

"Don't matter, Ilie. You know the rules." We all groaned because we hated Daddy's shoelace ritual and we couldn't escape it.

Wouldn't you know? Metta and Wava did fine but when he came to me it was another story. "Ila, untie those shoelaces this instant. You know you can't go outside like that. I won't tolerate it." Daddy believed that neat, polished shoes made the man, woman, or child. And second to that was the importance of shoelaces laid flat and straight. If shoelaces were twisted, we were not allowed to go out in public.

"Here, Honey, let me fix 'em." Daddy held my small foot in his lap and put my unruly laces right. One of my happiest days was when Mother bought me a pair of shoes with round laces, and I was no longer under the tyranny of the "straight" shoelaces edict.

Mother and I said goodbye to the two girls and Daddy as they walked out the front door, and Daddy drove them to school for their first day.

Unfortunately, their first day of school at Rocky Ford was the last day of life as I'd known it in the Armsbury family.

EIGHT

With Daddy off to work and the girls at school, everything was quiet and relaxed. I decided to play with the doll that Mrs. Hughes had given me. I wanted to make her some baby clothes from scraps out of Mother's rag bag. Wava and Metta had been gone almost an hour. I was sitting at the kitchen table with a needle and thread, some red flannel, and my doll when I heard the front door burst open followed by hysterical sobbing.

"Mother! Mother! Where are you? Mother!" Wava screamed, each word more piercing than the one before.

Mother had been outside in the privy and just entered the back door as Wava screamed, "I hate him—I hate him. I want to go home! Mother!" We ran into the living room at the same time. Mother walked over and grabbed Wava's left arm as she continued screaming and sobbing. Wava was standing just inside the front door, tears gushing down her cheeks. Her eyes looked wild and her hair was a jumble of tangles, her beautiful braids all undone.

"Wava, what is this? What's wrong?"

But Wava didn't answer. She looked at Mother for a moment as her legs crumpled under her and she collapsed in a heap on the floor. The hysterical sobs were replaced by the sound of heart-felt weeping as she put her hands over her face and moaned. In disjointed words, interrupted by hiccups Wava whispered between sobs, "Mother, he walked into my classroom and just sat down. As big as day."

"Who walked into your classroom? Daddy? Why would he do that? Why are you so upset?"

"No," Wava moaned. "Not Daddy. That boy. Mrs. Wilkerson's son, Earl! He's here in my class. She's here. She's followed us here." Wava stopped talking and began moaning and swaying where she was on the floor.

Throughout Wava's outburst I remained still, just inside the doorway of the living room. I'd never seen anything like this before. Oh, sure. Wava'd been upset at times in the past. She'd cry or yell, but never anything like this. I felt sorry for her and the only thing I could think to do was walk over and put my arm around her shoulder as her sobs grew quieter.

Mother's face looked ashen. She took a step or two back and collapsed onto one of the wooden chairs in the living room. Her head drooped and she stared at the floor. I watched as her lips parted and her breathing slowed. Although her shoulders and chest rose and fell, I couldn't hear her inhaling. After a couple of minutes of trance-like concentration I saw her shoulders straighten as Mother drew in a big breath followed by a bigger sigh. She placed her hands on her upper legs and stood up, took another deep breath then looked at Wava and said:

"Wava, get up off the floor. Go wash your face. If you feel bad, go lay down for a bit. I'm going to walk over to the school and get Metta. I want you to keep an eye on Ila. I'll be back shortly." Mother turned and walked into her bedroom to get her coat.

"But what if Daddy comes home?" asked Wava, the sound of tears in her voice.

Mother pulled on her gloves. "He won't come home before I get back. I'm sure he's with that woman someplace." Then Mother left.

CHAPTER EIGHT

Metta and Mother returned home just before noon. Mother had apparently told Metta about what had happened to Wava earlier in the day because Metta's eyes were red when she entered the house. I was glad to see them because Wava hadn't said two words to me since Mother had left and I was lonely and sad and worried.

"Mother, I'm hungry," I groaned. "Can I have something to eat?"

"Just give me a minute. I need to get my coat hung up before I can fix somethin.'" It turned out to be soup, but it was warm and filling.

After lunch, Mother did something that was out of character for her. She was not known for her warmth. If one of us had a scraped knee or a bloody nose, she'd tell us to stop fussing, clean ourselves up and go back outside or wherever we'd come from. It was Daddy who kissed the hurt fingers or the bruised elbows, who gave hugs and smiles and said, "Now be careful next time. Don't want any injured girls round these parts!"

So, we were all surprised when Mother said, "Girls, I think we need somethin' to cheer us up. I think I'll mix up some cookie dough, and you can help me cut out cookies and bake 'em." Even though it was mid-January, Mother got out her Christmas cookie cutters, a star, a bell, and a round that she used for making wreaths, and we spent the afternoon making sugar cookies. She even mixed up some frosting and colored it so we could have red, blue, and green frosted cookies. Supper that night was cookies and milk, and even though it was a terrible day, I still remember eating cookies for supper and how good they tasted.

To no one's surprise Daddy didn't come home that night. Nobody said anything about his absence—after all, what was there to say? The day had been so emotional that we girls went to bed early— around 7:30. The last thing I remember before I fell asleep was seeing Mother sitting at the kitchen table, staring off into space, with a cup of tea and her Bible nearby, and her head in her hands.

Daylight was coming in through our bedroom windows when I woke up the next morning and that was unusual because Mother woke us up while it was still dark to get the girls ready for school. When I rolled over, I saw Wava and Metta still sound asleep. I was sure something was wrong, so I jumped out of bed and ran into the kitchen only to stop short.

There was Mother, her back to me, standing at the kitchen sink washing the previous night's supper dishes.

"Mother, Wava and Metta are still in bed. Shouldn't they be up and already at school?"

"No, Ila. Yesterday was hard and I got things I need to do today, so I want you girls to stay here. That way I'll know where you are. Might as well wake 'em up though so I can get started."

With that, Mother dried her hands on her apron and walked out of the kitchen toward her bedroom.

"Metta. Wava. Wake up. Mother wants you to get up." "Mmmmm," mumbled Wava. She slowly opened her eyes, blinked and shot out of bed.

"We're late. We're late for school. We're going to get into trouble for sure. Metta! Get up, we're late."

"Wava, it's okay," I explained, trying to calm her.

By this time Metta was awake, too, and they both looked at me with confused expressions. Mother never let them stay home from school unless they were sick.

Metta stretched and yawned and Wava fell back onto the mattress and pulled her blankets up to her chin.

"It's cold in here and if we don't have to go to school I want to stay in bed," she announced.

"No, Wava," exclaimed Mother as she came bustling into the bedroom. "Sloth is one of the seven deadly sins. Now get up and get

CHAPTER EIGHT

dressed. You can go stand in front of the fire to warm up. I want you to eat some breakfast."

Wava muttered but did as she was told. Metta and I dressed in a hurry, too, and rushed into the living room where Wava was already standing with her backside toward the fireplace. If you've ever had a fireplace and been real cold, you know what a joy it is to stand in front of a warm fire, your backside to the heat, your hands rubbing your derriere. The only thing better is to wear a floor-length robe and stand over a floor vent while the furnace is blowing warm air up into your billowing robe. That's heaven!

"Scoot over! You're hogging all the heat," I complained.

"Am not. There's plenty of room."

"Mother, Wava's hogging…" I started to yell but Mother cut me off as she walked into the living room carrying her winter coat, hat, gloves, and purse.

"I don't want to hear it. I want you three to listen to me. As soon as you're warm, go in the kitchen, eat your breakfast—there's oatmeal on the stove—do the dishes and make your beds. Then you can play here in the house, read, whatever. No fighting."

"But where will you be and what're you going to do?" Metta asked.

"I'm goin' to walk over to the parsonage and talk with the pastor. Probably be back about lunch time. If I'm not, there's soup sittin' on the back porch." Winter's deep freeze worked great if you didn't have an ice box.

By this time Mother had her coat on and buttoned and was walking toward the front door. "What are you going to talk about? What are you going to do?" I was always an inquisitive child—Wava preferred 'nosy'—and couldn't refrain from asking.

"Ila…girls…just do as you're told. I'll be back as soon as I can," then she was gone.

When she returned, Mother explained that at her request the pastor drove her to the Western Union office, where Mother sent a telegram to Grandma Rosenie. All we knew at the time was that late on the same day, a messenger arrived at the front door with a telegram for Mother. We girls were excited because it was the first time someone in our family had received a telegram and it made us feel important.

After reading the telegram, Mother folded it up and put it in the front pocket of her heavy woolen dress.

"It's from Grandma Rosenie. She's sendin' us money and we're goin' home tomorrow. We're goin' back to Lucas, so girls, I want you to pack up your clothes and toys. Nothin' else. There's a train leavin' here at 8:30 tomorrow morning and we'll be on it. Now, I need to go over and talk to the pastor again. I'll be back soon as I can."

Mother woke us up early the next morning, around 5:30, so we could dress, eat, and get the rest of our things together. At 7:00 a.m. we carried our few possessions over to the pastor's house, got in his car, and he drove us to the train station. By 8:35 a.m. Rocky Ford, with all its painful memories, was a thing of the past, and, as far as we girls knew, so was Daddy.

NINE

Our train pulled into the Ellsworth station around 6:30 p.m. It felt like we'd been on it for weeks because we hadn't eaten a thing since breakfast; there'd been no money to buy food for a packed lunch or to purchase food on the train. We gathered our few belongings and stumbled off the train into the welcoming arms of Grandpa Newt and Grandma Rosenie who were waiting on the platform. Grandma held Mother in a protective bear hug as Mother sobbed.

Grandpa Newt gave Mother a couple of awkward pats on the back before he stepped forward, took his hat off and said, "Girls, I'm mighty glad to see you and even gladder you're home. Let's go."

"Grandpa," I said, "Daddy's not with us. We left him and didn't even get to say goodbye. How'll he know where to find us?"

"He doesn't care a whit about us, you can bet," Wava snarled. "I don't want him to find us 'cause I don't ever want to see him again." Her head shot up, her chin jutted out, her lips were compressed into one grim scowl.

I was shocked and so was Metta. I couldn't imagine never seeing Daddy again and we both started crying. "Mother," I sobbed, "you want to see Daddy, don't you?"

After a couple of minutes of continued weeping, Mother's tears subsided. She pulled a handkerchief from her coat pocket, blew her nose, and wiped her eyes. Turning toward me, she said, "This ain't the time or place to talk... I'm hungry. Ain't you? We haven't had nothing to eat since breakfast."

"Well," Grandpa Newt jumped in, "can't have growin' girls goin' without food. There's some fine restaurants here in Ellsworth and I think we could all use us a bite," Grandpa smiled as he turned toward the pile of crates, trunks, and luggage piled on the platform beside the baggage car. "But first let me get your trunks or what-have-you."

"That's okay," said Mother as she again wiped her dripping nose on her handkerchief. "This is everything."

Grandpa started to ask something, but I saw Grandma Rosenie stare at him and shake her head, so he clamped his mouth shut.

"Come on, girls. Mother," Grandpa said. "We got starvin' people here and we need to find some food quick." He set off at his usual brisk pace and led us toward the car. Because Grandpa's legs were so long, I had to run to keep up.

As we piled into Grandpa's car, Grandma Rosenie asked, "Newt, where we goin'? It's supper time and won't be many places open this time of night, or if they are, they'll be full."

"We're goin' to The Baker House. These girls need some good food and lots of it, and I can't think of no better place than that." It didn't take but a couple of minutes before Grandpa parked the car in front of the Baker House Hotel and Restaurant and we all trooped inside.

Talk about elegant! I'd never seen anything like it in my life. The dining room had huge windows which let in the light during the day. Because it was night, the room was illuminated by gorgeous, ornate chandeliers. The room was big—you could seat one hundred people easily and still have plenty of room to move around. The walls were covered in an elegant wallpaper with large cabbage roses of deep reds, pinks, purples, and yellows; blue delphinium, cheery white daisies with vibrant orange

CHAPTER NINE

centers; and lush green vines and leaves. The ceiling repeated the pattern of vines in embossed tin ceiling tiles.

I had never seen such a beautiful room in my life, and it was in little Ellsworth, Kansas of all places. What, I wondered, was it like in other places? Were there rooms even bigger and more elegant? I wanted to find out. As we were being seated Mother turned to us girls and said in a hushed voice, "Mind your manners."

Faces were grim around the table until a waitress began setting plates of hot steaming food down in front of us. No one spoke until after we'd each had a few forkfuls of meatloaf, mashed potatoes and gravy, smothered steak, or green beans. Grandpa Newt was the first one to speak up.

"Girls, how did you like riding on a train?"

Wava scowled as she replied. "I didn't want to ride on that old train 'cause I didn't want to move but Mother made me."

Grandma Rosenie cut her off. "Wava, that's enough. Your mother's had a hard row and done the best she could. Now eat your supper." That shut Wava up for the rest of the meal which was just fine with me because by that time I had lots to say.

"Grandpa, that train was the best one ever. I'd ride a train to the moon if I could," I couldn't help grinning as I told Grandpa and Grandma about everything we saw.

"Have you ever seen a mountain, Grandma? I bet mountains are taller than giants and if you climbed to the top of one you'd see the whole world, and that's what I want to do when I grow up."

Grandpa chuckled. "Climb to the top of a mountain or see the whole world?"

"Both. I want to do both," I grinned and laughed.

By the time we were done eating and Grandpa had paid for supper I could barely keep my eyes open. I noticed that Mother's head was drooping, too, and Metta and Wava were slumped down in their chairs,

Metta's head listing to one side, and Wava's head leaned back, her eyes closed and her mouth slightly open. Grandma Rosenie roused us from our stupor, and we stumbled out of the restaurant towards the car.

I staggered behind the rest of the family, fell onto the car seat and was asleep almost the minute the car door closed. I don't remember a thing about the drive to Lucas because when we got home, I went straight to bed. I slept with Maxine while Wava and Metta slept with two of our other aunts.

* * *

Lucas is located in north central Kansas, in the middle of the ancient North American inland sea—no ocean or beaches for swimming or sunbathing for millions of years—just miles of rolling hills and scenic valleys covered with prairie grass, streams—full of fish—which drew birds and other wildlife, and acres of limestone deposits, chock-full of fossils, which were mined and turned into fence posts by early settlers in the late 1800s because there was precious little timber. The weather was unpredictable. Hot, humid summers with temperatures of $100°$ or more, breezes that could turn into tornadoes with little warning, and arctic cold winters with winds that could freeze tears on your cheeks.

By 1900, Lucas had a population of about 500 souls, and farming was the primary business. Buildings on the dirt main street were made of limestone blocks while houses were either limestone or wood. Big families were common because of the need for lots of hands— cheap labor—for planting and harvesting—and Grandpa Newt's was one of the biggest families around.

* * *

CHAPTER NINE

When Max and I walked into the kitchen the next morning, we found Mother sitting at the kitchen table cutting up dough for noodles while Grandma was at the counter deboning a stewed hen for homemade chicken and noodles.

"Where's Wava and Metta?" I wondered.

"I took 'em over to the school first thing this morning and enrolled 'em so they won't be home 'til this afternoon. Now, you go play and stay out of our hair. We got cookin' to do and don't need no help from two little girls."

Our days quickly took on a predictable routine. Max and I played or bickered, as all children do, or helped Mother and Grandma Rosenie until my sisters and aunts arrived home after school. Once they completed their homework, we played until supper.

Grandpa Newt was an early riser and gone during the morning, so we only saw him for dinner at noontime, and late in the afternoons when he got home from working on the ranch.

One evening during supper, after we'd been at Grandma and Grandpa's about a week, Metta turned to Mother and asked, "When are we going home? I miss our house in Waldo."

Mother stopped eating, put down her fork, and looking chagrined, turned toward Metta. "I don't know. Don't have no money to pay for food or utilities. I 'spose I should get a job but how'd I get to one? Don't have no car." Mother looked defeated as she heaved a sigh and turned to look at Grandma Rosenie.

"Well, that's something to think about. Let's talk about this after the young'uns are in bed," Grandpa suggested.

The next evening, we realized the discussion about returning to Waldo was moot. We were eating supper when Grandpa Newt announced, "I was at the bank this afternoon and heard somethin' you should know. That woman, Mrs. Wilkerson, is back in Waldo."

Everyone stopped what they were doing and stared at Grandpa as he continued, "Heard that she's filed for divorce…or her husband has… don't know which." Not understanding the import of Grandpa's announcement, I started to say something but Metta piped in. "If Mrs. Wilkerson's in Waldo, Daddy must be there, too. Can we go see? I miss him and I'm sure he needs us."

"No! I don't wanna see Daddy and I can't ever live in Waldo again," screamed Wava. "Everybody probably knows she's his girlfriend. I'll never get over the humiliation and shame. People'll look at me and point and whisper and I just can't take it."

"What do you mean 'girlfriend'? What's wrong with having girlfriends?" I asked. I couldn't understand why Wava was so mad at Daddy. Wava and Metta had girlfriends, too, and I knew that because sometimes they came over to the house to play after school.

Wava started to sputter indignantly, "What's wrong with a girlfriend? Are you stupid?"

"That's enough," Mother proclaimed as she glared at Wava. Then she turned toward Grandpa and asked in a subdued tone of voice, "Is Ira there, too?"

"Don't know, but I don't think so. Otherwise I'da heard about it. I think it's just her and that boy of hers back at the Wilkerson house. Thought I'd drive over to Waldo in the mornin' and look around, check your house, see if everything's okay. I can tell in a minute if anybody's livin' there. I'll ask and see if anybody's seen Ira." Nothing more was said about Daddy until the next evening.

* * *

"I went over to Waldo," Grandpa said as he heaped food on his supper plate, "and went by your house. Ain't nobody livin' there far as I can

CHAPTER NINE

tell. The door was locked. I looked in the windows—there's dust on everything."

"Where's my Daddy?" I cried. "Something bad coulda happened to him."

Metta nodded in agreement, and even Wava looked concerned although she tried to hide it by taking a bite of a hot homemade biscuit dripping with butter.

"He's not in Rocky Ford," Grandma Rosenie said as she looked from Mother to Grandpa Newt. "I wrote Walter after Florence and the girls got here. If Ira was there, he'd a told me."

Now we had even more things to worry about. Where were we going to live? Where would Mother get money? And where was Daddy? But at that time adults didn't talk about problems or anything else of substance with their children present. So, after supper Metta and I slipped out of the kitchen and went upstairs where we could be alone, and I could ask her about Daddy's girlfriend.

* * *

Poor Metta. When we were both grown, we talked about that conversation and how uncomfortable it was for her, trying to explain to me the difference between a girlfriend from school, like her friends, and Mary Wilkerson, Daddy's girlfriend.

* * *

As hard as it was for Metta to tell me, it was equally hard for me to hear her explanation.

"Metta, are you mad at Daddy, too?"

She didn't answer me right away. She bowed her head and sat still for a minute before whispering, "Yes."

"You don't sound mad. You're not yelling like Wava."

"No, I'm not. What good would it do?" She looked up at me as she said that, and I saw a tear run down her face.

"Why are you crying? Are you sad, too?"

"Yeah, I'm sad."

"Why?"

"Because this isn't how it's supposed to be. Daddies are supposed to be home with their wives and their children and ours isn't. I want him to be like other daddies. To love us and come home and make Mother happy so she won't cry all the time, but he doesn't do that, and I don't understand why. Sometimes I think he doesn't really love us."

"Oh, Metta." It was my turn to put my arms around her and comfort her as tears fell into her lap.

"He is like other daddies. He does love us. I know he does."

"Maybe you're right, Ila. But he sure does get into trouble a lot." I nodded in agreement and that ended our conversation about why everyone was mad at Daddy.

My dad's adultery was just one more injury in a long line of transgressions against us. But for us girls, not including Eloise who missed so much of the family drama because she wasn't born until mid-1921, his abandoning us for another woman was the first of many open wounds we girls suffered before we were old enough to make our own decisions and control our own destinies. When I look back now, it's a wonder to me how well each of us healed…or didn't.

**

Talk at the supper table about Mrs. Wilkerson's presence and Daddy's absence ceased as did discussion about our living situation. So, I was

CHAPTER NINE

surprised when Max and I went down to breakfast a few mornings later and Mother wasn't there.

With the help of Grandpa Newt, Mother found a job at a small restaurant, a fixture at the north end of Lucas' main street. Farmers and businessmen gathered there every morning for coffee and gossip, and local families went for inexpensive home-cooked meals. The fare was hearty and simple, what you'd expect from a small cafe in rural Kansas in the 1920s. A typical breakfast was eggs fried in bacon grease, four strips of crispy bacon, and homemade bread slathered with butter and homemade preserves all for $.25 including refillable cups of strong, black coffee. Dinner and supper meals were just as filling and cheap.

"Grandma, where's Mother? She still in bed?"

"'Course not. She's at work—been there since 5:00 a.m."

I wish I could tell you that having a job and earning her own money increased Mother's self-confidence, but that wasn't the case. Instead, she was ashamed that she had to work, that she couldn't rely on her husband to support the family. In spite of her dismay, Mother toiled in the cafe's kitchen. She was up at 4 a.m. and at work by 5. She made her fabulous cinnamon rolls one day and her pecan sticky rolls the next—the cafe always sold out of both by 9:00 a.m. She cooked all the breakfast and lunch orders and never got home until after 2:00 p.m. when she took a nap 'til about 4:00 p.m.

Afterwards, she helped Grandma Rosenie with supper and was in bed by 7:00 p.m. only to get up and do it all over again the next day. The only variation to her work routine was Sundays when she cut up and fried over a hundred chickens, whipped heaps of mashed potatoes, and made her incredible cream gravy for the Sunday dinner crowd.

To the end of her life, Mother was embarrassed that she had only a fifth-grade education. She was never able to help any of us girls with our homework, something she found deeply humiliating. Little did she know how educational it was for me to watch her work.

So Wava, Metta and the older aunts were in school during the day. Mother was at work. I was at home with my aunt, Maxine, and Grandma Rosenie, and Grandpa worked at the ranch. Our days gave us comfort—no chaos—no excitement—no hurried moves from one house or one town to another. Just when I was getting used to the calm, a house guest showed up and everything changed again.

TEN

"Florence, you almost ready to go?" Grandpa asked as he stood up from the breakfast table on Saturday morning.

"Where you goin'? Can I go, too?" Grandpa was deluged by requests from his daughters and granddaughters, including me. If he was taking the car we wanted to go along for the ride.

"No. Nobody's goin' except Florence. We're drivin' down to Ellsworth to pick up her sister from the train station. She's gonna visit for a few days."

Aunt Lottie was closest in age to Mother at only two years her senior and married to Oat Trexler. She and Uncle Oat owned Trexler's Market, a grocery store in Hill City, Kansas. Although Mother and Aunt Lottie had been raised by the same set of parents, and had similar facial features, their temperaments could not have been more different.

Aunt Lottie had been in the house less than twenty minutes when she began her campaign to let Mother and everyone else know what she thought about the state of Mother's marriage. As she unpacked her valise Aunt Lottie, her face grim, said, "Florence, divorce him. Who knows where he is or what he's doin'. Whatever it is, it can't be good."

Mother, who was helping Lottie unpack, dropped the dress she was getting ready to hang in the closet, turned towards Aunt Lottie and gasped, "I can't do that, Lottie. What would people say?"

"What do you think they're sayin' now? You know as well as I do that some men just ain't made for marryin' and I'm afraid Ira's one of 'em." Mother's face lost all its color, and she was so upset she excused herself and went to lay down.

That night at the dinner table Aunt Lottie continued her campaign, skillfully directing the supper conversation to point out more of Daddy's weaknesses. Aunt Lottie had changed from her traveling dress into a simple, long-sleeved dark blue dress and re-done her hair.

"Well, I feel rested now. All unpacked. But, Florence, you look tuckered out this evening even though you laid down for a while. You okay?"

I hadn't noticed until Aunt Lottie pointed it out, but Mother's face did look drawn and pale, and there was a slight tremor in her hands. "I'm fine, Lottie. Just real tired tonight and my back aches more'n usual."

"My goodness I know just how that is. Thank the good Lord Oat helps me. That's the difference when you got a helpmate instead of some sluggard runnin' around drinkin' and carousin' all day."

Lottie looked over at Grandpa Newt, who nodded in agreement, and at Grandma Rosenie, who stared intently at a spot on the tablecloth.

At the time I worried that Aunt Lottie would hurt Mother and Grandma Rosenie's feelings and it wasn't until years later I realized her intent was to get Grandpa Newt's support because Mother respected him and his opinions. And Grandpa Newt had to walk a fine line because he didn't want to hurt Rosenie by saying that her oldest son was a drunkard and a philanderer, both of which were unfortunately true.

Living with a houseful of relatives—Grandpa, Grandma, our aunts, Mother, and now her sister—made it hard for Wava, Metta, and me to find a way to be alone so we could talk about the whole business of

CHAPTER TEN

divorce. But we managed one day after school because when they arrived home Wava told our aunts that we were going to make cards for Mother for Easter, so our aunts went outside to play and left us alone.

We went up to Wava's room and sat down on the bed. Metta was the first to say something.

"I don't know how I feel about Mother divorcing Daddy. I never thought of it until Aunt Lottie brought it up."

"Me neither," Wava chimed in, "but I hope she does it. Good riddance is what I say."

"Wava, how can you be so mean? He's our dad and he loves us," the words rushed out of my mouth.

"Oh yeah? Well, he has a funny way of showin' it doesn't he? He's embarrassed us, humiliated Mother, now she has to work and she's never home when we get home from school …"

Metta cut her off. "That's not true and you know it. She is too home before we get home. She's just in bed, taking a nap 'cause she's tired."

"Well, that's the same as not bein' home 'cause she's not there for me to talk to. Besides, there's never enough money and I hate wearing those hand-me-down dresses from our aunts. I want store-bought clothes in the styles I see in the papers and in the magazines. I want pretty things and a nice house, and we don't have any of that. Not like Grandma and Grandpa do."

Neither Metta nor I knew how to respond to Wava. This wasn't the first time she'd complained about her lack of new clothes and other finery.

"Well," I said, "I don't want them to get divorced. I don't know anybody whose parents are divorced. I don't even know what it means to be divorced. Do you?"

"It means," Wava said in a snotty tone of voice, "that they won't be living in the same house. We'll be with Mother and Daddy can live wherever he wants to and do whatever he wants to, and we won't be embarrassed by him anymore."

"I don't think it means just that, Wava." Metta replied. "I think it means that it won't be easy for us to see Daddy or for him to see us. And it might be harder on Mother although I don't really know how 'cause I don't know anyone who's divorced either."

We couldn't agree among ourselves but fortunately or not, our opinions weren't asked for and Mother did what she thought was best, the end result being that Mother finally decided to get a divorce. It was filed on May 9, 1921, on the grounds of adultery and gross neglect of duty. However, the filing contained our next big surprise—Mother was pregnant, and the baby was due in August.

ELEVEN

I wonder now what Mother felt when she discovered she was pregnant again and married to a man who didn't support the three children he already had? Despair? Fear? Hatred of Daddy? Self-loathing because she'd agreed to have marital relations even after she'd moved all of us into Mrs. Hughes' house? There are lots of things you realize, after the death of your parents, that you wish you would have asked or told them when they were still alive. You grieve over missed opportunities, insights you might have gained if only you'd thought to ask.

Praise you could have offered. I realized many years after her death that Mother was braver than I ever gave her credit for.

My baby sister, Eloise, was born on August 19, 1921, four weeks after my sixth birthday. Mother returned to work at the restaurant as soon as she could and with the help of all our aunts, uncles, and cousins, she rented a little house in Lucas and furnished it, so we were finally able to live on our own.

It was the tiniest house I've ever lived in—a living room big enough for a sofa and a table with four chairs and just enough room to walk around without bumping into each piece of hand-me-down furniture. The kitchen was behind the living room and was furnished with a decrepit and filthy gas range and a scarred cast iron sink with attached drain boards on either side of the sink. The whole thing was set on iron legs against the back wall—no hand pump for water so we had to fill a bucket from a pump outside the back door. Dirty water drained from the sink by a pipe that extended through the wall out to the far edge of the yard behind our house near the privy. The sole bedroom was off the living room and was just barely big enough for Wava, Metta, and me. Metta and Wava slept together in one bed and I slept on a cot. We had a dresser with three drawers, one for each of us and nails pounded into the dingy white plaster walls for our hanging clothes.

Eloise slept in the kitchen in an old cradle that Grandma Rosenie had used for her babies, and Mother slept in a claustrophobic little closet—it might have been intended as a pantry—off the kitchen. She kept her clothes and Eloise's in two wooden crates under her bed.

Mother's divorce hearing was held on October 3, 1921. I've rarely seen her look worse than she did that day. She dressed carefully in one of her few "good" dresses, a dark brown woolen with a high collar, long sleeves, and a set-in waist. You could tell she hadn't slept much the night before by the huge bags under her eyes. She wore a prim brown hat, white gloves—that's all she had—and sensible brown shoes. Her brown purse held a clean cotton handkerchief—just in case—and another was stuffed up her left sleeve ready for use at a moment's notice. Her face was pale and drawn and while she rarely smiled, that morning she looked positively grim and defeated.

Of course, we children weren't allowed to go but the following Sunday, after dinner at Grandpa and Grandma's, Metta and I overheard Mother telling Grandma Rosenie what had happened.

"Was Ira there, Florence?"

"No but his attorney was."

"How'd you feel about that, not seein' him?"

"Relieved…sad…tired."

"What happened?"

CHAPTER ELEVEN

"I had to tell the judge about what happened… you know… about that woman and Ira, and Colorado and such—no money, the girls doing without…" We could hear Mother sniffling, and once she stopped talking and blew her nose, as she told Grandma about the hearing.

* * *

When I think back to Mother's day in court, I can't imagine anyone less prepared for that than she. She had been raised to believe that marriage was for life and that her role in her marriage was to submit and endure, no matter how awful. Add to that her lifelong fear of being alone—it's a wonder she went through with the divorce.

When the hearing was over, the judge gave her custody of us children, possession of the house in Waldo, the Overland auto, and $50.00 per month in alimony. Daddy was ordered to pay attorneys' fees and the mortgage on the house.

And that's when Daddy's troubles really began.

TWELVE

Why can't every day be like this? I wondered as Wava, Metta and I walked home from school one late October afternoon two weeks after the divorce. I was six years old and had finally joined my sisters at school. I was learning the joys of the play yard at recess and putting faces to the names of boys and girls I had heard Metta and Wava talk about for so long.

The air was crisp, not too cool, just right for long sleeves or a light jacket. We were crunching leaves as we walked on the sidewalk toward home. I love the smell of fall leaves—a bouquet of dust, mold, and moisture. I wasn't paying much attention to our surroundings and was startled when Wava said, "Quick. Cross the street. Here comes Mr. Dinsmoor."

S. P. Dinsmoor was what you'd call a character. Years after the Civil War in which he fought for the North, Mr. Dinsmoor and his first wife and children moved to Lucas and Mr. Dinsmoor began working as a sculptor—in cement. He built a large twelve-room home—fashioned to look like a log cabin—from cement. After that, he began building the Garden of Eden, at least his interpretation of it, complete with concrete serpents hanging from the branches of concrete trees scattered around the property. His pièce de résistance was the mausoleum with two glass-covered sarcophagi, one for him and one for his first wife.

CHAPTER TWELVE

The good Christian citizens of Lucas were already unhappy with Mr. Dinsmoor's recreation of the Garden of Eden. Some thought it was blasphemy pure and simple. Mother called him "evil." After Mr. Dinsmoor's first wife died and he, at the age of 81, married his 20-year-old housekeeper and fathered two more children, the Lucas citizenry knew that Satan must somehow be involved. So even though we crossed the street as Mother instructed, we stared at Mr. Dinsmoor and pondered what life was like behind the closed doors of his peculiar home.

Who would have ever thought that over the years Mr. Dinsmoor's Garden of Eden would become so famous? People from all over the world travel to see it now because it is so incredibly fantastic. Closer to home, Lucas is known as the Grassroots Art Capital of Kansas and the Garden is one of the eight wonders of the state. It makes me proud to say I'm a Kansan!

* * *

As we turned the corner of our street, we saw that Grandpa Newt's car was parked in front of our house, right behind Mother's. It was unusual for Grandpa to be anyplace but the ranch in the middle of the afternoon, so we ran the last few yards home to see what had happened.

Mother was half sitting and half laying on the sofa, her face ashen and her eyes closed. Grandpa Newt was sitting beside her, watching her intently, his hat in one hand and a handkerchief in the other. Grandma Rosenie was walking the floor carrying Baby Eloise, but Eloise wasn't fussing at bit. In fact, she was sound asleep.

"Mother, what's wrong?" Wava asked, her voice trembling with fear.

No answer.

A little louder and more desperately sounding, Wava tried again.

"Mother, what's happened? Is something wrong?"

No answer.

Metta tried this time, a little different approach. Her voice was calm as usual, but her eyes were bright and flicked from Mother to Grandpa to Grandma and back again.

"Grandpa. What's wrong with Mother?"

He cleared his throat a couple of times before saying in a quiet voice that slowly increased in volume, "It's your father. He's been arrested. He's in jail." By the time he'd said the word "jail" Grandpa sounded like the thunderous voice of God, not a good sign at any time. No one said a word. We'd never known anyone who'd been arrested. There couldn't possibly be anything more scandalous than arrest, could there?

Finally, Wava was able to find her voice and in a shaky tone asked, "Why?"

"That's just it, honey," Grandpa said. "We don't know."

By this time Mother had sort of recovered from her shock. She opened her eyes and sat up straighter on the sofa, smoothed the skirt of her dress, and patted her hair, which was slipping out of the bun she'd made early in the day.

"It must be a mistake, I'm sure. Ira's done lots of things we disapprove of, but I can't imagine that he's done anything that would get him arrested."

After some discussion it was decided that Grandpa would take us girls and Grandma Rosenie to their house, before he and Mother drove to the county jail, in Russell, and find out what had happened.

Mother and Grandpa didn't get back to the house until well after supper. When we saw Grandpa's car park beside the house all us girls— our aunts, my sisters, and I—ran to the front door and crowded around it, anxious to hear what they had learned.

"Girls. Get back," Grandpa Newt ordered, his voice sounding tired

CHAPTER TWELVE

and strained. "We haven't had a bite to eat. Let's get somethin' in our stomachs and then we'll tell you what we know, which ain't much," Grandpa said as he hung his coat and hat on the hall tree and walked toward the kitchen. Mother, her shoulders slumped, trailed slowly behind.

After what seemed like an eternity, Grandpa pushed his plate to one side, wiped his mouth with his napkin, and turned to us girls who had been standing quietly near the kitchen table.

"Ira's been charged with white slavery," Grandpa said, his voice grave.

Mother's chin dropped to her chest and she began to sob.

Grandma Rosenie gasped but the rest of us just looked puzzled.

Grandpa swallowed hard once or twice and said, "It's like kidnapping. Mrs. Wilkerson says that your daddy kidnapped her and took her to Colorado."

The upshot of Daddy's arrest was that the Armsbury name was null and void in our part of Kansas. Not only that, but Mother lost the house in Waldo because with Daddy in jail there was no money to pay the mortgage.

It wasn't until we were adults that we finally uncovered the details of Daddy's arrest. After obtaining her own divorce and learning that Mother and Daddy were divorced, Mrs. Wilkerson started putting pressure on Daddy to marry her. When he refused, she went to the Russell County Sheriff and told him that Daddy had transported her across state lines against her will "for immoral purposes."

None of us girls, not even our aunts, were allowed to go to the trial and we never heard any discussion about it from Mother, Grandma or Grandpa. Our knowledge of what happened, who said what to whom, and the court testimony came from classmates whose parents attended the trial and talked about the salacious details in front of their children.

ILA'S WAR

The trial was held in Russell.

The first person to testify was the Russell County Sheriff, W. H. Sellens. His testimony was brief and straightforward.

"Mrs. Mary E. Wilkerson of Waldo, Kansas, came to my office on ____, 1921. She said that the defendant, Ira Ray Armsbury, took her to Colorado against her will and forced her to have sexual relations with him." Snickers from a couple of men and gasps and moans from some of the ladies—ladies who wouldn't be caught dead in public without their hats, gloves and other finery, but who wouldn't miss the gory details of a sex trial for anything—emanated from the audience.

Mrs. Wilkerson was the next witness and boy did she spin a tale. "Although I am a respectable divorced woman," apparently there was a lot of snickering and laughter at this point, at least that's what I was told, "I have made the acquaintance of several men because of my job," she explained.

"And what is your job, Mrs. Wilkerson? Please tell the judge." instructed the prosecuting attorney.

"I work at the cream station in Waldo. We sell fresh cream, milk, and butter. Sometimes eggs, but not usually."

"Go on, please. Tell the judge what happened."

"Well, you know there's the big Decoration Day gatherin' at the Delhi Cemetery every year. We do a lot of business just before Decoration Day what with people buyin' cream and milk and such for homemade ice cream."

"Well, Mr. Armsbury, he come in and bought cream and milk. Said he was makin' ice cream for the celebration. We talked about ice cream, the price of cream and milk, it's goin' up you know, and I guess that's about all."

"Mrs. Wilkerson, please tell the court about how you wound up in Colorado with the defendant."

CHAPTER TWELVE

"Yeah, I'm sorry. You see, one evenin', I don't exactly remember when, but it was chilly out, so's I had to get my jacket, Mr. Armsbury come to my house. Said his wife had made some homemade ice cream and would I like to come over and have some seein' as how we had talked at the beginning of summer about ice cream. Had his car, you see, had drove over to my house and said he'd take me to his house and bring me back home, I wouldn't of walked in the dark which I don't want to do seein' as how it's easy to trip and fall and besides that it was cold and I catch cold easy."

"So's I said, 'well, okay. I love ice cream and it's mighty nice of you and Mrs. Armsbury to think of me' so's I fetched my wrap, and we went out to his car, and I got in and we drove off."

"It didn't take but a minute afore I knew somethin' was wrong 'cause he didn't drive toward his house. He drove out of town headin' west and he just kept on agoin' and he didn't stop, even when I said I needed to iron my shoelaces."

"Beg pardon? Mrs. Wilkerson what does that mean, 'iron your shoelaces?'"

"You know…you know. Iron my shoelaces! The john? The bathroom? He wouldn't stop even when I said I needed to go to the bathroom. He just drove all night, just drove clean through. Even if he'd a stopped what was I goin' to do? We was out in the country in the dark someplace I don't know where. I'd a had to get back in the car with him so he took me to Colorado, and I didn't want to go."

It wasn't Daddy's testimony that demolished her story. It was Mother's. That's right. Even though they were divorced. Even after everything Daddy had put her through, Mother testified on Daddy's behalf at the trial. She told the judge that it simply wasn't true that Daddy had taken Mrs. Wilkerson anyplace against her will.

"That woman followed him every place he went, and he tried to get away from her. He went to Lincoln, to Natoma, to Osborne, to Luray, and I don't know where all. Finally, we decided…"

"Who's 'we,' Mrs. Armsbury?" interjected the prosecuting attorney.

"Me and Ira. We decided that he'd have to go away a lot farther than he'd done before. So, he went to Colorado Springs. Everything seemed okay so he asked me and the girls to come visit and we did. And it was shortly after that that she showed up… I don't know how she found out, and Ira swears he didn't tell her…"

"Your Honor. I object. The witness cannot testify as to what the defendant said."

"Sustained. Mrs. Armsbury, please refrain from repeating what your husband said to you. We'll let him tell us himself."

"Yes Sir. I'm sorry, sir. This is just so hard." According to some of our classmates' parents, that's when Mother started crying on the witness stand and the judge offered to stop the questioning for a bit, but Mother said no.

"Please continue, Mrs. Armsbury."

"Well. She, umm Mrs. Wilkerson, showed up in Colorado Springs so after a while, Ira took me and the girls and we went to Rocky Ford, Colorado, to where one of Ira's uncles lives and wouldn't you know it? She showed up there, too."

"How do you know 'she showed up there'? Did you see her?"

"Well, no, I didn't. But her son, he's the same age as my Wava, who's 13 now. Her son walked into Wava's classroom on her first day of school in Rocky Ford and that's how I knew she was there.

"She just followed us everywhere and we couldn't get away from her. Ira's done lots of things I don't approve of, but he never kidnapped that woman. He never took her against her will to Colorado." Mother's testimony brought the trial to a halt. The judge scolded Daddy from the

CHAPTER TWELVE

bench—told him to go home to Lucas, to his wife. Make up with her, get remarried, and stop chasing skirts. Then he turned to Mrs. Wilkerson and threw the book at her. Called her a liar and a whore. Said he'd put her in jail just for the hell of it if he could. Said he was damn sorry for her husband and understood why he'd divorced her soon as he could and good riddance.

The judge dismissed the charges, told the sheriff to release Daddy, and ordered the court records destroyed. And that was the end of Daddy's three-year affair with Mrs. Wilkerson.

∗ ∗ ∗

"Wava, do you think the trial is over yet?" I asked as we—Wava, Metta, Maxine and I—walked toward Grandma Rosenie's house after school.

"I don't know, and I don't care. Just so long as he stays away from me," Wava grumbled. "Everybody's talkin' about it, and it's so embarrassing. I wish I could just crawl into a hole and pull it in after me."

Maxine ran up the stairs of the back porch ahead of the rest of us, opened the back door, and hollered. "Your dad's right here, and so's your mother."

Metta and I ran past Wava up the steps and into the house, crowding around our folks who were sitting at Grandma's kitchen table drinking coffee. Grandpa and Grandma were there, too.

It was like Christmas, only better, and my gift was my dad, sitting there as big as glory. I started to ask what had happened but Wava, who had stopped and was standing in the doorway growled, "What're you doin' here?"

Daddy turned toward her and offered her an embarrassed smile as he replied, "Hi, Honey." Wava bristled when he said "Honey" and glared at Daddy. He pretended not to notice and continued, "It's good to see you—it's good to see all you girls. I've missed you."

At this, Wava turned to Grandpa Newt and asked again, "Grandpa, what's he doin' here? Is the trial over?"

"Yeah, it's over. The judge dismissed the charges and told your dad to go home and make up with your mother so …"

Wava didn't wait around to hear any more. She just stomped through the kitchen into the dining room. We listened to her heavy footsteps as she walked into the front hall and climbed the stairs.

"Are you coming home with us now, Daddy?" I asked, hopeful that we could now resume what passed for normal in our family life.

Daddy didn't get a chance to answer because Mother jumped right in. "'Course he ain't coming home with us. We're not married, and I ain't livin' with him in sin." So, we—Mother, Wava, Metta, Baby Eloise, and I returned to our house just after supper that night and Daddy took up residence at Grandma and Grandpa's.

**

Wava, Metta and I had, not surprisingly, very different reactions to the divorce, arrest, and trial. Wava was absolutely humiliated and didn't want to be seen in public with Daddy—anyplace—any time.

Metta continued in her role as the overachieving, good daughter. She tried to help both Mother and Daddy in everything they did. But Metta watched and listened as everything unfolded. One of the things that most affected her was hearing Mother say over and over how she wished she'd stayed in school. Metta took that to heart and decided that after high school she would go to college.

As for me, I was very unhappy about the divorce when it happened and very frightened when my dad was arrested and jailed. That's probably

CHAPTER TWELVE

a pretty normal response for a kid. But watching my dad's exploits, even though I didn't completely understand everything, and seeing the enormous pain on my mother's face, made me angry. The end result was that over the next few years, I started talking back to my dad and that didn't always go well for me. I also resolved that when I married, I would marry a man unlike my father—someone who would be true to me and to our wedding vows.

* * *

Daddy took the judge's admonition about remarrying Mother to heart and immediately began courting her. Each evening, Daddy called on Mother bringing one of his sisters to act as a chaperone at Mother's insistence. After all, what would the neighbors say—that was Mother's big worry. She should of, in my opinion, been worried about what would happen if she took him back. But her fear of being alone far outweighed her fear of Daddy's future transgressions. So, on Tuesday, January 10, 1922—unbeknownst to us—and while we were at school and Eloise was at Grandma's, Mother and Daddy drove over to Lincoln, Kansas, got married again and returned home before school let out for the day.

Once Mother and Daddy remarried, Daddy insisted that Mother quit work at the restaurant because Daddy didn't want anyone to think he couldn't support his family, which of course he couldn't. He began job hunting in earnest which was the beginning of a whole new set of problems.

THIRTEEN

The day started out like all our school mornings. Wava, Metta and I were seated at the table in our tiny house eating breakfast. Eloise was tied with a dish towel to a small wooden chair so Mother could feed her cereal. Daddy walked into the living room from the kitchen. He was sporting his gray flannel long-sleeved work shirt with his gray wool work pants, and he had his gray and dark blue plaid overcoat draped over his left arm. His black newsboy cap was set at a rakish angle on his head. Mother had given him a fresh haircut and shave and he smelled of his favorite fragrance—Tappan's German Cologne.

"Daddy, you look real handsome," I said. He always took great care when he was going out in public. "What are you going to do this morning?"

"Well, Ilie," he explained as he sat down on the sofa with a cup of coffee, "I need a job and I'm going out today to look for one. Need some money comin' in, you know." Mother didn't say anything, just looked at Daddy before turning back to feed Eloise. We girls left for school before Daddy left so we didn't see him again 'til we got home in the afternoon.

When we returned, Daddy was sitting in one of the wooden chairs by the table. His overcoat, one sleeve torn, was tossed on the sofa and his gray shirt was covered in dirt with specks of blood down the front.

CHAPTER THIRTEEN

The knees of his pants were stained with mud and grease. One eye was swollen almost shut with red, blue, and purple all around. He was holding a damp cloth under his nose and his face and knuckles were covered with scrapes and bruises.

"Daddy, what happened?" we all screamed at the same time, even Wava.

"Nothin', girls. It's nothin'."

"Girls, go to your bedroom and do your homework. If you got no homework, go outside and play a while," Mother instructed. "I'll call you when dinner's ready,"

They wouldn't tell us what happened. So, we were unprepared for the barrage of comments we heard at school the next day.

"Your ole man finally got what's comin' to him, my old man said."

"You can't take advantage of a lady and get away with it in this town."

"Your ole man better watch out or next time it'll be worse."

I don't know that the beatings were any worse, but there were a few more before Daddy realized that he couldn't go outside during the daytime and be safe. Mother worried about money, and Daddy became despondent—something none of us girls had seen before. And that began a new chapter in my education about life.

We girls had never seen our dad drink or, as far as we knew, had never seen him drunk prior to his arrest and trial. But now, since he couldn't go out publicly to drink his bootleg booze—remember this was during Prohibition—he drank at home. Don't ask me where he bought the stuff—I have no idea.

Usually, he wouldn't start drinking until after we'd eaten supper. He had a bottle hidden where Mother couldn't find it and he'd pour himself a jelly jar full of whiskey, sit at the table, and drink. He wasn't a mean drunk. He just got louder and more talkative. Sometimes he'd tell

ILA'S WAR

jokes that we girls didn't understand, and he'd be the only one laughing. Other times he'd pull out his harmonica and play a tune or he'd sing. Whereas Wava reacted with disgust and Metta with sadness, I was scared when his behavior changed. When I was older and understood what alcohol could do to someone, I decided I didn't want to be a drunk and I didn't want to marry one either.

Mother's reaction was predictable and always the same. She'd pull out her Bible and quote scripture. "And be not drunken with wine, wherein is riot; but be filled with the Spirit." Ephesians 5:18. Or, "Wine is a mocker, strong drink a brawler; and whosoever erreth thereby is not wise." Proverbs 20:1.

She also preached to us girls about the evils of drink. "Remember, girls. Alcohol is the devil's drink and once it's caught you, you're trapped and damned for all eternity. I hate to think that I would never see you again once I die and go to heaven while you languish in Hell. I want us to always be together in the bosom of the Lord."

I don't know how long we could have gone on like this if Grandma Rosenie hadn't stepped in to help.

"Girls... Wava... Metta... one of you. Answer the door. Don't you hear that knock?" It was evening, after supper and we were all doing homework at the table. Daddy was asleep on the sofa, or he'd passed out—I don't know which. Wava rose, grumbling the whole time, and went to the front door to open it.

"It's Grandpa Newt and Grandma Rosenie," Wava shouted as she walked back toward the table still grumbling. "I have math to do. Don't interrupt me."

"Why, Mother and Dad. We wasn't expectin' you this evening. Come on in. It's cold outside. Can I get you some coffee or tea?" Mother walked past Daddy averting her eyes from his limp body while drying her hands on her apron. Metta and I followed her to the front door. I

CHAPTER THIRTEEN

was happy to have an excuse to stop working on my spelling words. Besides, I was always curious whenever the grownups talked together. Thankfully, this time they didn't send us out of the room, so we stayed and listened.

"No, Florence. Set yourself down. We've got some good news that's going to solve all your problems." Grandma was beaming as she hugged Mother.

"My goodness. What is it? We could sure use some good news around here. Let me wake up Ira. He's just restin'."

The smell of alcohol wasn't as strong as usual, but you could still tell that Daddy had been drinking. I don't think Grandpa Newt was fooled and if Grandma Rosenie noticed, she didn't say anything.

"Irie. Irie, wake up." Mother shook his left shoulder as she roused him. "Irie, your folks is here. They got somethin' to tell us."

"Huh?... Wh... a... What?" Daddy mumbled.

"Irie. Get up. You folks is here." Mother repeated. "They want to tell us something."

"Okay. Sorry." I watched as Daddy sat up and stretched both arms over his head before running his fingers through his hair, which mussed it more than when he'd been napping. He sighed before rubbing his hands down his trouser legs to straighten his pants. "Well, folks," he said as he gave Grandma Rosenie a smile, "this is a pleasant surprise. Sit down, sit down. What can we do for you this evening?"

"Ira. Florence. We've found you a business. It's all set. We bought a restaurant over in Lincoln. The owner has agreed to continue running it until May when school's out when you can take it over. Now, what do you think of that?" Grandma Rosenie's face was lit up like the kerosene lantern we used to go from the house to the privy late at night.

Everyone was silent for a few moments before Daddy spoke. It was clear he wasn't entirely awake and hadn't grasped the meaning of her words. "A restaurant? I don't have the money to buy a restaurant. Lord, knows…"

Mother interrupted. "Do not take the Lord's name in vain, Ira."

"I'm not. I mean, ah, I want to work. I need to work but you know it hasn't been safe for me to go out of the house. I don't see how this is gonna change things."

"Ira, listen to your ma." Grandpa Newt commanded in his deep, gravelly voice. "The restaurant's already paid for… and it's in Lincoln. They don't know you there. So, you can go to work. Nothin's going to happen… unless…" and Grandpa's voice trailed off as Grandma Rosenie glared at him and shook her head.

"Lincoln, huh? Lincoln. That might not be so bad. That might just work out." Daddy turned to Mother and said, "Florence, what do you think?"

"Well, now. This is a surprise. I wouldn't a thought of this that's for sure. A restaurant. Well, I can cook. Ira, you're a pretty good cook, too. And the girls could help. It'ud be a lot of work, and there's things we'd have to learn but I 'spose we could."

And that's when Wava spoke up. "I'm not moving to Lincoln or anywhere else. You all can go if you want, but I'm staying here." She paused for a moment before adding, "I bet folks do, too, know about Daddy. I don't want them knowing I'm his daughter. So, I'm not going."

And nothing that anyone could say would budge her. So, when school ended in May we left Wava behind and we moved to Lincoln, optimistic about starting anew.

FOURTEEN

The house Daddy rented for us was at the north end of Lincoln next to the water tower. It was the biggest house we'd ever lived in—so large that we didn't use all of it—a two story affair with an outside set of stairs to the second floor. Daddy decided if we needed extra money, he'd rent out the second story.

Lincoln, Kansas, was a farming community of about 1,600 people, bigger than Waldo and Lucas combined. All the buildings on main street were made of native limestone which gave the town a feeling of substance. The end of World War One saw the return of many of the town's young men who married and started their own businesses. As a result, the business community was bustling with at least six grocery stores, four attorneys-at-law, a thriving dairy, eight garages, three drug stores, at least two banks, gravel streets, and city-wide telephone and electrical service. A large flour mill was located on the Saline river, just south of town, near the dam where you could catch some mighty fine catfish for delicious eating. And the best thing about Lincoln as far as I was concerned was that it was far enough away from Lucas that Daddy's reputation did not precede him, so he could leave the house during the day without fear of getting beat up.

Mother joined the Methodist Church as soon as we were settled in. She made friends with other church ladies and—no surprise—joined the Women's Christian Temperance Union, which held their meetings at the church.

Our restaurant was located on main street, just five doors east of the Saline Valley Bank. Mother and Daddy decided to call it Armsbury's. Grandma Rosenie gave Daddy $25.00 for the till, and we were in business.

Mother was the day cook and Daddy worked at night. Metta and I, at ages eleven and six respectively, and baby Eloise went to work with Mother every day. Metta learned how to peel potatoes and wash dishes. I was in charge of caring for Eloise who played and napped behind the lunch counter. When Eloise was asleep or absent from the restaurant, I was also the backup dish washer. If we weren't busy midmorning I waited on customers at the counter.

The building was long and narrow with a cramped aisle running the length of the room. Customers entering the restaurant could sit on either side of the aisle on one of the ten stools at the oak counter or at one of the two-person tables on the other side. A huge oak and glass cooler with heavy brass handles sat behind the counter, some of its doors covered with beveled mirror which allowed customers to look at their reflections and see who was sitting behind them. A long white marble bar with a foot rail extended the oak counter by several feet. Customers in a hurry could stand at the bar and eat while visiting with my dad who held court every day in the same spot once he showed up.

The floor was covered with linoleum sporting a pattern of flowers in faded blues, reds, and purples. Ceiling fans resembling huge airplane propellers were suspended from the 16-foot ceiling, which was covered in large, gray embossed squares. The high ceiling and hard surfaces made everything sound tinny unless the place was packed with diners, when the noise level changed to a deep, dull roar.

We couldn't afford fancy, printed menus so each morning Metta

CHAPTER FOURTEEN

or I pulled the heavy, old Royal typewriter out from under the lunch counter and typed up the day's menu.

Dinner Menu

Veal Stew with Dumplings----------30 cents
Roast Beef--------------------------30 cents
Roast Pork--------------------------35 cents

with

Mashed Potatoes & Gravy
Creamed Peas
Rice Pudding

Plate Lunch (choice of meats)-----25 cents
Head Lettuce-------------------------10 cents
Fresh Tomatoes----------------------10 cents
Chili   cup---10 cents   bowl---15 cents

Pies
Apple, Cherry, Raisin, Pineapple, Chocolate
Coffee   Milk   Tea

We spent the summer developing a routine. Daddy arranged to purchase most of the groceries and bakery products for the restaurant from Zink's Grocery, one of the many thriving businesses on main street, and before long Daddy and Porky Zink were best friends and drinking pals. Daddy didn't want to play favorites with the Lincoln business community because he wanted the families of all those businessmen to eat at the restaurant. So, we also bought from other Lincoln stores and Daddy became friends with most of the businessmen up and down main street. Many of these guys became Daddy's drinking buddies so he didn't drink at home anymore, much to my relief.

We three girls began learning the restaurant business from the ground up—or in our case from the dirty floors up. Mother also began to learn the restaurant business—as an owner. That meant she trained any newly hired girls and put in long hours when someone didn't show up for her shift. Daddy no longer objected to Mother working, probably because he didn't pay her and because it gave him freedom to drink and carouse when he didn't want to work.

When it came time to enroll us girls for the fall 1922 semester at Lincoln, Wava refused to return home. Her reason was the same old one—she was humiliated by Daddy's past behavior and she didn't want to be around him. Mother was upset, but there was nothing she could do, so Wava started classes at Lucas while Metta and I began school in Lincoln.

It was in early 1923 that some of Daddy's friendships with a few Lincoln businessmen began changing. The Ku Klux Klan was organizing all over north-central Kansas, including Lincoln. Because no Blacks or Jews lived in that part of Kansas, Catholics were the focus of Klan hatred. When the Klan failed to persuade Daddy to join up, they started a new campaign—trying to get Daddy to switch from the Catholic baker, Porky Zink, to the KKK baker, Herman Knoch. We weren't Catholic, and I don't think Daddy cared one way or the other about anybody's religious freedom, but he wanted the restaurant to be successful, and he thought that the bread and buns made by Porky Zink were better than the bakery products made by Herman Knoch. Daddy refused to switch which made for some tense times for him around town and at home.

One thing that always relieved the tension was getting a letter from Wava telling about school, her friends and her activities. Her letters were

CHAPTER FOURTEEN

infrequent so when one arrived Mother made an occasion of it, waiting 'til Daddy got home to read it out loud to all of us. One March evening in 1923, we were all anxiously awaiting Daddy's arrival so we could hear the news from Wava's most recent letter. When Daddy walked in the back door, he was grumbling.

"Those Kluxers. Bunch of idiots. Herman Knoch's buns are like rocks. Nothin' but damn rocks."

"Ira," Mother interrupted him, "We got a letter from Wavy today. Been waitin' for you so's we can read it."

"Okay, Mother. That'll be good… make me forget my troubles, as they say." He sat down at the kitchen table, pulled his reading glasses out of his front pocket, and settled down to read to us.

> *Dearest Mother, Daddy, and girls:*
>
> *I have a beau. His name is Nolan Farrington, and he is the son of a successful rancher near here.*
>
> *You should see his clothes. Daaapper! When he comes to town, he escorts his older sister, and he is quite the gentleman. Always gives her his arm, walks on the outside, removes his cap to greet a lady.*
>
> *Now don't worry. We were introduced at a church function, so it's alright. And he owns a car. Not his father's car, but one that Nolan bought with his own money. I think he's swell, and he thinks I am, too. Maybe when school's out in May, I can bring him to Lincoln to meet you. You'll think he's swell, too.*

Neither Mother nor Daddy thought there was anything "swell" about Wava's beau. "By, God. She's too young for a beau." Daddy spat out.

"Ira, she needs to come home. I don't care how much a gentleman he is." Daddy agreed and this time put his foot down. No crying, no pleading, nothing could persuade him or Mother to let Wava remain in Lucas. So as soon as school was out in May Daddy drove to Lucas, packed up Wava and her things and brought her back to Lincoln where she worked in the restaurant with us all summer.

Life in our family seemed to calm down after that. Mother opened up the restaurant every morning and did all the cooking for breakfast and dinner, Daddy did the cooking for supper and stayed to close. We three older girls headed for the restaurant as soon as school was out and worked there 'til 8:00 p.m., when we could go home for the night. The conflict between the Klan and Daddy remained about the same, so life went on pretty quiet until one Saturday in October 1924.

It was a beautiful, crisp fall morning, almost lunchtime. All the stores on main street were busy, and the sidewalks crowded. The restaurant was full with customers who were taking a break from shopping, all hungry and wanting food. Wava and Metta were waiting tables, and I was at the counter refilling coffee cups when a stranger walked in, sat down near me, and said, "You must be little Ila." I was just getting ready to ask, "Who are you?" when Wava rushed up from behind and grabbed the stranger by the shoulders, pulling him around as she blurted out, "Why, Nolan. What are you doing here?"

"Happy belated birthday, Miss Armsbury. I'm sorry I couldn't make it down here before now to give you my best wishes."

So, Nolan Farrington hung around Lincoln for the afternoon and came home with us that evening to meet the folks. He seemed nice, was real polite, and when it was time to leave, we all said "goodbye" with smiles and hugs to boot.

But the next morning, when Wava showed up at the restaurant to work the Sunday morning breakfast rush, she was wearing a ring on her left ring finger. Mother was the first to spot it. She grabbed Wava by the arm and hauled her into the kitchen.

CHAPTER FOURTEEN

"Wava Irene Armsbury, where did you get that?" I was washing dishes, and I could hear the trembling in Mother's voice—she was furious.

"It's my birthday present from Nolan. It's just a friendship ring. Isn't it beautiful?" It was a tiny diamond set in white gold. I thought it was pretty, too.

"You take that off right this minute and give it to me." When Wava didn't move, Mother's voice increased in volume and in rage. "I said, take that ring off. Take it off now." And Mother almost pulled Wava's finger out of its socket as she tugged on the ring. Tears rolled down Wava's face like raindrops off a steep roof, but she took the ring off and handed it to Mother. Later that day at home, once the restaurant was closed, Mother stood over Wava's shoulder and supervised as Wava wrote a tear-stained letter to Nolan explaining that she could not accept a diamond ring as a birthday present since she was only 16 years old. Not trusting Wava to complete the task, Mother took the ring and the letter to the post office the next day and mailed everything back to Nolan.

FIFTEEN

Things were still tense at home—Wava moped about returning the ring to Nolan. In addition, the Klan was putting renewed pressure on Daddy. It was Friday night in early January 1925, and Metta and I were working at the restaurant. I was glad to be up to my elbows in warm soapy water as I stood at the sink scraping pots. I preferred washing pots to being at home, caring for Eloise. At nine, my haunts were limited to the restaurant, home, school, and church. Metta was out front waiting on tables. Suddenly she burst into the kitchen through the swinging door, saying, "Daddy, there's Klansmen in front of the restaurant with more marching this way and somebody's calling your name—I don't know who." Most Friday nights the Ku Klux Klan paraded right by, but this time, they stopped.

Daddy turned from the huge black gas range and swore, but that didn't bother me—I was used to it. A gigantic metal pot full of Daddy's famous chili gave off to enticing odor of cumin and garlic and I could see beads of sweat on Daddy's forehead. The griddle popped with the grease of hamburgers frying and I could smell onions already cooked and ready to be served up.

"They'll just have to wait a minute. I've got food cooking here." He turned back toward the stove as I quickly dried my chapped hands on my apron and walked out into the dining room.

CHAPTER FIFTEEN

Like most Friday nights, the place was packed with Lincoln High School kids wolfing down hamburgers and cokes before the basketball game, and Catholic families enjoying the blue-plate special: Mother's fried fish with a side of macaroni and cheese. I hurried over to the steamy front window, wiped clear a peephole, and watched the Klansmen shuffle along in their pointy-hooded white robes. Metta was right behind me, "Move over," she said. "I want to see, too."

Electric streetlights and a waning crescent moon provided eerie light, so the marchers looked like ghosts huddled in the street in front of the restaurant. Behind the Kluxers, straight across the street from the restaurant, the one-story limestone buildings gave off a dull white light while their big black windows looked like unblinking eyes. A few cars were parked diagonally at the curb on both sides of the street.

One of the Kluxers stood on the sidewalk about four feet from the front door. He was shuffling from one foot to the other, trying to keep warm, but probably nervous, too. Daddy could be a monster when he was angry. I could hear murmured voices coming from outside.

The men stamped their feet on the frozen gravel street as they hopped around, trying to ward off the bitter cold. One looked down as he lifted his left boot, then recoiled in disgust. Horse manure: not everything was frozen!

"Ira!" the man on the sidewalk called; I thought it was Mr. Hundertmark, the owner of The Hundertmark Store and a local KKK bigwig.

Daddy came out of the kitchen, and as he stomped by the lunch counter, untying his stained white apron, he said, "Metta, Ila, you stay in here." He smacked the apron down on the counter and pushed through the front door, planting himself on the sidewalk with his hands on his hips. Even though Daddy had his back to us, I could tell he was furious. His arms were taut, his hands balled into fists, his head cocked to one side

ILA'S WAR

and his back straight as the yardstick Mother used to paddle us with when we disobeyed. Over to one side, we could see an American flag and a big wooden cross, each one held up by strong men in robes and hoods. The flag made a snapping sound as it flapped in the cold winter wind.

"Ira, we know you're a loyal American...," said the man who'd called Daddy's name a minute ago. Now I was sure it was Mr. Hundertmark.

"Damn right I am!"

"Now don't get riled... nobody's saying you aren't. But it doesn't look good doing business with someone who's loyal to Rome and the papistry." We could see white-hooded heads bobbing up and down.

"Porky Zink is as good an American as any of you—probably a damn sight better. And he's my friend, just like many of you are my friends."

That was one thing about living in a small town—everybody knew everybody else and there was precious little you could hide from your neighbors. Why, every Monday morning when the clean laundry was put out you could see Klansmen's white sheets with the holes cut for their heads, hanging on the clothes lines, and white pillowcases made into hoods with two eye holes hanging nearby.

"Porky has the best bread around. I've told you before and I'll tell you again—I'm not switching bakers and that's it."

"It's not just your baker that's the problem. It's serving breakfast to those Catholics on Sunday morning after they've gone to their church. Makes it look like you're supporting Catholics over your own kind."

"My own kind?"

"You know. It just doesn't look good."

I noticed suddenly that the restaurant was completely quiet behind me. Everybody sat still, some with forks halfway to their mouths. A glass shattered, bursting the silence like a gunshot. Jack Donley, the son of a local farmer and a regular attendee at St. Patrick's Catholic Church,

CHAPTER FIFTEEN

shakily set the tray of glasses he was holding on the counter and stooped to pick up the shards. Jack, tall with dark hair and a quick smile, was a classmate of Wava's and he helped us out on busy nights.

"So, you want me to close on Sunday?" Daddy barked.

"No, no need to do that. Just don't open up so early."

"And who's going to make up for my lost income? You fellas all planning to start eating your Sunday dinner at my restaurant?"

Silence.

"I didn't think so. Well, I can tell you this. Folks who want a good breakfast at a decent price can always find it at Armsbury's, and I'll set my hours so I can get as many of 'em as I can because in my book a Catholic quarter and a Protestant quarter—they all spend the same."

The Klansmen murmured to each other and moved off down Main Street. Slowly, the restaurant came back to life. I got a broom and dustpan to help Jack. As we knelt by the mess of broken glass, he kept his eyes turned from mine.

"It's okay, Jack. Daddy says they're all just talk," I said as I tried to reassure him.

Daddy went back to the griddle, and I to the sink. "I told you, Ilie. Those Kluxers are just a bunch of blowhards. Trying to interfere in a man's own business when it's none of theirs. Don't you worry, honey. I can take care of myself and the restaurant, too."

I was still shaken from everything I'd seen, but other than some talk, nothing bad had happened so I figured Daddy was right, and I went back to washing dirty pots and pans. The dishwater had cooled, but it felt good on my wrists. I put all my concentration into chipping melted cheese off of Mother's big rectangular baking pan, trying to shut out the scene I'd just witnessed. Don't think about it; I told myself. Just do your work and keep your eyes down. That was the Armsbury way, at least for us females.

Suddenly, shouting voices came from the dining room. "What's going on here?" "For God's sake, get out of here!" Then the sound of furniture tipping over and dishes breaking. By the time Daddy and I got to the swinging kitchen door, two Klansmen had Jack Donley by the upper arms. He wriggled as they dragged him toward the front door of the restaurant. They lifted him clean off his feet, and with one great effort threw him through the big plate glass window that faced main street—with a sound like my whole world exploding, which it did.

You can't imagine the fallout. Wava had a conniption fit—she was mortified by the Klan's attack at the restaurant. "What will people think? You've shamed me in front of my friends." Those were her exact words. She immediately dropped out of school at Lincoln, bought a one-way train ticket and went back to Lucas to return to high school there.

And as for Daddy? His rage was as cold as an arctic winter. He sold the restaurant—said he wasn't going to let the Klan or anybody else tell him how to run his business or who to hire. He told Mother that as soon as school was out in May we were moving to Fairport, Kansas, about 75 miles west of Lincoln. And that's exactly what we did.

* * *

My dad did a lot of bad things in his life—I won't deny it for a minute, but I have always been proud of him for standing up to the Klan. Daddy taught me some important lessons that night: that sometimes you have to go your own way when the majority is wrong. He also taught me that it was good to fight for what's right, even if you have to fight alone. And he taught me not to back down, even when the going gets tough. Neither Daddy nor I ever imagined that a few years later I'd apply those lessons in a fight with him, and that ultimately, I would win.

* * *

CHAPTER FIFTEEN

The blows just kept coming. We were still trying to come to terms with the attack at the restaurant, Wava's move to Lucas, and our impending move when a letter from Wava arrived, informing us that she was dropping out of school in Lucas where she was a junior and that she and Nolan were getting married in May. Mother and Daddy blew up. We drove to Lucas and met with Wava at Grandma Rosenie's house. Daddy demanded to know if she was pregnant, but she was vehement in her denial, insisting instead that she and Nolan saw no reason to wait.

Mother pleaded with her to finish high school. "Wava, look at me. Look at my hands, how rough they are, how my knuckles are swollen from all the years of hard work. Look at my back. It's bent and hurts all the time. See these varicose veins? My legs ache after standing at a stove for hours on end, cooking. I don't want this for you," Mother cried as she pointed to her own body, begging Wava to wait.

Mother even tried bargaining with Wava: if she'd return to school in Lucas, she could continue living with our relatives there, and as soon as she graduated from high school, Daddy would pay for a nice wedding.

"Nolan has money, and he can buy me nice clothes. I'm not goin' to have to work like you. And folks think well of the Farringtons. They're a good family and I'll be happy there." Wava was haughty in her response, almost sneering at Mother.

Metta tried talking to her, too, her voice quiet but her anger unmistakable. "Wava, you're breaking Mother's heart."

"Daddy's broken my heart—more than once. Why can't he be like other fathers—just go to work and go home. But no, he has to be a big show-off. Everywhere he goes he gets in trouble and before long people know who he is and what he's done. When I marry Nolan, people will respect me and say, 'There goes Mrs. Nolan Farrington. He's that fine young farmer who works a ranch with his dad,' not 'There goes Ira

Armsbury's oldest girl. Wonder if she's like her old man?'"

Even Grandma Rosenie put in her two cents. "Honey, I know you love Nolan, and he is a fine young man. But as a school marm, I've always taught my girls that education is the most important thing a young woman can bring to a marriage. You don't have much longer to go. Can't you just wait a few more months?"

But Wava was adamant...Nolan would provide the security, the money, and the respectability that she craved. So, on May 27, 1925, just a few days before our move to Fairport, Wava and Nolan were married at the office of the Russell County Justice of the Peace. Mother and Daddy remained adamant in their opposition to the wedding and refused to attend, but they did allow Metta to be an attendant. They also refused to help Wava buy a wedding dress. Nolan did that—a gown of blue crepe with long, ivory gloves that buttoned at the wrist. No cake, no presents, and no other family, while in Lincoln Mother spent the entire day crying. Wava was 16 and Nolan was 23.

SIXTEEN

Fairport and Lincoln could not have been more different. Whereas Lincoln was a bustling farm community, Fairport was literally an oil patch in the middle of a dusty Kansas field. Oil had been discovered in 1923, and drilling commenced shortly after that. You could hardly even call Fairport a town—it was unincorporated, and the "houses" were little more than tar paper shacks and old boards slapped together in haste for the drilling crews. The sole restaurant in Fairport, owned by the Sparks family from Lincoln, was open twenty-four hours a day. Daddy and Mother were hired to work as cooks there. Our new home was a trailer parked behind the restaurant.

The only one who seemed to like Fairport was Daddy, who found a whole new group of drinking buddies in the oil field hands working on the rigs. Mother cooked for eight hours during the day and Daddy cooked at night and drank with his new friends before coming home for a few hours' sleep.

Mother hated our life there, and she hated Daddy's drinking. When she was upset, I was, too, and then I'd get into fights with my dad.

"Daddy, you didn't come home last night, and Mother was upset." Daddy was hunched over a cup of black coffee at the table in our tiny trailer.

No comment.

"Daddy," I said in a louder voice, "You made Mother cry again last night. Where were you?"

"Ila, leave me alone. Can't you see I don't feel good."

"And whose fault it that?"

"That's enough, Ila."

Summer in Fairport dragged by for Metta and me. Metta passed the time by helping in the restaurant. The Sparks family lived nearby and had a teenage son, Paul, who was Metta's age, thirteen, soon to be fourteen. My only playmate when Metta was working was Eloise, who was four. We didn't see Wava at all, but her frequent letters told us about how much she loved her new life.

Mother became increasingly worried at the approach of the fall 1925 school semester because Metta was ready for her freshman year in high school and there was no high school in Fairport. The closest one was in Russell. Paul Sparks offered to drive Metta to and from school every day, but Mother wouldn't hear of it. After what had happened with Wava, Mother wasn't about to allow Metta to spend time alone with a boy.

So, Mother wrote to her best friend in Lincoln and asked if Metta could live with them for the school year. Naturally, the answer was "yes" so Metta was shipped back to Lincoln over the Labor Day weekend of 1925 and started school September 8.

The first years of my life were full of chaos, courtesy of my dad, but the dullness of life in Fairport was almost too much for me to bear. Metta had been a bright spot in my otherwise long and boring life in Fairport, but with her gone I was miserable. At my ten years of age to Eloise's four there was little that I could do with her other than read to her or watch her play. It was a lonely time for me. Even starting school didn't help because I could never stay after class to go to someone's house or have a friend come play at our house since I was needed at home to watch Eloise or help at the restaurant.

CHAPTER SIXTEEN

One Saturday morning in early November 1925, just as I was preparing to feed Eloise her breakfast, a big black touring car pulled up in front of our trailer and four men emerged. I didn't know any of them except for the Lincoln County Sheriff. My first reaction was "Ah Oh. What's Daddy done now?"

But I'd jumped to the wrong conclusion. After knocking on the door of the trailer and being let in, the four men introduced themselves as a delegation from Lincoln.

"Ira," said one of the men dressed in a black suit with a heavy wool overcoat and wool hat, "We want you to come back to Lincoln and reopen your restaurant."

Daddy looked at them like they were aliens. "Hell No. After what I been through. I'm not goin' back. Not gonna fight with the Klan or anybody else."

"Don't worry, Ira. Won't be no more fighting. The Klan's gone. We run 'em out of town and there won't be no more trouble from them."

Daddy didn't believe them at first. He just shook his head.

"Well, if that's true, don't make no difference 'cause I don't have the money to open a new restaurant," he explained.

"We figured that, Ira. We'll take care of it. We're gonna fix up a big building, turn it into a first-rate restaurant. New tables and chairs, new counters and stools. We'll finance the whole shebang including your move back to Lincoln."

Daddy looked astonished—his eyebrows shot up and he grabbed a handkerchief from his back pocket and wiped his forehead—a sure sign of nervousness.

"Why're you fellas so all-fired het-up about a restaurant. Aren't there already some in Lincoln?"

"Yeah, but they ain't as good as yours. We need a good restaurant 'cause an oil and gas pipeline is coming through right near Lincoln, and we're gonna need a restaurant that's open twenty-four hours a day, seven days a week, and we think you're the only one that can do it. Will you come?"

After staring at the group for an instant, Daddy said, "Let me go talk to Florence for a minute. Be right back." He was gone about twenty minutes which left me alone with Eloise and the Lincoln delegation.

I was nervous I can tell you and didn't know what to do. So, I just kept an eye on Eloise and tried to pretend that there was no one watching me.

Finally, Daddy returned. "Well, fellows, I guess you got yourselves a new restaurant."

They shook hands all around. One man handed Daddy a key, "Ira, this is the key to the front door of your new restaurant," and then they left.

I could hardly wait to leave Fairport. I resolved that when I grew up, I was going to travel and see the world outside the confines of rural Kansas, and I was never going to live in a small town again.

SEVENTEEN

We moved back to Lincoln just before the end of 1925, and I started school and the new year with renewed optimism. Metta was home; I was with my old friends; I knew most of the teachers, my way around the school building, and the town already; and we were making money hand over fist.

We moved into an old, rented farmhouse on the northwest edge of town, just inside the city limits. It had three bedrooms, one small room that could be reached only by stairs right inside the back door—that was Metta's bedroom—a larger bedroom off the kitchen for Eloise and me, and Mother and Daddy's bedroom off the living room. We even had electricity and running water in the kitchen, but we still had to use a privy for our toilet.

If there was one room in the house that was Mother's favorite, it was the living room. The floor, unlike all the other floors in the house, was wood, but it had seen a lot of abuse: deep gouges and scratches where previous renters had carelessly dragged furniture across the floor. Big windows facing south and east let in bright morning light through faded rose-patterned curtains and Mother covered the floor with oval area rugs she'd braided from scrap material so that the room felt and looked homey even if impoverished.

Our new restaurant, named the Popular Cafe, was open 24-hours a day because the men putting in the pipeline worked three eight-hour-shifts. Daddy even had to hire one woman whose only job was to pack sack lunches! The workmen came in for breakfast at 6:00 a.m., picked up their lunch sacks, and came back for supper at 5:30 or 6:00. The money rolled in!

And Daddy spent it, too. He bought us a new Dodge sedan. Mother bought all new furniture, and I got a coat with a real fur collar.

Some of the money even came my way. Because I was older now, ten-and-a-half, I had more responsibility at the restaurant, being in charge of the gum and match machines and, when I wasn't in school, working at the lunch counter. During the day most of our customers were businessmen, but nights and weekends we served families and young couples courting. One of my favorite customers was Judge Joslin. He came in every day for coffee and conversation with other businessmen, but he always took a moment to inquire about my day, encourage me in whatever I was doing, and when he was done drinking his five-cent cup of coffee, he'd leave me a five-cent tip. With his encouragement, I opened a savings account at the Farmers National Bank. I dreamed that one day I'd have so much money I could take a trip around the world, ride on a train again, and have adventures. Those tips and his friendship eventually came to the rescue of my sister, Metta, but I'm getting ahead of myself.

Yes, life was going well for the Armsburys and for Wava and Nolan. Wava's letters kept us up to date about the goings-on at the ranch, and also about their two babies, LaDonna, born in 1926 and Phyllis born in 1929.

The only problem we faced, and we would have faced it no matter where we lived, was that Daddy had renewed his friendships with his old drinking buddies, and he was drinking even more than when we'd lived in Fairport. He and Mother would fight, she'd cry, and I'd get mad at

CHAPTER SEVENTEEN

my dad.

"Daddy, I heard you last night, and I heard Mother crying. You were drinking, weren't you?"

"Ila, that's none of your business. I'm a grownup and don't answer to you."

"I hate it when you drink. Mother gets upset and cries. You fight. Sometimes I feel sad because I can't make her happy and I can't make you stop."

We went around and around. I didn't realize how angry my dad was with me and my comments about his drinking until the day I hurt myself while playing in the restaurant.

"Here, put this on," I said as I handed my school friend a cap and apron. I was in the sixth grade and eleven years old. School was out for the day, and we were going to help Mother.

"Betcha can't carry more than two plates of food through that swinging door," my friend commented as we were heading toward the kitchen from the dining room.

"Betcha I can. I been doing this a long time now and I'm real good at it," I boasted.

I don't know how it happened. We were both trying to go through the swinging door at the same time. She was a bit ahead of me, and charged into the kitchen. She whirled around and shoved the door closed so I couldn't walk through. One second I was pushing and the next I'd put my right hand through the glass window of the door and my wrist was gushing blood.

"Mother," I hollered as my friend yelled, "Mrs. Armsbury! Help."

Mother was in the kitchen cleaning off the grill when she heard our screams.

Mother gasped when she saw all the blood. She grabbed the towel that was hanging from her waistband and wrapped it around my wrist.

"Ila," she commanded, "Sit here on this stool and hold your hand above your head. Your dad's next door and I'm gonna run get him."

Mother was out the front door at once and back almost as quick with Daddy right behind her.

"Let me see, Ilie," Daddy said as he unwrapped the towel from my wrist. "Good Lord, that's quite a cut you got there." Then he noticed the broken glass and blood on the floor and on the swinging door.

"What happened here?" he asked looking grim. My friend started to cry so I spoke up.

"Daddy, we were playing, and I accidentally put my hand through the window. It was my fault."

He looked mad but he also looked worried because now that my wrist was below my shoulder the blood was gushing again from the deep wound.

"Well, we'll talk about it later. We need to get you to Dr. Newlon right now."

Dr. Malcolm Newlon was a physician and surgeon in Lincoln. He'd built his own hospital up at the north end of town. That's where we went.

"Come in, come in. Let's see what we have here," Dr. Newlon said as he ushered Daddy and me into his examination room.

"Climb up here, please, Miss Armsbury," he directed. "Here" was a big, cold white enamel and black cast iron exam table. Dr. Newlon wore a long white coat and looked serious as he unwrapped the blood-stained towel from my wrist. He peered at the cut for a minute before saying, "Well, Ira, this looks pretty bad. I think it needs some stitches. I'll give her some anesthetic, so she won't feel the pain."

"Oh, she doesn't need a shot for pain," Daddy said. "She's tough. She can take it." He looked at me, his eyes glinting, and I noticed a vein throbbing in his right jaw. "You can take it, can't you?"

CHAPTER SEVENTEEN

I didn't know what to say. I'd never had stitches before and didn't know what was in store for me. I also was taken aback by the look on his face—challenging?—menacing?—angry? Maybe all those.

Dr. Newlon looked puzzled, moving his eyes from Daddy to me and back. "Well, if you're sure?"

"Yep, go ahead. She'll be fine."

After another glance at my dad Dr. Newlon turned to me and said, "Miss Armsbury, lay down on this table and let your dad hold your arm still so I can put in the sutures. Do you understand?" I nodded, leaned back, and laid down. Daddy grabbed hold of my right arm and held it straight and tight as Dr. Newlon plunged a needle into the skin of my wrist.

Let me tell you it hurt like hell. I could feel each burning stab of the needle as Dr. Newlon inserted it first into one skin flap then the other, and the tug of the thread as he pulled the two pieces of skin together over the cut. I struggled to pull my arm away from the torture and broke out in a sweat even though it wasn't hot in the room. All the time Daddy kept saying in a stern tone of voice, "Ila, lay still. It'll be over in a minute." When Dr. Newlon was finished I sat up, cradling my right arm and wrist with my whole upper body, and glaring at my dad. Tears burned in my eyes, but I was determined that he wouldn't see them, no matter what.

Daddy and I rode home in silence. I couldn't even look at him I was so furious at his refusing any anesthetic for me. On a deeper level I was devastated that he'd allowed me to feel such withering pain.

By the time we got home after the doctor's visit my dad was feeling pretty ashamed of himself because he offered to go to the restaurant and bring me back some ice cream. I turned him down. Some things just couldn't be made better even by an apology.

* * *

ILA'S WAR

Here I am now, approaching the end of my life, trying to understand what happened to me during my growing-up years. When I think about this incident I wonder, did he really believe it wouldn't be too painful? Or did he deny me anesthetic as a means of punishing me for talking back? For breaking the window? Maybe he was a sadist. How do I figure it out? To this day I haven't come up with a satisfactory explanation for what he put me through. There's just some things, I guess, I'll never understand, no matter what.

* * *

Metta graduated from Lincoln High School in May 1929 and in the fall went to Emporia State Teacher's College. I missed her a lot, but Eloise was older and more interesting at age eight, so Metta's absence wasn't as painful as when she'd been sent to Lincoln from Fairport. Plus, I had all my friends in Lincoln, Grandpa Newt and Grandma Rosenie and my aunts who regularly came to visit from Lucas. So, I wasn't lonely. And I was busy with the restaurant.

Business was good, not only at the restaurant but all over Lincoln, until the pipeline was completed, and the money just dried up and the unthinkable happened. The stock market crashed, and everybody was broke. Business at the restaurant slowed to a trickle. Our only customers were a few businessmen who came by in the mornings to have coffee and commiserate. And even they cut back on the number of mornings each week they came in. The families who ate breakfast or dinner at the restaurant all but disappeared. Yet somehow Daddy kept the doors open so we always had something to eat.

In the meantime, what with the collapse of the stock market, we saw an increase in the number of hoboes who stopped at the back door of the restaurant. If a man offered to do a little work, he was guaranteed

CHAPTER SEVENTEEN

a meal. Whenever I see Red Skelton in his Freddie the Freeloader hobo costume, I always think of the men who came to the back door of the restaurant. Occasionally as I stood at the sink washing dishes and daydreaming, my thoughts would be interrupted by a knock on the back door.

"'Scuse me, ma am, I been traveling a spell and sure'm in need of a hot meal and a place to sit myself down for a while. Any work needs doing? I'm real handy with tools and I can worsh them winders for you quicker'n you cun say 'Step right in here and set yourself down.'"

"Wait, here, sir while I go get my Mother or Daddy and you can talk to them. I'll be right back, sir."

Both Mother and Daddy had soft spots for those men, Black or White, who were hungry, tired, and dirty. I never saw them turn a single soul away. Daddy kept a table complete with tablecloth and napkins in the kitchen where we fed many a hobo and where we also served Lincoln's sole Black resident, James Mitchell.

As I see it, when you commit to telling the story of your life, you're committing to tell the truth. And the ugly truth is that back in those days I was a racist—everyone was. We children used "the N-word" without thinking, just like our parents. And once we were older, if we thought about it at all, we thought of it simply as a way of identifying people who weren't like us—not our skin color, not our intelligence or capability, certainly not our status in life.

So, it should come as no surprise that we didn't refer to Lincoln's Black resident as Mr. Mitchell, but as "N-Jim". Jim was born in the deep south and had lived in Lincoln since the 1880s. During the early years he'd supported himself by working for area farmers, but the last thirty-plus years of his life he worked for a prominent family and lived on main street, in an apartment over the Saline Valley Bank. And he took all his meals at the restaurant at that little table in the kitchen.

ILA'S WAR

* * *

Thinking about James Mitchell makes me think about my own racism. How I hurt Jim, whom I loved when I was a kid, listening to his stories about the old South and his travels, without even realizing that I was belittling him. And how I hurt others as well. For instance, I used the "N" word to describe my patients on the "Negro Ward" of the teaching hospital where I went to nursing school. I even used it in a few letters home when I wrote about patients I helped treat during the war.

It wasn't until after the war that I began experiencing an awakening—a realization that we—Americans, I mean—had separated folks based on color and went further, demonizing certain skin tones and the people who had them. But as small incremental changes occurred, like working with a Black nurse or seeing my first ever Black physician and how capable he was, I had to start challenging my beliefs. Once I did that, I had to start asking myself the hard questions like, where did I get the idea that African Americans weren't as smart or capable as whites? Why did I think it was okay to use an insulting and degrading term as a name for someone?

I realized that I said and did what others did, including my folks, without any consideration of the meaning or the consequences. But as I saw the changes around me, read newspaper stories, and watched the horrific violence like that in Birmingham and Selma on TV, I realized that I had to challenge every single belief I had, couldn't just let them go without examining each one to see if it still held up in light of my new awareness. I couldn't let myself off the hook by saying, "I was just a product of my times," because now I knew better.

I'm not proud to admit my racist beginnings, and sometimes a racist idea just seems to pop into my head from outer space. When that happens, I have to look at it, call it what it is—free-floating racism—and flush it out of my mind just like flushing sewage down the toilet. God,

CHAPTER SEVENTEEN

how I wish there was an inoculation we could all get right after we were born that would destroy the racism virus before it ever takes hold.

* * *

Metta came home for Christmas of 1929, and that's when I learned how bad our family finances really were. We were all at the restaurant, working. With fewer customers we had more time for cleaning and Daddy decided that all three of us girls should help while Mother cooked, and he worked at the lunch counter and waited tables.

"Put some elbow grease into it, girls. I want all those glass shelves behind the counter washed with ammonia water—make 'em shine," Daddy directed us as he sat on one of the lunch counter stools and oversaw our work. "I want to be able to see my reflection clear from the front door."

Finally, he decided that the glass was clean enough. "Take a break. Go into the kitchen and have some cocoa. I'll be there in a minute. We need to talk anyway."

When Daddy came into the kitchen a few minutes later, Mother was sitting on an old wooden chair we kept near the stove, her feet propped up on an empty wooden vegetable crate. Eloise was sitting on the floor, leaning against the wall. Metta was washing up a few dirty dishes in the sink, and I was pouring myself some hot cocoa. "Metta, honey, I'm sorry to tell you this, but your mother and I have decided that you're going to have to stay home. We don't have the money for you to go back to Emporia after Christmas."

The dish Metta had been washing dropped into the dirty dishwater with a thud as she turned around and stared at Daddy, a look of shock on her face. She didn't say a word. Her eyes grew big and silent tears began to stream down her cheeks. "I love school. I want to be a teacher," she stammered, her voice breaking.

"We know, honey," Mother said quietly. "But nobody's got money right now and we don't neither. We're just tryin' to keep the restaurant doors open."

The stunned silence seemed to go on forever. My mind was racing, trying to think of a solution. Suddenly I realized I could help.

"Metta," I was almost giggling I was so excited and proud of myself, "it's okay. You can stay in school. I have money and I'll loan it to you."

"What the hell are you talking about, Ila? This ain't a time for joking. Can't you see you're breakin' your sister's heart?" Daddy demanded.

"But, Daddy. I can help. I do have the money—I've been saving it for a long time, and I have $250.00 in the bank. It's all the nickel tips I've saved from Judge Joslin, plus some other tips, too. Metta can have it and when she's done with school, she'll pay me back, won't you, Metta." It wasn't a question; it was just a simple declarative sentence—I knew she would.

So that's what we did. I went to the bank the next day, closed my account and gave Metta all my money.

This experience became one more piece of my life's philosophy—my guide to understanding the world. I realized I could have power if I had money. I liked knowing that with money I could make a difference in my life or someone else's—in this case my sister. Second, and maybe even more important, Daddy didn't control everything. He may really have believed that making Metta drop out of college was the right decision—I think he did. But he wasn't the only one who could make things happen. By loaning Metta my $250.00 I made things happen, too.

Those realizations came just in time to help me through our next crisis—courtesy of my dad.

EIGHTEEN

It was about two weeks before Easter, 1930. Eloise and I had been asleep for hours. Something woke me but it was quiet for a few seconds, so I thought I'd been dreaming when I heard mumbling, then louder voices. I couldn't make out what they were saying, but they sounded like they were right on the other side of the bedroom wall. I punched Eloise. "Listen," I whispered. A moment later we heard crying. I pushed Eloise to get out of bed and we both ran through the kitchen and living room to Mother and Daddy's bedroom.

The lamp on the bedside table was on, the shade off-kilter, tipped so that most of the light was shining on Daddy. Mother was sitting up in the bed, crying and looking horrified. She was tugging at the collar of her faded blue flannel nightgown as though she needed to cover up to protect herself from some unseen threat. Daddy was propped up on his elbows, the tan and white striped sleeves of his pajama top pushed up almost to his elbows. His hair was rumpled from just waking up, and his eyes bugged out of his head in a look of panic I'd never seen before. Daddy was yelling, "Mother, I can't move my legs! I can't move my legs!" as both he and Mother stared at his lifeless legs like they were aliens preparing to strike.

I gasped as I inhaled, and stared—first at Mother, then Daddy—and burst into tears. I was terrified. How could someone as big and strong as my dad suddenly be unable to move his legs? A selfish thought popped into my head: what would this mean for me? I was already working at the restaurant after school and on weekends. Did this mean I'd have to do even more? Just the realization that something bad was happening *again* was overwhelming and almost more than I could take. But guilt for thinking of myself and not Daddy wiped those thoughts away in a second. My body and mind went numb.

Eloise just stood there, staring.

Mother stopped crying when she saw us. Her face changed in an instant from fear to consternation, her brow wrinkled, and her lips tightened into a straight line as she said, "Girls, go back to bed." That's when Eloise began to cry.

"Mother! Please! I'm scared. Please don't make us go. Can't we sleep in here?" Eloise begged as she sobbed.

Mother sighed and was quiet for several seconds. I thought sure she was going to point towards the door and tell us to "git," but she surprised me.

"Eloise, Ila. Stop crying. Get your blankets and pillows... you can sleep on the floor at the end of the bed, but I don't want to hear a peep—not one sound from either of you or it's back to your room and I won't argue."

Daddy cleared his throat. "Ahem, Mother. I still need to go to the bathroom..." and his voice trailed off.

Mother's face changed in an instant from a penetrating stare at Eloise and me to disgust as her eyes narrowed and she shifted her gaze to Daddy's face. At least he had the decency to look embarrassed as he stared at his lap.

"Girls," Mother hissed, "go to your room ..." Eloise began to cry again and sputter, "but, but you said ..." Mother cut her off and raised her voice.

CHAPTER EIGHTEEN

"Go to your room," she said sternly, "and get your blankets and pillows. I'll call you in a few minutes and you can come back in and sleep on the floor. Don't argue. Just do it."

Mother rose from the bed and spoke to Daddy as we turned to walk out of the door. Her voice was quiet, low, and harsh. "I have an idea. I'll be back in a minute."

As Eloise and I hurried back to our room I heard Mother's quick steps behind us. She stopped in the kitchen, and I heard a cabinet door open followed by a clinking sound like glasses or jars being moved around on a shelf. Then Mother's rapid steps back to her bedroom and the door firmly closed. I heard her say, "Here, use this." Then nothing 'til the bedroom door opened again, and I heard Mother walk back to the kitchen and out the back door. A few moments later, she returned and called out, "Eloise and Ila. It's okay. Let's get some sleep. Tomorrow's going to be a long day." And it was.

It felt like I'd only been asleep a few minutes when Mother woke Eloise and me early the next morning. Mother was already dressed for work as she said, "Get dressed, Eloise. You're going with me to the restaurant. I need you to help me with the breakfast crowd before school. Ila, you stay here and take care of Daddy." I tried to protest, "But, Mother, I have school, too." She cut me off before I could continue.

"Daddy still can't walk. He isn't any better than he was last night but I'm sure it won't last long—we just have to get through the day. The Bible says, 'Children, honor your parents,' and that's what I expect you to do." I gathered up my blankets and pillow and started out the door. I thought Daddy was asleep because the covers were up over his head, but as the bedroom door closed, I heard Mother say, "Here, Ira. Use this." A moment later she walked through the kitchen and out the back door only to return a few minutes later.

I didn't want to miss school and I didn't want to stay home alone with Daddy either. I was scared that I wouldn't know what to do if something else happened.

After we were both dressed, Eloise and I walked back into the kitchen from our bedroom at the same time. Mother shooed Eloise out to the car. As she steered me toward the bedroom, I asked, "Shouldn't we take Daddy to the doctor?" She shook her head. "No, this'll pass in a couple of days I'm sure. Probably just strained muscles. Now don't give me any sass, just listen and do what I say." She looked me straight in the eyes, her voice dropped to a whisper and she said, "There's a quart jar sitting on the bedside table by Daddy. If he has to a …" she stammered before starting again, "if he has to…to relieve himself, he will use that. If that happens," her face was red with embarrassment, "use newspapers to pick up the jar and empty it outside in the privy. Be careful and rinse it off with water and bleach before you take it back into the bedroom. Use lots of newspapers and be sure to wash your hands with soap and hot water."

My chin began to quiver, and tears welled in my eyes. I tried to look brave but inside I felt queasy—like you feel when the car you're riding in goes over a hill too fast, and your stomach drops—only it wasn't a good feeling, and I thought I might faint. I was only fourteen. "It's just for a day or two," Mother said again as she walked out the door.

I didn't know what to do with myself, so I went into the living room and sat on the sofa, right outside the bedroom door, and looked out the window. It wasn't long before I heard Daddy calling, "Ilie, Ilie come here." I stood up and walked to the door so I could peer in not sure whether I should enter. Daddy was laying on his back, the blankets drawn tightly up under his chin. His face was pale and his voice so soft I could barely hear him, but he gave me a warm smile and gestured for me to enter the room.

CHAPTER EIGHTEEN

"Come in, Honey. It's okay. It looks like we've got some trouble here, don't it?"

I nodded and walked slowly towards the bed. "Daddy, what's wrong? Why can't you walk?" Tears were welling in my eyes, but I tried not to cry so I wouldn't upset Daddy.

"Well, Honey, that's what we need to find out. I don't feel good, that's for sure."

"Are you in pain, Daddy?"

"My legs hurt—kind of like cramps in the muscles—a couple of days ago…"

"I remember that," I interrupted. "You rubbed on some Sloan's Liniment. Daddy, that stuff smells awful. Does it work?"

My dad chuckled. "It does smell bad, don't it? And at first, after you rub it in, it kinda burns but not for long. But it makes the pain go away and that's all I care about."

"So do your legs hurt now?"

"No, now they're numb so I don't feel a thing. Could be I've hurt my back and need a little rest. But I surely do feel tired all over like I haven't slept in days. I think I'll take a little nap now. Don't you worry, I'll be okay in a while."

"But, Daddy" I didn't feel reassured, "how do you know you'll be okay?"

"Ilie, it's just one of those things. Worrying won't help. Now you run along and let me rest."

I spent my time reading and ate some lunch. About two hours later, Daddy called me again to say he had used the jar. His face was bright red, and he stared at the floor when he mumbled, "Do what your mother said, and take this outside."

Now I have to tell you, I worked as a nurse for a lot of years, taking care of patients whose diseased and damaged bodies excreted substances that were sickening to look at and worse to smell and that didn't bother me. But I felt queasy when I had to walk over to Daddy's bedside and pick up that jar of urine. It was something that no child should ever have to do for her parent.

But I did it, and I didn't throw up 'til I was outside.

Mother and Eloise got home around six o'clock that evening bringing supper from the restaurant with them. Eloise brought me my assignments for the next day and told me about school happenings, and Mother went in to take care of Daddy.

The rest of the week was just the same. Each morning I asked Mother about having the doctor come out and each morning she replied, "Not yet. Let's give it a little more time." So, I spent my days with Daddy. We talked about my homework, about trips we wanted to take, about what I wanted to do when I grew up—travel and see the world, visit big cities, buy fancy clothes, eat in elegant restaurants, and go to the theater and museums—in other words, do all the things I'd read about in school.

Around midweek, Mother told Daddy that he was missed. "Ira, several folks have asked me about you. Porky Zink was in and wanted to know why you was playing hooky? I just told him you was under the weather but we expected you back at the grill in a few days." Daddy smiled, pleased that folks had noticed his absence, his eyes glowing with a mischievous spark.

But Daddy didn't get better. By Palm Sunday evening, Mother was so exhausted she couldn't eat supper. I was upset because I didn't want to miss another week of school and I told Mother.

"You're right, Ila. We can't go on like this that's for sure. Tomorrow morning, first thing, I'll call Grandpa Newt and Grandma Rosenie as soon as I get to the restaurant and tell them what's happened. Maybe they can come down and help." We didn't have a phone at home—couldn't

CHAPTER EIGHTEEN

afford it.

I nodded and asked, "What about a doctor, Mother? Shouldn't you call the doctor, too?"

"I guess I'll have to."

True to her word, Mother called the doctor and Grandpa and Grandma the next day. After hearing about our troubles, Grandpa Newt decided he'd come because he was the only one big enough to lift Daddy in and out of bed.

I was relieved when Dr. Kerr came to the house. "Now," I thought to myself, "Daddy's bound to get better, 'cause Dr. Kerr can fix anything."

But I was wrong. He was as puzzled as the rest of us.

"Don't know what it is but you need to take precautions, just in case it's polio. Florence, can you send the girls away for a while?"

"I can send Eloise to Wava's, I guess, but I'm going to need help at the restaurant so Ila's going to have to stay here. I don't know what else to do."

Dr. Kerr nodded gravely but explained, "Be sure she washes her hands good with soap and hot water any time she touches Ira or any of his things."

The plan was that Grandpa would take over Daddy's care and I would go back to school. Grandma Rosenie drove Grandpa to Lincoln two days later, helped pack up Eloise, and turned around and went back home. But things didn't go smoothly between Daddy and Grandpa, let me tell you.

Grandpa hadn't been in the house but a few minutes when I heard Daddy say, "What the Hell are you doing here?" He sounded furious, too.

"Florence called and asked me to come." Grandpa didn't sound happy, either.

"We don't need you here. We're doing fine."

"Listen to me, boy, and listen good." Grandpa sounded really mad now. "You're not doing fine, and Florence isn't either. You can't walk, can you? She's cookin' your meals, helpin' you with your private things, takin' care of Ila and tryin' to run a restaurant because you sure as hell can't. Somebody's gotta take care of the restaurant. And Ila isn't strong enough to turn you. Besides, she should be in school. Florence called me and I'm here to help her, not you. You and me—we'll just have to put up with each other and make the best of it." And that's pretty much how all their conversations went—hostile and brief. I tried not to be around when Grandpa was in the bedroom with Daddy because I didn't want to hear it. Every time they'd argue I felt my stomach begin to knot up with pain and I'd get nauseous.

I hated seeing Eloise go, too. She and I were five years apart and while she was younger than me, we slept together, played together, confided in each other about everything. I knew when she left, I'd be home with only adults to talk to, and because of the troubles we were facing, I was pretty sure they wouldn't have time to talk to me.

NINETEEN

The day that Grandpa arrived to help us is the day Mother first heard that there were other men in Lincoln just like Daddy.

That night at home Mother told Daddy, "Ira, there's five other men besides you who are crippled now."

"What are you saying? Someone else besides me? Who?" Daddy's eyes were big, and the look of fear had returned to his face.

"You know them all. S. C. Page, Fred Noon, Fred White, Herman Zier, and that Olson fellow."

I watched Daddy's face. He seemed to be thinking, concentrating on Mother's words.

"They didn't all stop walking on the same day you did," Mother explained. "You were the first. What if Dr. Kerr is right and you got something contagious? I'm going to call Metta soon as I get to work tomorrow and tell her she can't come home for Easter. No use takin' any more chances than we have to."

Everybody in town was scared. Folks stopped in at the restaurant to ask how Daddy was doing and bring Mother the latest updates on the other five men who were down. Folks said that Daddy was worse off than the rest of them. I was afraid Daddy might die, or that Mother would become crippled, too. And I wondered if the same thing would happen to me? I tried to get some answers one evening as we were riding home from the restaurant.

"Mother, do you think Daddy will die?" Mother kept her eyes on the street and both hands gripped on the steering wheel. She frowned as she answered me.

"Hush, Ila. Don't talk that way."

"But, Mother, what if Daddy dies? What will we do?" She still didn't look at me and I wasn't sure she was really listening.

"He's not going to die."

"But how do you know? Will he get better? Maybe we should take him to K.U. to the big hospital there." Mother exhaled loudly as she answered.

"There's no money for anything like that and I don't want to hear another word about it."

I was frustrated because I couldn't get any more out of her. It took me years to realize that Mother was afraid talking about something bad might make it come true.

In the meantime, I did my best to help my dad. Mother worried, and sometimes in the evenings she sat by his bedside and held his hand, something I'd never seen before. Even Grandpa Newt treated Daddy as gently as Grandpa Newt knew how.

It didn't take long to find out what Daddy's getting crippled meant for me—more work at home—even with Grandpa Newt there. I washed Daddy's hair, changed the sheets, did the dishes, and helped Mother with laundry. Then I either went to the restaurant to help or on to school.

On Monday afternoon, the day after Easter, Mother was waiting for me outside the back door of the restaurant by our car. Her presence there surprised and worried me. "Mother, why are you out here instead of inside cooking?"

"The night cook came in early. Let's go, Ila. I need to get home."

"Why? Has something happened? Is Daddy okay?" She didn't

CHAPTER NINETEEN

answer me except to gruffly say, "Get in the car."

"But, Mother, what's wrong?" Still, she refused to answer me, just slammed the driver's side door, started the car, and drove down the alley toward home, staring out of the windshield straight ahead. She seemed angry but I couldn't figure out why and thought maybe she was mad at me.

Grandpa Newt was sitting at the kitchen table, drinking his afternoon cup of coffee. The minute we entered the kitchen Mother dropped her purse on the table, rushed past him without saying a word and stormed into the bedroom. I followed her as far as the living room, hoping I'd finally learn what was wrong. She fixed Daddy with eyes that looked like they were shooting the flames of Hell straight into his heart and screeched:

"Jamaica Ginger! You drank poisoned Jamaica Ginger and that's why you're crippled! Why you're all crippled." From where I stood, I could see them both through the open bedroom door. Mother stood in the middle of the room, and even though she was only 5'2" she towered over Daddy who was struggling to pull himself up on his elbows so he could respond. While Mother screamed, I looked over my shoulder at Grandpa Newt to see what he'd do. Grandpa Newt stood up, stiff and straight, his hands clenched into fists at his sides. He didn't move and he didn't look at me: he just stood and listened; his face grim.

"Florence, calm down. What are you talking about?"

"There's hundreds of men in Oklahoma, all crippled just like you, and all the papers say it's because of poisoned Jamaica Ginger. Alcohol! Alcohol! How could you?

"The devil has captured you, Ira Armsbury, and is dragging you to Hell and he's using alcohol to do it. You have defied God and defiled the sacred temple that is your body and now God is punishing you for it.

"Your harlot wasn't enough to shame me? Your arrest and

that trial. Now this... this plague you've brought on all our heads. Everyone will know that you're a fornicator **and** a drunkard." And with that she turned and marched out of the bedroom and stalked past me into the kitchen.

I was stunned. I'd heard Mother and Daddy quarrel before, but I'd never heard Mother spit out such words of venom, condemning Daddy for all eternity. But, I wondered, was it true? Was this all Daddy's fault? I looked at Daddy whose face had turned white. His eyes met mine and he weakly called, "Ilie?"

But I couldn't...what? Look at him? Listen to another excuse or lie? I left the house... I couldn't stand any more. A big field with several old trees extended from the back of our house to the next street. I liked to explore back there and this particular day, I needed some time to think, so I walked toward the tree line that bordered the road and sat down under a huge old cottonwood tree which had taken root in a small gully. No one could see me from the house, but I could hear Mother if she called.

I'd worried about Daddy, prayed to God to make him well, helped him with his personal needs as best I could. I'd stayed home from school for him, got behind in my studies, cried with fear 'til there were no more tears. And suddenly we'd learned that this entire tragedy could have been avoided? For the first time I saw my dad as selfish and self-centered, interested in his own needs and desires, and heedless of any consequences.

I was shocked to think that Daddy had done this to himself— and to us—enraged that this was Daddy's own fault. How could he do this? We had all pleaded, cried, yelled, and prayed with him and at him various times over the years to stop his drinking.

I don't know how long I sat there, crying, and thinking, but finally I decided I'd cried enough for one day, so I quit and walked back

CHAPTER NINETEEN

to the house. Things were quiet. Food from the restaurant was sitting on the kitchen table. Mother and Grandpa Newt were sitting there eating supper and talking about the Bible. The door to the bedroom was open but the light was off. I wondered, for an instant, whether Daddy was sleeping, but just as quickly thought to myself, "I don't care even if he's awake. I don't want to talk to him anyway." So, I walked into the kitchen, fixed a plate of food, and sat down at the table.

"Mother, I heard you tell Daddy that Jamaica Ginger made him crippled and that it's alcohol."

"A good Christian doesn't imbibe in any alcoholic drink. It's a sin against God and man." She was quiet for a minute before adding, "Ila, I don't want to talk about it anymore—not now—not ever," and as far as I know, she never did again.

That night—when we'd first learned that Daddy had poisoned himself by drinking Jamaica Ginger—I didn't go in to tell Daddy good night before I went to bed—I just couldn't—I was too angry. My next chance to talk with him didn't come until the next night, after Mother and I finished supper. Grandpa Newt had carried Daddy's dirty supper dishes into the kitchen, so I went into the bedroom and closed the door.

Daddy's face lit up when he saw me. He was wearing a big smile as he pulled himself up on his elbows. "Hi, Ilie. I missed saying good night to you last night. Everything okay?"

"No," I growled. "How could everything be okay when you're crippled because you drank Jamaica Ginger and Mother said that's poisoned alcohol." Tears began streaming down my face as I stood near the bed, but far enough away he couldn't reach me, my arms crossed over my middle as I hugged myself to keep from flying apart into a million little pieces.

Daddy's face changed in an instant from a big smile to sadness and his eyes dropped from my face to the floor. His voice was quiet and sounded sorrowful as he said, "Ilie, I'm so sorry. I just don't see how it could be the Jamaica Ginger. Why, I've drunk that stuff for years and nothing bad's ever happened before."

"But Mother said ..." I sobbed but I couldn't go on.

"Ilie, come here. Please." I moved over by the bed and Daddy reached his arm out and gently laid his big hand on my back as he gave me an awkward hug. His hand moved slowly up and down as he gently rubbed my back and I leaned into the bed soaking up the comfort. When I looked up Daddy's eyes were teary, too. I leaned forward and gave him a hug. We stayed like that; Daddy balanced on one elbow with the other arm stretched as far as he could go around me and me leaning into the bed hugging him. Finally, he pulled his arm back gently and said, "Ilie, it's bedtime. I know this is hard for you and I am sorry, but we will get through this."

* * *

Mother and Grandpa didn't rush to help my dad after they learned what had caused him to be crippled. Mother no longer sat by his bedside holding his hand, even when he asked her to. And when Daddy, albeit reluctantly, called for help from Grandpa Newt, Grandpa was slow to respond.

One evening I overheard Grandpa refuse to help Daddy sit up in bed.

"Boy, you better figure out how you're gonna take care of yourself, 'cause I got my own family to take care of and I'll be goin' home to Lucas here pretty shortly." Grandpa walked out of the bedroom and joined Mother and me in the living room where I was doing homework and Mother was reading her Bible.

The next evening, Daddy asked me to bring him one of the

CHAPTER NINETEEN

wooden chairs from the kitchen.

"Set it down right here, right by the bed. That's right. Ah, no, no, a little closer, that's the ticket, so it's touching the bed and I can reach it. That's it. You can go back to what you were doin' now." He smiled and winked at me as I turned to go back to the living room.

It was hard to concentrate on my homework because of the noise coming from the bedroom. First, I heard the rustling of bed clothes followed by grunting, panting, heavy breathing, more grunting and the chair scrapping across the floor. Finally, the noise subsided but I was curious, so I peeked into the bedroom and there was Daddy sitting on the chair, his pajamas mussed, but he smiled when he saw me and motioned me in.

"Need to learn how to do things for myself. I been thinkin' how I was gonna do it, and by golly I think I figured it out. Took a bit of time, but I made it to the chair." He was beaming like I would if I'd just walked on a tightrope across the Grand Canyon.

"Won't be long now and I'll be back to work. Yes, Siree. Won't be long."

Daddy's restlessness increased once he'd taught himself how to sit up and move from the bed to the chair.

He dedicated himself to relearning how to walk. He'd sit up in bed and use his arms and hands to lift and swing first one leg and then the other, so his feet were flat on the floor. Next, he'd pivot his whole body so that he was sitting on the side of the bed. Then, grabbing the back of the chair, he'd pull himself upright to a standing position and push the chair ahead of himself, shuffling his feet. It was slow and arduous for him and painful for me to watch. But it wasn't long before he'd graduated from a shuffling walk with the chair to walking with a pair of crutches.

To increase his upper arm strength Daddy spent hours each day hitting a punching bag suspended over a table on our screened-in back porch. He became so proficient that he looked like a prize fighter ready to go into the ring.

All his sweat and exercise paid off: he was driving his car by the first part of June and back at the restaurant by the end of the month.

In a weird twist of fate, the Lincoln chapter of the Women's Christian Temperance Union held its regular meeting at the end of July and had one of the largest turnouts in its history. I imagine they had a lot to talk and pray about since so many Lincoln men had fallen under the spell of demon rum. Mother attended and came home singing the words to a song she heard performed there—"Where is My Wandering Boy Tonight?"

I look back at that time—when it would have been so easy for my dad to act like a martyr, feel sorry for himself, or give up—and marvel at his optimism, persistence, and courage. It was one more lesson for me and I tucked away what I learned from watching him so that if and when I was confronted with a crisis, I'd know how to get through it. Mother's solution to every crisis was prayer, and while I still believed in prayer, I liked Daddy's approach which I added to my life philosophy—"Ila, don't whine. If you don't like what's happening, get up and do something!"

TWENTY

Metta's classes were out for the summer of 1930. She was working at the restaurant, but of course, Daddy wasn't paying her, just like he didn't pay me or Eloise or Mother. The lunch rush hour was over. Metta had been waiting tables all morning, and I was washing dishes because Eloise hadn't felt good and had stayed home. Mother had been standing at the old, hot gas range for hours, and you could tell, just by looking at her that her back and feet ached.

Metta walked into the kitchen through the swinging door and said, "Mother, there's no one out there. Why don't you take a break and sit down?"

Mother looked around the kitchen, nodded her head once and said, "I believe I will. You girls can go outside and sit in the sun if you want. I'm going to get me a cup of coffee and sit at the counter. If anyone comes in, I'll let you know."

So, I dried my hands, got a glass of water, and Metta and I went out the back door to sit on the slanted wooden door that covered the steps down to the dirt floor cellar that ran the length of the restaurant. I was curious about college and why Metta had decided to become a teacher.

"Don't you get lonely away from home?"

"Oh, I was lonely at first, even a little bit scared. But I wasn't really alone. The other girls and my teachers were always around. And I was so busy with my studies, you know, that I just didn't have time to feel sorry for myself. And I knew I'd be coming home for Thanksgiving and Christmas and that helped a lot."

"But why a teacher? Do you like children that much?"

"I like children, but I love teaching. I love knowing that I can make a difference in someone's life. I can open up the world to someone who may never leave Kansas but will still know about Egypt, or Scotland, or Hawaii simply because I helped him learn to read. Why, I truly believe I will be doing God's work when I start teaching. And what could be more important than that?"

Before I could ask anything else, Metta added: "And think about it, Ilie. You've seen how hard Mother works in the restaurant and how little she has. Do you want to work that hard? I don't. You know there're nights that she can barely stand, her back hurts so much. No, I've worked in that restaurant all I care to. Once I have my teaching certificate, I'm going to earn my way, but without the backbreaking labor that Mother does."

Have you ever had that experience where a lightbulb goes off in your brain and suddenly you know something that you hadn't known just a moment before? Well, that's what happened to me as Metta talked. I realized if I didn't get more education—not just a high school diploma—I'd be stuck in Lincoln at that restaurant, just like Mother, caught up in Daddy's craziness, and I'd never have a life of my own. I decided I had to go to college.

My sophomore year in high school started right after Labor Day. With Metta back in Emporia and Eloise only in fourth grade, my work schedule became even more exhausting. I got up every morning at 5:45 so I could help with the breakfast crowd, grab a fast bite to keep me going and run a mile to the high school for classes. At 11:50 a.m., I ran back to the restaurant and helped with lunch before rushing back to school for

CHAPTER TWENTY

afternoon classes. When school let out at 3:50, I had to hightail it to the restaurant and wait tables 'til 8:00 p.m., when I finally got to go home for the night. You can see why I wanted to go to college.

I just had to convince my folks, especially my dad, to let me go. That became my project for the next two years.

It was quite a campaign because my folks made their expectations clear. Mother wanted me to marry some nice young man from Lincoln, settle down near the folks, and have babies. Daddy was fine with all that, but he also wanted me to work in the restaurant, for free, so he could cut down on his labor costs. His selfishness no longer surprised me. I'd already confronted it on more than one occasion. Remember when I cut my wrist? or when he crippled himself because of his drinking? The problem was that I decided I wanted to go to nursing school at the University of Kansas in Kansas City.

My dad's response? "No, Ilie. You can't go to K.U. Al Capone runs Kansas City, along with Chicago and New York, don't you know that?"

"What?" I know I sounded shocked. I knew who Al Capone was, but I'd never heard that he ran Kansas City.

"It ain't safe for a young girl. I won't allow it." I was reeling from this pronouncement when he continued, "You can go to Salina to Wesleyan Hospital."

I was livid, and almost screamed my response. "If I'm going to work hard in school for three years, I want to be able to go wherever I choose in the whole wide world. So, if I can't go to K.U., I'll just stay here and work in this dirty old restaurant the rest of my life!"

"Suits me," he replied. "As soon as school is out in May I'll lay off the day waitress and you can take her place. You can keep your tips, if you make any, but that's it." Which meant no pay from him—I'd still be working for free.

ILA'S WAR

It was one of the worst periods of my life. I couldn't see any way out from under my dad's thumb—stuck in that god-forsaken restaurant with no income of my own other than the money from the candy and match machines and tips, and my dad's refusal to allow me to apply to K.U. for nursing school. When Daddy entered the restaurant in the late afternoon to work the evening shift, I left. When we were at home at the same time, I stayed in my room. We didn't speak to each other. I think he expected me to back down, but I couldn't resign myself to a life of drudgery. Our battle of wills continued even after I graduated from Lincoln High School in May of 1933.

Things came to a head the Sunday after Thanksgiving. The Sunday dinner rush was over. Eloise and Daddy had already finished their clean-up jobs and gone home. The closed sign was hanging on the front door and Mother and I were the only ones left to finish the last of the dirty dishes before we headed home, too. I felt so bad that while Mother was finishing up her last-minute tasks, I wandered out the back door. I intended to go sit in the car and wait but instead, much to my surprise, I started sobbing but didn't know why. I didn't want Mother to see me crying, so I went down into the cellar and sat on the bottom step when I heard Mother.

"Ila what're you doing down there in the dark? There's cobwebs in your hair. What in the world is goin' on?"

I didn't know how to answer her. All I could think to do was shake my head, but Mother's stare was unremitting. Finally, after what seemed like an hour of quiet, I tried to explain.

"Mother, I'm sorry," I sniffled. "I know you've taught us that there are always others whose burdens are bigger than ours. And I know I ought to count my blessings and remember that I have a warm place to sleep at night and good food to eat every day, but I'm so miserable, I... I..." and I started crying again.

CHAPTER TWENTY

"Ila, stop it! Now! Just stop it! You're going to make yourself sick. It can't be all that bad."

"But Mother, it is. I can't stand the thought of spending the rest of my life in this town, working in this restaurant. I've got to leave. You know I do. I want to be a nurse and I want to go to K.U. and I want to live in a big city and work in a big city hospital, and I want…"

Mother cut me off and said, "I know. I know. But what prompted this now? The way you were actin', I thought you were gettin' used to the idea of stayin' here and settlin' down."

"Haven't you heard that new song on the radio? I can't stand to listen to it. Every time it comes on, I start to cry."

"Ila, stop all this foolishness. What song? Why would a song make you cry?"

"It's the words. 'Boulevard of broken dreams… awake to find their eyes are wet with tears…' Mother, that's me. I wake up sometimes at night or in the morning, and I can tell I've been crying in my sleep. I just don't think I can do this," and I started sobbing again.

"I see."

We were both quiet as I rose, adjusted my blouse and skirt, wiped my hands across my dirty face, and slowly climbed the stairs. I took the door handle from Mother and carefully lowered the cellar door to its closed position. I turned to Mother and looked at her with tears in my eyes.

"Ila, I'll think of something, I will, but I want you to pray. And pray hard, cause it's going to take a lot of prayer to make everything turn out okay."

* * *

Sometime after the first of the year, January of 1934, a rumor—one that

ILA'S WAR

I now think was started by my mother—began circulating around town that the K.U. nursing program received 700 applications per year but only accepted 40. Daddy heard the rumor and when I again broached the idea of applying, he agreed. I think he figured I wouldn't be accepted.

Daddy was shocked when I got an official letter of acceptance from K.U. *I* was overjoyed, laughing and crying at the same time, as I read and reread the acceptance letter. I had a path out of Lincoln and away from the restaurant and my dad's craziness. I had only four weeks to prepare and my first act was to go to each of the businessmen who had written letters of support for me—Mr. Hollingsworth the jeweler, the school superintendent, and Judge Joslin—and thank them personally for their help and encouragement. In my remaining time, Mother and I sewed dresses, skirts and blouses, nursing uniforms, night gowns, even undergarments, so that when I went off to school I'd be supplied and ready to study.

Finally, the day I'd dreamed about for so long—leaving Lincoln—arrived. Early Monday morning of Labor Day, September 3, 1934, Daddy and Mother drove me to Kansas City.

I heard snatches of conversation between Mother and Daddy. "Haven't drove... long drive... good day to be out... them trees is..."

My mind raced as we approached Kansas City. I was still in shock, realizing that I had won the war with my dad over my future. Everything had happened so fast. Now, I was starting down a new path, one that I had feared might elude me forever. I couldn't focus on the scenery as I replayed the previous night's conversation in my head.

"Ilie, I'm gonna miss you working nights with me at the restaurant. Won't get real lonesome though, 'cause I know when you finish and come back home I'll have me a first-rate nurse to look after these old bones. Yes, sir! Things are gonna work out swell." I didn't want

CHAPTER TWENTY

another fight, so I ignored his comment about me returning to Lincoln. I figured, there'd be time enough later for that battle.

Daddy's voice roused me from my daydreams sometime later. "Ilie, we're here. Let's get this stuff into your room." So Mother, Daddy and I unloaded the car and moved me into my new home, Hinch Hall, the nursing students' residence at K.U.

TWENTY-ONE

Living in a residence hall was like living at home, only this home was more luxurious, and I had more than three sisters. I shared a room with another nursing student. Our room had two clothes closets side-by-side and our own bathroom complete with toilet, lavatory, and tub. I pretended I was living at the Waldorf Astoria because I had to share the bathroom with only one other person—my roommate— rather than home where I had to share with three, Mother, Daddy, and Eloise, and four if Metta was there.

We could add little touches to make our rooms more homey, so I brought photos and a rag rug that Mother had made. My roommate, a girl from a wealthy family in eastern Kansas, brought matching twin-size bedspreads. We were quite proud of our room and were sure it was the prettiest in the building.

About two weeks after school started, I received a letter from Mother.

Your dad's taking the credit for you being in nursing school. Says it's because you're smart like him.

I could just picture him. Sitting on a stool at the end of the lunch counter, facing the front door, a mug of hot, steaming coffee sitting on the counter in front of him. I knew exactly what he'd say, too. "Didja, hear

CHAPTER TWENTY-ONE

'bout Ila? Accepted into nursing school at K.U. Mighty smart girl, I'd say. Takes after her ole man." I could only shake my head in wonder and think, what a *character*.

Nursing education was a combination of classroom lecture and hands-on training. I studied at least twenty hours a week in addition to working six ten-hour days for a total of 60 hours per week at Bell Memorial, the teaching hospital associated with K.U. In exchange for my work, I received free room, board, and laundry at Hinch Hall and was paid $8.00 per month. We also had to provide our own equipment: scissors, metal syringe, tweezers, and a thermometer.

I was too busy to get homesick, and those few times when I wasn't working, in class or studying I made new friends and even attended parties and dances, always with other nursing students and a chaperone. I'd always been athletic so during the summer months I played tennis, swam, and went for long walks around Kansas City, especially the beautiful Kansas City Plaza with its fountains and ornate Spanish-style buildings. Every day I considered myself the luckiest girl I knew because I was pursuing my dream. How many people can say that?

***

I was making beds and giving baths on one of the men's wards when I first heard it—a soft "click" followed by the sound "uhhhhh." Nowadays we call it the death rattle, but it didn't mean a thing to me at the time—until I looked over at the patient in the next bed, a young black man with a severe bladder infection who had been unconscious for five days.

"Click—uhhhhh" again. As I stepped to his side, he vomited bright green fluid. I grabbed a towel and an emesis basin from the small table by his bed and began cleaning him up, but it rolled out faster than I could catch it.

"Miss Rose," I called to the second-year nursing student, who was attending another patient five beds from me. "Miss Rose. I need some help here."

She looked up, nodded and headed toward me when my patient vomited again. After a quick look she said, "I'm going to get Miss Lewick," and I nodded in relief. Miss Rose walked quickly out of the ward, leaving me to try again to clean up the mess and comfort my patient. I put my arm under his head and shoulders and a hand on his wrist, taking his pulse, when his breathing changed again.

"Click—uuuuhhhhhhh." then nothing. His eyes rolled back, his tongue protruded, he jerked once or twice, and stiffened out. I knew he was gone. I pushed his tongue in and closed his mouth and eyes. There was nothing else I could do.

"He's dead," I said in a soft voice to Miss Lewick and Miss Rose as they walked toward me. The words were hardly out of my mouth when Miss Rose hit the floor—out cold.

Miss Lewick grinned like a chessy-cat and said, "Miss Armsbury, you'll have to help Miss Rose prepare the body."

"But Miss Lewick, I'm only a probie and haven't learned how to take care of a corpse," I explained. Probies—the title given to nursing students during their first 18 months of school—could get into big trouble if they performed a task for which they had not been trained, and I'd worked too damn hard to get thrown out of nursing school.

"It's all right, Miss Armsbury. Miss Rose will be in charge, and you will observe and assist when asked."

By this time Miss Rose had come around and was sitting up, her face as white as the walls of the hospital ward.

Miss Lewick walked off and I stood at the foot of the bed, looking at Miss Rose expectantly.

Nothing happened.

CHAPTER TWENTY-ONE

I waited, still looking at Miss Rose and giving her what I hoped was an encouraging smile.

Still nothing happened. Finally, I said, "Shall we get started?" thinking that would snap her out of whatever daze she was in—but it didn't work.

"Ah, Miss Armsbury," she stammered. "I believe you are going to have to do this... but I will sit right here and tell you what to do and how," and that's what she did.

I bathed him, removed the tubes that had been inserted in his legs and wrists and body openings, took off all the adhesive plaster marks, tied his mouth closed, cleaned his fingernails, and wrapped him in a sheet. When Miss Lewick returned, about thirty minutes later, she said, "Miss Rose, that's a nice, neat job." I didn't say a thing, but I didn't need to because Miss Rose said, "You'd better tell Miss Armsbury that."

"Miss Armsbury?" Miss Lewick sounded surprised as she turned to me. "You did a very good job here. Is this your first dead body?"

"Yes, ma'am, it is."

"Well, how do you feel? Queasy? Weak in the knees? Frightened?"

"No," I replied after a few seconds of thought. "I feel fine. I'm sorry this man died, and I wish there had been something more I could have done. But I feel okay."

"Good," Miss Lewick said as she nodded her head and gave me a smile of approval. "I have no doubt you'll do well the next time."

She was right. I did do well the next time I lost a patient, but not at supper the evening of that first death when they served peas that were the same color as my dying patient's excretions...after two bites, my stomach took a leap, and I left the table.

* * *

ILA'S WAR

I learned quickly that to be a nurse you had to become hardened to the sights and smells and sounds, but not to the patient. We saw patients with skin grafts, deep and horrific smelling bed sores, amputations, surgeries, and deliveries. Some of the girls fainted and some vomited, but I stayed right in there and loved every minute of it—not the gore but the skills shown by doctors and nurses who knew how to help and how to heal. This was the calling for me.

I believe that one of the most amazing sights in medicine is a live birth. I observed and even assisted a bit in one when I'd been in nursing school only five months. A young woman gave birth as we were preparing her for the delivery room! After the baby was born—a little girl—the doctor handed her to me and I cleaned, dressed and weighed her. What a miracle! That's when I decided obstetrics was for me.

* * *

Mother wrote me at least once a week to tell me how everybody in the family was doing. Metta was in her second year of teaching and dating one of the Wilson boys. Eloise was in the eighth grade and doing well in her studies. Daddy wrote, too, giving me all the latest gossip about the folks who worked on main street. Much of the talk was about the horrible dirt storms that seemed to be worsening in central and western Kansas.

In early spring, 1935 I received a chilling letter from Metta, who was back living in Lincoln, teaching at the junior high school. She wrote, "I'm keeping a journal of the things that happen. Maybe I'll write a book someday. Who knows? Anyway, here's a copy of my entry for last Friday."

Friday, March 15 I witnessed the most severe storm known

CHAPTER TWENTY-ONE

to my 23 years of life. In the early evening, the wind began to rise. It increased in velocity and carried great quantities of silt from unknown sources. The air was so filled with dust particles that electric lights could not be seen across main street... The blinding, choking hurricane raged on for hours. A thick layer of silt gathered on every object that presented a surface.

An incredible amount of dust collected in houses and other buildings. Few buildings were able to withstand the impact of wind-blown sod. Breathing was difficult inside because a dusty fog pervaded in each room. It was almost impossible to sleep without a damp cloth over one's nose and mouth. Dust collected on pillows where one's head lay. By morning, a white spot on a grey background marked the place where an object lay.

Stories told of the following morning are incredible to those who have not seen [this]. In many houses, the colors in upholstery, rugs, and curtains could not be identified. Some 300 pounds of dirt were removed from one room in the Junior High School building.

Shortly after getting Metta's letter, I received bad news from Wava. Both LaDonna and Phyllis had developed asthma because of the dust. Wava said that every night she put wet bed sheets over the little girls' beds to try to keep out the dust, but by morning the sheets were dry and covered with dirt as was the girls' bedding. The only place in their whole house that was dust-free was the breadbox, which was kept inside a drawer in the kitchen.

To make matters worse, the ranch had produced no wheat or cattle for the previous three years and Nolan had borrowed money from a bank in Lucas to offset the financial losses. But he hadn't been able to repay the loan, so the bank had taken the farm. Wava, Nolan and the girls had moved to Lincoln and were working in the restaurant with Mother and Daddy. It was a hard adjustment for Wava. No more store-bought dresses and fancy undergarments. And worst of all, she had to wait tables and cook—tasks that she felt were beneath her.

In the late spring of 1935, the aunt of one of my classmates, a nurse working in Manila, came for a visit to the nursing school and spoke to a group of us girls. It was just an informal gathering, we sat around a big table in one of the classrooms and listened with rapt attention.

"Have you given any thought to what you want to do after nursing school?" she asked. "As you know, I live and work in the Philippines. I've been teaching there for five years. My boss is a member of the Board of Directors of the Manila Hospital, and he's told me many times that American nurses are in great demand over there. American nurses work as supervisors or superintendents. You'd never have to do general floor duty. If travel and living in a foreign country are for you, think about coming to Manila after you graduate in 1937. I can get each and every one of you a job."

I tell you my heart almost pounded out of my chest. Travel and work in a foreign country were two of my life's goals and here was someone who could make it happen. I could hardly wait to graduate.

* * *

Early summer, 1936, after I'd just completed the first two years at K.U, I got a letter from my dad.

> *Honey, I'm sorry to have to tell you this but you're going to have to come home. Mother and I don't have the money for your last year.*
>
> *Now, Ilie, I know you had your heart set on this, and maybe*

CHAPTER TWENTY-ONE

we can come up with the money in another year or two, but not right now. Let me know when you'll be arriving, and I'll pick you up at the train station."

I was furious. He'd done the same to Metta—committed to help her with school expenses but didn't do any planning or saving ahead of time. I'd helped Metta and after her graduation from Emporia State in 1931, she'd gotten a teaching job and started selling ladies suits on the side as a way to pay me back. But she didn't have a lump sum she could send me now when I needed it.

I agonized over what to do, coming up with several ideas but eventually rejecting them as being unworkable.

Maybe I should just defy the folks and refuse to go home. But if I do that, how would I pay for school?

Maybe I should ask Grandpa Newt for the money. But if I do that, Daddy would be so furious and so humiliated that he and Mother might never speak to me again.

Maybe I should go home and beg Daddy for the money—or offer to work for free in the restaurant for a year after graduation if he'll borrow money for me to finish school. But would anybody loan him money? They all know Daddy in Lincoln, so that's out.

Suddenly I had a brainstorm: I would borrow the money myself. Why not? They knew me in Lincoln. They knew I was a hard worker and I always kept my word. Why wouldn't they loan me the money? The more I thought about it the more the idea appealed to me. Judge Joslin had always encouraged me to do well in school, he'd even sent me money on occasion, and he'd offered to help me any way he could. I didn't have anything to lose, so I wrote him, explained the problem, and asked if he could loan me the money for a round-trip train ticket to Lincoln. He sent the money straightaway.

The next day I got up early, dressed with care, and took the early morning train home. I didn't tell anybody I was coming. I walked from the train station, which was at the west end of main street, to the Lincoln State Bank, walked right in like I was as good as anybody, met with the bank president, and sat right down to ask for a loan. It was one of the hardest things I'd ever done, and I don't mind telling you my heart beat like a metronome set at *prestissimo*. But I walked out of that bank with a check large enough to pay for my last year of school, and all the extras I'd need to graduate.

My next stop—home to tell my folks. Mother was already home from work when I walked in the back door. She was sitting at the kitchen table with a cup of coffee. Eloise and Daddy were working at the restaurant.

"Why, Ila, what are you doing here? We wasn't expecting you. Is everything okay?"

"It's great, Mother. I'm great, too. How are you? When will Daddy be home?"

"You know he won't be here 'til after 8:00. Where's your things? We didn't know you was coming home so soon. Eloise hasn't moved her things out of the dresser to make room for you yet."

"That's okay, Mother. I've been up since before dawn. I think I'll just lay down for a bit. When Daddy gets home, we can sit down and talk."

* * *

I was up from my nap, sitting at the kitchen table drinking a cup of coffee when Eloise and Daddy walked in the back door. "Why, Ilie. I didn't expect you so soon. How'd you get here? Somebody give you a ride?"

He gave me a quick hug as he walked by. "Let me get a cup of

CHAPTER TWENTY-ONE

coffee and we can sit and visit. You probably got lots on your mind."

His piddling around in the kitchen gave me a few seconds to collect my thoughts, but once he sat down, my mind went blank, and I just blurted out my news. "Daddy, I don't have to leave school. I got a loan from the bank."

"You did what?" Daddy roared. "That's the stupidest thing I ever heard of in my life. Borrowing money you can't pay back."

I wanted to say, *"How would you know? The only investment you ever made was in your girlfriends or your booze."*

He sat and glared at me. I turned toward Mother, hoping she'd come to my rescue, but she didn't say anything, just started crying, shaking her head and wiping her eyes with an old handkerchief she kept poked up the sleeve of her dress. Finally, she said, "No man wants a wife who doesn't know her place, Ila. There are just some things a woman doesn't do."

In that moment I realized just how far apart we were, Mother, Daddy, and me. I knew while they might love me, they'd never understand me. I couldn't change them and I sure as hell wasn't going to let them change me, because I didn't want what they had to offer. It was one of the lowest points of my life. I couldn't think of anything more to say so I said good night, went to bed with Eloise, and caught the early train the next morning back to Kansas City and my future. I didn't see my folks again for a year, until graduation, in 1937.

A month prior to my graduation Miss Froehlke, the head of the nursing program, called me into her office. My only thought was "what have I done now?"

"Sit down, Miss Armsbury," she said in that commanding voice of hers.

"Yes ma'am. Is there a problem? Have I done something?" my voice quivered as I asked.

"Yes, you have Miss Armsbury. Yes, you have. I'm delighted to inform you that you have been awarded the next post-graduate course in obstetric nursing here at K.U. It's given to only one out of every class, the girl is chosen as to her scholastic record, practical work, interest, and efficiency. It's a new course and you are only the 4th student to receive it."

I felt faint. "I don't know what to say, Miss Froehlke. Thank you... aaahh... Thank you."

"You're welcome, I'm sure. Now you know this doesn't pay a great deal, but after you get out, there'll be more money and a job waiting for you, too."

TWENTY-TWO

"Marguerite," I mumbled as I yawned into my coffee cup, "I don't know how much more of this I can take."

Marguerite Coffman, my work supervisor, best friend from college, housemate, and confidante nodded and put her head in her hand, her elbow resting on the kitchen table. "I know, believe me I know. I don't think I've ever been so tired in my whole life, not even when we were in school," she said with her eyes closed.

Since we'd graduated from K.U. two years previously, Marguerite and I had worked for the same maternity program but in two different agencies—she was a nursing supervisor at the Kansas City Health Department, and I was an assistant supervisor at the Kansas University Hospital Maternity Center. In those days, most people didn't see a doctor until they were practically dead. Same with poor pregnant women who didn't get prenatal care and had their babies at home.

Home births didn't always go well. Sometimes babies, or mothers, or both, died during the birthing process. That's why the school opened the Maternity Center. Teams from the Center went to homes in the Kansas City slums, where doctors delivered babies. But it was emotionally and physically exhausting work because of the conditions we saw.

I thought my family was poor, but I didn't know poverty until I worked in the slums. People living in wooden crates, cockroaches so thick that they covered the light I used to see by, malnourished women who could not produce milk to nurse their babies. I couldn't do anything about the horrible living conditions, but thankfully I could show new mothers who couldn't nurse how to feed their newborns.

"Miss Armsbury, ma'am, how'm I gonna feed this baby when I don't have no milk? This baby gonna starve and all I can do is pray."

"Well, praying is good, and I never discourage anyone from prayer, but there is something you can feed your baby."

"But I can't buy that 'spensive formula so what'm I gonna do?"

"You don't need formula. You can use navy beans."

"Navy beans? How a newborn baby ain't got no teeth gonna eat navy beans? I never heard such a thing."

"You take navy beans and boil them until they're mush. Mash them up, like you were mashing potatoes, but even more until the beans are real fine. Add a little bit of sugar and some sterile water, just until it's liquid. Put it in a sterilized bottle with a nipple—you'll probably have to make the nipple hole a little bigger—and there you have it. That will feed your baby."

After 22 months of work without a break and being on-call all hours of the day and night, I was pooped.

In early 1940, Margie and I each got letters from the Red Cross offering us a year of active training with the Army, but we'd just laughed. Neither of us could see ourselves taking orders from an Army officer. But as time passed, and we became more exhausted and depressed by our jobs, we decided to reconsider the offer.

Circumstances outside our control helped us make the decision. The Maternity Clinic moved to a new facility, and Margie and I had to help with the packing and the move as well as remain on-call for home deliveries. The move was finally completed after days of bone-and-muscle-weary work. Margie and I were thrilled to have the whole weekend

CHAPTER TWENTY-TWO

off—unless we got called in for a home delivery. It was a Saturday morning in early September 1940, and we were sitting, dressed in our pjs and bathrobes, at the kitchen table going through the mail.

"Margie, look. Here's a letter to you from the Red Cross," and as I handed it across the table, I spied another letter to me. Before I could open my envelope, Margie began laughing.

"I don't believe it, Ila. It's another offer of a year of training with the Army."

"Wait. Let me see what mine says." I tore open the envelope and scanned my letter.

"Mine, too. You know? A year ago, I wasn't interested. But I wasn't so damn tired either."

Margie piped up, "And depressed."

"And depressed." I concurred. "Now I can see some advantages to this. It'd be a break, great training that I wouldn't have to pay for. And the war..." my voice trailed off as I thought about what was happening in Europe. A few days earlier the Nazis had begun air raids on central London. I worried it wouldn't be much longer before we entered the war, too. "If the U.S. enters the war, they're going to need a lot of nurses."

Margie and I talked for hours that weekend debating the pros and cons of joining. In the end we decided that we'd join the Army at the same time. That way, we thought, we'd be sent to the same base and could continue working together. We filled out the paperwork, sent it in, and waited for a response. A couple of weeks later we heard back. On November 1, 1940, we drove to Leavenworth, passed the Army's exams, and signed up. All that was left was for me to go to Lincoln and tell the folks.

I decided the best course of action was to tell them together, and the best time to do that was on a Sunday afternoon after the restaurant was closed for the day. So, I got up early on Sunday morning, November 10, and took the train to Lincoln. I arrived at the house about an hour before the folks got home.

"Why, Ila. We didn't know you was comin' home. Somethin' wrong?"

"No, Mother. I just wanted to see you and Daddy, and thought I'd make a quick trip. Margie's covering for me today and tomorrow morning, so I'll leave early and be back by the afternoon. I made coffee so you'd have some fresh when you got home. Let me get you a cup."

Daddy walked in about that time, so I poured a cup for him, too.

"Sit down, Folks. I've got something I want to tell you."

"I knew it. I knew it. There's somethin' wrong isn't there. What is it, Ila?" Mother looked frightened, like she feared I was going to tell them I had an incurable disease.

Daddy reached across the table and patted her arm. "Now, Mother. Give our girl a chance to tell us what's goin' on." He turned to me, "Go ahead, Honey. Why are you home?"

"Well, Mother. Daddy. I've quit my job with K.U. I was so tired, and depressed, seeing all that poverty and filth. I just couldn't take it anymore. So, I've joined the United States Army... actually, the Army Nurse Corps. Margie and I decided we'd both join and take advantage of the training they're offering nurses. It's free and it's only for one year." I looked from one face to the other as I gave them each encouraging smiles that I hoped would result in their understanding and acceptance of my decision.

"The Army? The Army?" Daddy exclaimed excitedly. "Hear that, Mother. Our girl would be a nurse in the Army. You know your Uncle Dwight was in the Army in World War I. Always wished I coulda gone with him, but I was already married and had you girls. They wouldn't let an old reprobate like me join. Why, I couldn't be prouder, honey."

CHAPTER TWENTY-TWO

Sadly, Mother didn't feel the same. Her eyes—it's hard even now to describe how they looked—glaring but frightened at the same time?

Her voice so low I had to lean in to hear her, Mother asked, "Why you, Ila? I don't want you to do this."

But Daddy jumped in before I could respond. "Mother, don't you understand? Training! Make her a better nurse. And free room and board when you think about it. Plus, they'll be payin' her, too."

I was pleased with Daddy's enthusiasm and support, but not surprised by Mother's opposition. Mother feared change of any kind, and when you added the possibility of war to the mix, I knew I wouldn't be able to change her mind.

Mother slowly shook her head. "No. It's not okay. Ila, I don't want you to go. What about the war in Europe? I'm dead-set against this."

"Daddy, your support really means a lot to me." I paused and continued. "Mother, I'm sorry you're upset. But I've given this a lot of thought. I need to make a change, and I think this is the right decision for me. Besides that, a lot of my friends from high school have enlisted and I want to do my part. I hope we don't get into a war. But if we do, I want to be ready."

Pause.

"And, I want to be there."

So, on December 9, 1940, Margie and I were sworn in as Second Lieutenants. But there were a couple of hitches: female Second Lieutenants were considered by the Army to be a notch lower in prestige than "real" Second Lieutenants, so we received less pay than our male counterparts. The other hitch was that we weren't assigned to the same Army base. Margie was sent to Jefferson Barracks outside of St. Louis and I was assigned to Fort Leavenworth.

TWENTY-THREE

I hadn't been in the Army very long, a couple of weeks at most, when I started getting the attention of Miss Ella M. Miller, the principal chief nurse at Fort Leavenworth. She asked me to join her for dinner frequently, sit by her, and talk about my future with the Army. I hadn't considered that I had much future beyond my one year as a reserve nurse, so I was curious.

"Miss Armsbury, have you ever stopped to think what a career in the Army might hold for you? Just imagine. You can see the world on Uncle Sam's dime—beautiful and exotic places you'd never even know about if it weren't for the military. You can meet the most interesting people, famous doctors, politicians, military leaders. And you can be taken care of for life. Health care, education, housing, a clothing allowance. The best training to be the best nurse. If you do well, there's no telling how far you can go in this woman's Army."

"No, I haven't considered it, but I don't think I'm interested in anything beyond my one year."

Miss Miller, however, wasn't dissuaded. The dinner invitations became more frequent along with an implicit message that she wouldn't take kindly to me saying I had other dinner plans. So, after about six months of brainwashing I finally said "okay" and took the oath of office to join the regular Army for one year as a Second Lieutenant in the

CHAPTER TWENTY-THREE

Army Nurse Corps with the relative rank of Nurse.

And that's when Miss Miller revealed her diabolical plan.

The day I was sworn in, Miss Miller took me over to the Women's Ward where all the officers' wives were hospitalized when they gave birth. She introduced me to Miss Allen, a regular Army nurse, hard-bitten and weathered, who ran the ward.

"Miss Allen, this is Miss Armsbury. She's going to be in charge now, and you will be her assistant," Miss Miller announced in a firm voice. My eye lids flew up, my hand went to my throat, and I swallowed and choked in surprise at this new development. Miss Allen looked from Miss Miller to me with an unsurprising lack of warmth in her eyes.

"Miss Armsbury," Miss Allen said, as she nodded. I could tell from her tone of voice—decidedly cool—that it would not be an easy transition. And, in truth, I didn't blame her. Miss Allen was career Army, had years of experience and was much older than I. Then I appeared— an upstart, a girl, by Miss Allen's standards—and was suddenly made her supervisor.

But worse than that was my realization that Miss Miller knew I had joined the Army specifically to get away from the 24/7 routine of being on-call for labor and delivery of newborns. I was back where I'd begun, but now I was in charge of an entire hospital ward.

My life rapidly got worse after Miss Miller began my training. She came onto the ward every morning, ostensibly to offer me her guidance. But her ideas about training were unique—and probably against the Geneva Convention.

"Miss Armsbury, has the maid swept room 302 yet?"

"Why, I don't know, Miss Miller."

"You don't know? You don't know?" Her voice grew louder and more shrill as she grilled me. "Why don't you know??? You're the nurse in charge of this unit." After that she'd whirl around on her heel and stomp off down the hall. She had white hair and wore an Army nurse's cape which flew around behind her as she hurried down the hallway. All she needed was a broom.

Every morning it was something else.

"Miss Armsbury, how many patients were discharged and how many admitted in the last 72 hours?"

"Why, I don't know, Miss Miller."

"You don't know? You don't know? Why don't you know??? You're in charge of this unit."

I remember one particularly awful day when Miss Miller put in her early morning appearance. My period had started, and I was kind of weepy. Miss Miller waltzed onto the ward. I was standing at the nurses' station, reviewing a patient's chart.

"Miss Armsbury, how many clean sheets do you have in the linen room?"

"I don't know, Miss Miller.

"You don't know? You don't know? Why don't you know??? You're in charge of this unit." And she turned and marched off down the hall.

I went into the linen room, closed the door, and started crying. About five seconds later, the door flew open and there stood Miss Miller, scowling.

"Miss Armsbury," she growled, "we do not have room in the Army for crybabies," and she slammed the door shut.

She hounded me every day until I became so efficient, I knew the count of sheets, pillows, towels, patients admitted and discharged almost by the hour, number of babies born per day, per month, where my staff was, when, and why.

I worked for almost six months without a single leave, so exhausted many nights that I couldn't fall asleep. By the early part of December 1941, I was ready for some time off, so I invited Margie to come up

CHAPTER TWENTY-THREE

to Kansas City for the weekend of December 5, 6, and 7. We had big plans—sleep late, enjoy leisurely shopping and dining in some of Kansas City's swankiest stores and restaurants and see the sights including the Christmas light display on the Plaza. Margie brought along one of her nursing friends from Jefferson Barracks. We each got three-day passes, and as soon as they picked me up at the front gate of Fort Leavenworth, we were off and running. By Sunday late-morning we were tired and winding down from our three days of play. We decided to go for one more spin around Kansas City before Margie and her friend dropped me off back at the front gate of Fort Leavenworth and headed back to Jefferson Barracks.

One of us, I can't remember who, decided to turn on the radio so we could listen to NBC Red and the Sammy Kaye Sunday Serenade. The program was almost over—Sammy and his orchestra had just finished playing "Kaye's Melody" and the announcer had closed the program with, "This is the National Broadcasting Company." We heard the unforgettable three-tone chime we all associate with NBC, dead air… for about 30 seconds, then this:

"From the NBC Newsroom in New York. President Roosevelt said in a statement today that the Japanese have attacked…"

* * *

My Dearest Mother and Daddy:

I feel that I must write some words of condolence, but I hardly know what to write. I must be cautious, and many things I cannot write.

It looks as though that trip next summer is 'gone with the wind.' Undoubtedly, I shall be far away by then, but we cannot plan always as we would like.

I hope it isn't too much of a shock. I know that surely, in your hearts you knew and felt it was coming but facing the reality of the thing is much different.

I can find no words to describe my mental reaction when the news broke...

It's no use asking for a leave now. It's too late. I suggest your coming down, if possible, as soon as you can. It may be unnecessary, but since people are leaving with 6 hrs notice — you couldn't possibly make it if that should happen to me. I don't want to scare you, nor do I want to leave without seeing you. You aren't allowed to come on the post now, so I would have to meet you in Leavenworth.

Oh! It's all so uncertain, I don't know what to tell you. You and Daddy talk it over and do what you feel in your hearts. I can't think that God would take me without my seeing you first, however, we can't see ahead.

In facing the situation, I feel quite calm, and pray that I shall always have the courage to do my duty to God and my country. I'm so sure that I'm safe wherever I go, that I can't seem to be afraid. I'm so sure I'll come back, (as all bad pennies do) and I guess I'm the only one who feels that way. The rest say, "Well, I won't come back — if I go, I know I won't." But — not me — I'm going with my chin up, and a smile, and when I come back, I'll be the same old crazy kid.

Seems funny doesn't it? I mean, well, here it is — I can't believe it yet. Of course, they need nurses here, and I have just as much chance of staying as I do going, so I see no use of worrying. If I could feel that all was well in the hearts and minds of my family, especially you and Daddy, if you can see this as I do, and not say

CHAPTER TWENTY-THREE

"Why must you go?"—or "can't you get out of it?" or "I don't want you to go"—or anything else on that order, then I can go and have much more courage, and faith. You and Daddy mean more to me than I can say, and I love you dearly.

More than anything else in the world. You are the finest parents a girl ever had, and I know you'll always help me. And in this hour of need, I do want help. Just a lot of letters, and not just from you, but from all of you—Eloise, Metta, and Wava.

...Tell everyone hello, kiss them all for me, and now, let's all laugh good—It's a swell world anyway.

All my love to you

* * *

Two days later I received a letter from Wava. Even a tiny town like Lincoln, Kansas, was already experiencing the direct effects of the war.

> *Several Lincoln County boys are in the danger zone. Mary Bird's brother is on the ship, Oklahoma. The Dyer boy from Beverly was killed. Our Christmas program was discontinued by an order from the Federal Government stopping all activities connected with shortwave broadcasting.*

We were at war.

TWENTY-FOUR

"Thank you all for being here this cold January morning," the speaker said. All of the nursing staff of the Women's Ward had been ordered to attend a seminar about bacteriology and our speaker was a new arrival at Fort Leavenworth, Captain Emmett Bird Settle, a physician with the U. S. Army medical corps, specializing in pathology.

One of my classmates leaned over to me and whispered, "He's cute, don't you think?" He was taller than me, about 5'9, thin, with wire rim glasses, a square face, brown eyes and dark brown, wavy hair. But it was his mouth and lips that caught my attention. His mouth was oval with a full lower lip and a slightly less full upper lip. But, oh that upper lip. He had the most beautiful cupid's bow I'd ever seen. It was obvious he knew his stuff and knew how to explain it. I listened carefully throughout his presentation, took notes, and tried not to stare. There was no doubt about it, he was smart!

Apparently, I caught his eye, too, because when the seminar was over, he got Doctor Smithallen, with whom I'd worked, to introduce us.

"Dr. Settle, may I present Second Lieutenant Ila Armsbury, one of our fine nurses. Miss Armsbury is in charge of the obstetrics ward at

CHAPTER TWENTY-FOUR

the base hospital."

"Miss Armsbury, I'm delighted to meet you. How did you like my presentation?" Dr. Smithallen quietly withdrew as Dr. Settle and I exchanged pleasantries and chatted. I felt my heart racing, hoping he'd ask me out. Finally, he popped the question.

"I have two tickets to a concert in Kansas City this coming Sunday afternoon. Would you be interested in accompanying me?"

We saw each other almost every day after that because of our work at the hospital, and we had a date every night. I fell hard for Emmett—I called him E.B.—and he fell for me, too. He was older than I, 36 to my 25, but the age difference didn't matter a whit. Our courtship was hot and heavy but within the bounds of propriety based on my upbringing as a good Christian. And I got to know a lot about him in a short time reinforcing every belief I held that he was the one for me. He was Harvard educated and a doctor, and not *just* a doctor but a pathologist and fifth-generation doctor. He played the organ in his church and was an upstanding Episcopalian. And he was sweet and kind. I thought I was the luckiest girl in the world to have found this incredible man in the midst of the madness of war.

It was our Valentine's date on February 14, 1942, where we finally admitted our feelings to each other. And to think that date started out so badly.

We were supposed to meet at the Officer's Club, but E.B. was over two hours late. When he finally walked in, he looked rough—his dress jacket was rumpled, his hair mussed, and I smelled alcohol on his breath.

"Ila, I'm so sorry. I really am. I got caught in the lab and time just got away from me. One of the doctors who is visiting—you know about that conference?—well he wanted to talk and we went to my office. I thought it would just take a couple of minutes, but he wanted a drink. I just happened to have a bottle of whisky in my desk drawer so we each had a drink. All the time I sat there thinking, 'I could be with Ila instead of this clown,' but you know you can't say that to a superior officer. Can you imagine? 'Sir, my girl's waiting for me and I'd really like to get out of here.'"

Deep lines furrowed his brow and his red eyes looked glazed from exhaustion. How could I stay mad, especially when he held the biggest bouquet of long-stemmed red roses I'd ever seen?

"That's okay, Honey. I know how those things go. But you're here now and we have all the rest of the evening to celebrate our first Valentine's together." It was almost three years before I learned the real reason E. B. was so late for our date.

In the meantime, I was awaiting my orders. It was anybody's guess where I would be sent—Europe? The southwest Pacific? Someplace in the States?

Finally, I got my orders. I was to report to the 166th Station Hospital at Camp Callon, San Diego, California, by the end of April 1942. Turned out that those orders were wrong and after two weeks of waiting in San Diego, I was reassigned to the 155th Station Hospital and sent to San Francisco, where I departed on the USS *West Point* for parts unknown.

TWENTY-FIVE

"Watch out, Ila. You keep looking to your left and you're going to get hit. Remember, this is Australia and they drive on the wrong side of the road."

Who'd a thunk it—Ila Armsbury, world traveler, living and working in Melbourne, Australia. I was still in shock over my good fortune—I really was seeing the world, or at least part of it—at Uncle Sam's expense.

Mary Francis, a fellow nurse—my roommate and best friend in Australia—and I were hurrying back to our quarters after a morning of shopping in Melbourne. The head nurse for our unit had called a mandatory meeting for one p.m. in the mess hall.

"Good afternoon, ladies." You could hear the murmur of women's voices as Miss Harper called the meeting to order.

"Welcome to Australia. It was a long trip over here, but we made it. I know you are still getting used to this new land, so similar to, and yet so different from, home. It's the differences that will take some time getting used to. Like, the driving ..."

Laughter and head nods greeted her comments. We could all recount stories of close calls when we'd forgotten which way to look.

"But you'll notice some other big differences, the timing of the seasons has certainly been hard for me, personally," Miss Harper said.

More head nods and murmurs. We'd arrived in Melbourne on

June 4. Back home in Kansas, it was late spring, and the weather was heating up. In Australia, June is like our November, and July is the coldest month of the year. We'd been issued seersucker uniforms for summer but thank God for my good wool cape. It kept me from freezing!

"Nurses, the reason for this brief meeting is not to illuminate the similarities and differences between the U. S. and Australia. It's to give you a preview of what the next few weeks are going to look like." With that, all whispers stopped. Everyone wanted to know what was in store. After all the Army was not paying for us to enjoy shopping and sightseeing in Melbourne.

"Our assignment here at Travancore Hospital is temporary. You probably already guessed that because the number of patients in the hospital is so low—73 today—and most of them are convalescents. The 155th is a station hospital, not a convalescent hospital. Our job is to receive battle casualties and fix them up or to treat troops who are sick with diseases like dengue, malaria, pneumonia, or VD. So, I expect we will be moving out shortly. The problem is I can't tell you how long 'shortly' will be—not because it's classified, but because no decision has been made. So, in the meantime, I need you to do your assigned jobs to the best of your ability, settle in, but don't get too comfortable because I assure you, we will be moving to a permanent location sometime in the next few weeks. Any questions?"

There were none. But Miss Harper had confirmed what many of us suspected—we wouldn't be staying in Melbourne—it was just a matter of time 'til we found out where we would be going and what we would be doing—other than shopping, eating out, enjoying the scenery.

* * *

It was July 17, 1942. I had turned 27 the day before, and I was feeling

CHAPTER TWENTY-FIVE

kind of low. I'd gotten cards and letters from home and a wonderful photo of E. B., but my heart still ached because he was half a world away at Fort Leavenworth as far as I knew and I was here in Australia, still at Travencore, working in a VD ward. The number of cases of troops with venereal disease was growing and we now had close to 70 patients.

I was just finishing up a bath for a patient when I heard my name called.

"Ila? Ila Armsbury, is that you?"

"I know that voice," I thought to myself as I turned to see who had called.

"Craig?" I almost knocked over my basin of dirty bath water as I recognized Major Craig Olsen, a friend of E. B.'s and mine from Leavenworth.

"What in the world are you doing here?"

"You know the Army, Ila. I've been assigned to a medical unit here in Australia. I just stopped in here for a brief visit, but I had no idea you were here," Craig laughed as he waited for me to dry my hands and give him a hug.

I was trying to think of a place where he and I could go for a cup of coffee and a quick visit, but before I could get the words out Craig grabbed my hands, grinned, and said, "Ila, I have the best birthday present in the world for you… "

I knew instantly what he was going to say and suddenly I felt weak. "No, Craig. It can't be."

"Yes, Ila. He's here, not 30 miles from Melbourne. He was on the same boat as me. He's safe and sound and right up the road with the 3rd Medical Battalion."

I tell you, I almost fainted at the news.

"I'll call E. B. as soon as I leave here and let him know where you are."

TWENTY-SIX

"Does my hair look okay? Are my stockings straight? Dammit, Mary Francis, I can't get the cap off this bottle of perfume. I'm going to be late."

"Ila, my gosh, slow down. Your hair looks great, your stockings are fine. Here, let me open that bottle before you break it and cut yourself."

Thank goodness for friends. Mary Francis helped me finish getting ready for my date—my Australian reunion—with E. B. I took several deep breaths as I walked down the stairs to the lobby, hoping I'd get there first so I could sit down and stop my legs from shaking so badly.

But no such luck. E. B. and I spotted each other at the exact moment I walked through the archway into the lobby of the old hospital that had been converted into nurses' quarters. I played it cool, smiled and walked towards him with my right arm outstretched to shake his hand. I didn't want to seem too anxious or unseemly. E. B., however, wasn't concerned about appearances.

He grabbed me by the upper arms and pulled me to him so tight I couldn't move.

"Ila, for God's sake, give me a kiss," he growled as he pressed his lips against mine—and not in a gentle way.

CHAPTER TWENTY-SIX

His strong arms around me ... I felt safe and sensual at the same time. For a few seconds, I forgot where I was and got lost in that kiss. Suddenly I heard a door open and I pulled away. "E. B.," I gasped. "Not here. Everyone will see."

"I don't give a damn who sees. I've been so worried about you, and I've missed you like the blazes." Then he kissed me a second time—softer, more gentlemanly.

As we walked out to his car, I noticed how good he smelled. I'd recognize that spicy-scented aftershave anywhere. There was something else—a scent that took me a minute to recognize—alcohol. I couldn't resist teasing him. "A little nervous before our date, honey?'

"What?"

"The alcohol. It smells like you've been drinking," I explained.

"Oh, no, Honey. Well, yes. Well, maybe. I was so damn excited about this date and seeing you again I took off work early, went to the officers' club and had a couple of drinks just to kill time. But I'm fine, don't you worry."

"I'm not," I giggled. "It's nice to know that I have that effect on you. You get nervous just thinking about me."

"You have no idea!" he replied as he laughed.

Both of us were quiet as E. B. drove to the officers' club located in an upperclass residential area of Melbourne. The building had been a private residence at one time and still exuded an air of luxury. As we took our seats at a quiet table at the back of the dining room, the band began playing "September Song." In an instant I was back in Lincoln at the restaurant, helping Mother bake apple pies for the fall harvest celebration.

In spite of the war, food rationing, and the delicious-sounding menu offerings, I was so nervous I could barely eat a thing. E. B. had no such problem, however and ate enough for both of us. After the meal was cleared away, we sat and drank coffee as friends and acquaintances came to our table to say hello. They all had just one topic in mind—our reunion.

"Some people have all the luck."

"So, you decided to travel all this way just for a date? Wouldn't it have been cheaper to stay in Kansas City?"

"Everything good always happens to you, doesn't it, Ila?" There was nothing either of us could say so we just smiled and nodded in agreement.

It was fun to talk and laugh with old friends but after a few minutes, E. B. stood, and speaking softly, he leaned over me and said, "Ila, we need to be going."

"Where?"

"I thought we'd go see a movie at the Athenaeum Theater. They're showing 'Lydia' with Merle Oberon."

"Oh, I love her. She's beautiful. What's it about?"

"Who cares. I just want to be alone with you someplace where we won't be disturbed."

"Alone? Alone? We'll be in a movie theater for goodness sake. That's not alone," I snickered.

"Ila," then he paused for effect, "they have a balcony." His eyes looked lustful and my heart began racing at the thought of us being alone.

The theater was old and elegant with its plush carpet and heavy velvet drapes framing the movie screen. And it did have a balcony—three in fact, but only the first one was used by movies goers. The upper two were for ritzier productions like the symphony or opera.

The lights were already low as we found our way to two seats in the back row. I looked around and realized that E. B. was right— kissing, hugging, snuggling couples were scattered around the balcony with several

CHAPTER TWENTY-SIX

empty seats between each pair of lovers. E. B. helped me remove my outer coat, but I was hardly settled in my seat before he put his arms around me and gave me a kiss for the ages.

I wasn't inexperienced in dating—I'd gone out with lots of boys from Lincoln, Beverly, and Tescott, but nothing prepared me for E. B.'s deep, open-mouthed kiss.

After that I didn't care one whit about the movie. We spent our time making love—that's what we called kissing and caressing back then. E. B.'s kisses let loose a flight of butterflies in my stomach: I felt hot all over, and my skin tingled everywhere he touched me.

Much as we might have liked, our date couldn't go on forever, so when the movie was over E. B. took me back to my quarters. The dark and deserted street in front of the building allowed us a few more minutes to say our goodnights—abbreviated with kisses, deep sighs, and hugs—and then I went in.

TWENTY-SEVEN

As it turned out, our time together in Melbourne was very short—just two weeks before the powers-that-be decided that the 155th was needed someplace else—they just weren't quite sure where. So, we spent almost eight weeks wandering around the state of Queensland. Finally, just after the first of October 1942—springtime in Australia—we arrived at our final destination—Camp Cable, 30 miles southwest of Brisbane.

Camp Cable was the Australian home of the U. S. Army's 32nd Infantry Division, The Red Arrow Men, who had arrived there a few months ahead of us. Our job was to provide hospital and dental care for them.

Three units of the 32nd Division, the 126th, 127th, and 128th Infantry Regiments, were in New Guinea fighting the Japanese. The remaining elements of the Division were still encamped at Camp Cable. Strenuous training, sprained ankles, a few broken bones, jeep accidents and bar fights kept us supplied with a steady stream of patients.

The hospital consisted of ten wooden ward-type buildings connected with partially enclosed ramps. The hospital complex was located at the south end of the camp near the Albert River. We nurses were housed in two of the wooden buildings, but ward tents were erected within a few days of our arrival, bringing our bed capacity up to 432 although we had

CHAPTER TWENTY-SEVEN

only 141 patients at the time.

After weeks of temporary lodging, it was a relief to arrive at our home away from home, although the countryside was unlike the wheat fields of Kansas. The camp boasted tall eucalyptus gum trees and underbrush. Kansas has tall trees, too, but no eucalyptus.

The biggest scourge, however, were the mosquitoes which carried dengue fever, a virus for which there was no treatment. The symptoms of dengue were terrible headaches, a rash and body aches, high fever and vomiting. Most folks recovered, but in its most severe form, patients could develop dengue hemorrhagic fever and leak blood plasma that could end in death.

I had only been at Camp Cable about three weeks when I received a telegram from E. B. that he was coming through and would be there the next afternoon.

Just my luck, I had no leave when E. B. arrived, so we were confined to the grounds. After a moment's thought I said, "Let's walk over to the mess tent. We can sit and talk."

The mess tent was almost empty, just kitchen staff preparing for the next meal. We found a table where a soft spring breeze blew in, warm now but cooling as evening approached, and we sat down. The scent of eucalyptus and cooking food—nothing we could identify— provided an unusual backdrop for our conversation.

Although we were both excited to spend time together, our first minutes felt awkward and our conversation was halting: the strange scenery, the surprise and fascination of seeing wallabies, spiny anteater things, and those god-forsaken stinging ants. We talked about all the mundane stuff of our new lives in a new land, but not the important stuff.

After a few minutes of talk about me getting settled in, E. B. grinned and said, "Ila, I'm being sent up to Townsville on the coast.

We're going to be setting up a new pathology lab, and after it's up and running, we'll be working there so I'll be able to see you pretty often, even though I won't be as close as Brisbane. So, I thought we should celebrate, even if we can't leave here." E. B. laid a canvas Army shoulder bag on the table, lifted the flap and pulled out three bottles of Bulimba Beer.

"What a treat!" I exclaimed. "I wasn't expecting such great news, a celebration, or beer." E. B. produced a church key, opened two bottles, and handed one to me. I took a drink.

"Mmmm. Not bad, but I sure would love to be back home, drinking a Schlitz right about now," E. B. commented. He finished his and opened the second bottle while I was still enjoying my first.

"My goodness, E. B. You must have been thirsty!" I exclaimed.

"I was. You know I'm so busy that I rarely have time to sit down and enjoy a relaxing drink.

Ahh." E. B. sighed in contentment. "That was so damn good! Want another? I have one more here in the bag if you want it."

"No, I don't think so. This is plenty," I replied, relaxed and happy just sitting by the man I loved.

"Okay. I'll have that last one," E. B. said as he reached into the bag to pull out the bottle. I leaned my head against his shoulder, closed my eyes, and enjoyed our quiet closeness.

"Now," he said as he set the empty bottle on the table, his voice dropping lower, "Ila, I want to be alone with you. I *need* to be alone with you. Don't you feel it, too?"

I knew what he was driving at, and I shouldn't have been surprised. Even so, I gasped because I didn't know how to answer him. I wanted to be alone with him, too, and the sensations caused by his words were enough to make me squirm on the hard wooden bench. But I couldn't think of a place where we could go to be alone. And, I could

CHAPTER TWENTY-SEVEN

hear my mother's voice—all the way from Kansas—loud and clear, quoting scripture.

"Ila, when a man says he loves you, what he's really sayin' is ... he wants ... well, you know what he wants. Don't let 'em trick you with that sweet talk about love and such. Remember the Lord's words when he said, 'to the unmarried and the widows I say that is well for them to remain single as I do. But if they cannot exercise self-control, they should marry. For it is better to marry than to be aflame with passion.'"

I looked him in the eye as I squeezed his hand. "E. B., I know how you feel—I feel the same way. But I aah ... aah..." I stuttered as I looked at the floor. I could feel my face heating up, and I was sure that I was blushing from the roots of my hair down to my toenails. I couldn't think of another word to say. I felt awkward as the silence between us expanded like a rising cake and E. B. just sat there not saying anything to relieve my discomfort or his own. I glanced up at him and could tell he was unhappy—his jaw muscles were clenching.

Fearing he'd leave I suddenly blurted out, "Would you like to take a walk? There're some lovely spots down by the river. We might even be able to find a place to sit in the shade." His jaw muscles immediately relaxed, he took a deep breath and in a soft voice said, "I'd like that, Ila."

The sloping banks of the river were covered with a dense forest of exotic trees and shrubs which provided a thick, green privacy screen interrupted by rocky patches. We found a large fallen tree situated close enough to the river that we could see the glistening water rushing over partially submerged rocks and hear its soothing sound, but we were far enough away that someone walking along the bank couldn't see us. The main trunk of the tree rested on the ground and worked as a bench. A smaller branch ran parallel to the trunk but extended up at a diagonal and made a perfect back for our wooden sofa.

E. B. sat down at the vee and leaned back. As I took my seat beside him, E. B. put his arms around me and pulled me close.

"Ila, look at me."

E. B.'s eyes had a look of hunger in them, yet his lips barely brushed mine as he pulled me to his chest and began gently caressing my back. I felt loved and protected and thought to myself, "these arms are the ones I want to hold me for the rest of my life." We spent well over an hour there in the forest by the river—one of my most romantic memories.

TWENTY-EIGHT

Patients trickled into the hospital during November—men who got sick or were injured in training exercises. I was busy but not so much that I couldn't see E. B. It seemed like each day we fell deeper in love. Then on the 12th of November, 1943, we had a date—and a fight that ended our relationship.

It started out innocuously enough. E. B. sent me a telegram that he would be in Brisbane for a two-hour meeting and planned to drive out to Camp Cable to spend a couple of hours with me before he had to return to Townsville. I wasn't scheduled to work that afternoon, but I didn't have a pass to leave camp, so we walked down to the river, to our tree, with the intention of talking about where we'd live after we were married. I had no warning that this was going to be contentious. Boy, was I naïve!

After some general conversation and some hugging and kissing, E. B. said, "I hate these separations. Sometimes at night when I can't sleep, I pretend that we're already married. I close my eyes and think to myself, 'Ila's in the other room. She'll come to bed in a minute.' Then I fantasize about what we'll do once you're by me."

I laughed as I interrupted him, "And that helps you get to sleep?"

"Well, no, not that part," he grinned as he answered me and hugged me to him. "But after I relax…" he stopped and gave me a devilish grin before continuing, "eventually I get to sleep. I'll tell you what I look forward to the most, though."

"What's that," I asked as I tickled his ear with a piece of grass.

"I'll see you every day. You'll be the first thing I see in the morning, the last thing I see at night. When I come home for lunch you'll be there. Imagine that—how different it will be from the way things are now ... it's catch as catch can."

"Well," I replied laughing again, "You can certainly go home for lunch each day, but I won't be there. I'll be working somewhere, maybe the hospital where you're working."

E. B. removed his arm from my shoulders as he turned to look me in the eyes and asked, "What do you mean you'll be working? You're joking, right? I don't want you to work at the hospital where I am, or anyplace else. I'll make plenty of money and besides that, you'll have lots of work at home, what with kids and servants and the house to run."

His comments startled me. "Surely you can't be serious," I responded, my tone mocking. "I can't see myself with servants for God's sake. That's ridiculous. I don't want a bunch of sneaking servants in my house. Hell, I don't even know anybody who has servants."

"My mother has servants," E. B. replied, his voice low but firm. "We've always had servants as long as I can remember ... a cook, a housekeeper, and a gardener. There's nothing wrong with servants. They'll just make your life easier."

"E. B., I don't want servants." I know I sounded irritable—I couldn't decide whether he was serious or if he was just teasing me but carrying the joke too far. "*I* want to do the cooking and the cleaning, and *I* want to plant a garden just like my mother's. She grows the best tomatoes and corn, and you should taste her watermelon pickles. There's nothing better in the summer."

E. B. moved away from me and his voice hardened as he explained, "Ila, Mother has always impressed upon me that the Settle and

CHAPTER TWENTY-EIGHT

Bird families have a special position to maintain in town and I think she's right." He paused for a moment before continuing. "You've heard of the Emery, Bird, and Thayer Department Store, haven't you?" I nodded. Everyone I knew had heard of Emery, Bird and Thayer, a ritzy, five-story department store in downtown Kansas City. It was a fixture in K. C. and had been there for fifty years or more. The EBT Tea Room was famous for its elegant and restful afternoon teas.

"My mother is related to the Bird of EBT. Mother's always been concerned about how things look. She wouldn't like it if you worked and besides that, it wouldn't look right for the wife of a doctor, especially a doctor related to one of the Birds, to work. And planting a garden? Only someone low class does that. You understand, don't you?"

"Low class? You're calling my mother low class?" I was furious and my tone of voice reflected it. But before I could say another word E. B. interrupted me.

"No, Ila. For God's sake, no, I'm not calling your mother low class. I just mean that ... if you want a garden, the gardener will plant it for you." He gave me an ingratiating smile, trying to get himself out of the hole he was rapidly digging.

My voice took on a harsher tone. "E. B., who cares what other people think or how something looks as long as it's okay with you and me."

"Besides," I continued, "I need to work. My folks are poor and my dad's crippled. And just for your information, I don't think that makes them low class—that's just the way things are."

"Anyway," I continued, "they've scraped and scrimped all their lives just for the basics. And they sent me money for school when they could. I owe them and one way I can repay them is by working and sending them money every month, like I do now. I have a monthly allotment sent home to Mother and Daddy from my Army pay."

I was quiet for a moment, but by this time I was on a roll. "And anyway, I want to work. I didn't do all that studying in school for nothing. I like working. And what if something happened to you, God forbid, and I had to work to support us? You wouldn't want your mother taking care of us, would you?"

E. B.'s tone of voice was firm, his jaw muscles were clenching—I could tell he was angry, too, but was trying to control himself. "Of course, I wouldn't want Mother to support us. Don't be ridiculous. But Ila, *I* care what other people think. You know how some people talk. You've heard it yourself being in the Army. 'Women who join the Army are just husband-hunting.' 'Women who join the Army are loose women just looking for a good time.' And there's even worse than that said, and you know it. I won't have my wife working or people talking about you, thinking I can't provide for my family. And that's all there is to it."

I stood up, my hands on my hips as I glared down at him. "Who do you think you are? You're not my father, you're not my husband, at least not yet, and you don't have the right to tell me what I can and can't do. I'll work if I want to and nobody, not you or your mother or anybody else, is going to tell me otherwise."

With that E.B. jumped up, glared back at me, and said, "Goddammit! I won't *be* your husband if you don't change your mind."

"**Fine!**" I yelled. "That's just fine with me because I wouldn't want to be your wife and have you telling me what to do all the time. You just want a sniveling little girl, someone who will be so damned impressed by your family's money you can just snap your fingers and she'll jump. Well, let me tell you something, buster, I'm not a dog." With that I turned on my heel and stalked back to camp and my quarters. I didn't see E. B. when he left but I knew he was right behind me and that he went straight to his jeep and took off. All I could think was "Good riddance."

TWENTY-NINE

I was a mess—my emotions swung from boiling rage to despairing pain. I replayed our argument over and over in my head, as though it was a riddle to which there was an answer if I could just find it. I had moments when I forgot that we'd broken up—moments in which my world felt okay until I suddenly remembered the fight—then confusion settled over me like a cloud of mist floating above a lake at sunrise, dulling my senses and making me feel lost and alone.

Saturday evening, a week after our breakup, I was in my quarters catching up on my letter writing when one of my friends who had taken a 24-hour pass, came in.

"Ila, you're just who I was looking for. Have you heard about E. B.?"

"No. Why?"

"He's very ill. He's been in the hospital for days and they're just now moving him to a convalescent hospital in Townsville."

I was paralyzed with fear. "What's wrong with him, did they say?"

"I think pneumonia. I heard he was in an oxygen tent. It sounds pretty bad."

I hate to be afraid, and I hate to feel helpless. I was both. What if he died? What if he lived but they sent him home? I was in the dark, imagining the worst. I guess that's human nature. I had lots of questions, but no answers, and no one to ask. From that moment my days and nights dragged on. I worked, ate, and slept in a constant state of fear and anxiety.

Our hospital workload had been slow and steady, soldiers with injuries from training or fighting. Illnesses that we could treat with medication, bed rest, and good food. December started out slowly and none of the medical staff expected anything different in our workload, but we got a surprise on a quiet Sunday morning in mid-December. Almost everybody, including the chief nurse and the commanding officer for the 155th had taken the weekend off to go to Brisbane. I had volunteered to stay behind and be the charge nurse for the day shift.

Around 9:00 A.M., I met up with a first sergeant and we took a coffee break. We were sitting in the office of the main hospital building, gossiping when I looked up and saw an enormous cloud of dust on the horizon.

"What's coming in, sergeant?" I asked.

"Nothing that I know of ma'am."

"Well, something is, 'cause look over there." I pointed toward the road. We both turned to get a better look as a line of troop trucks and ambulances appeared out of a cloud of dust and snaked towards us. As the first truck pulled up in front of the office, we could see the rest of the line of vehicles stretching back. A corpsman, his clothes rumpled and dusty, jumped from the back of the lead truck and ran into the office, announcing that we were getting a convoy of sick Marines from Guadalcanal.

"Sergeant, get on the phone! Call Brisbane and get our people back here." I directed, as I headed out the door with the corpsman.

"How many Marines, corpsman, do you know?"

"No ma'am. But it's a lot. And I can tell you, there's more coming."

CHAPTER TWENTY-NINE

I ran toward the closest hospital building and began rounding up staff to help.

You should have seen those poor boys. Their clothes, what was left of them, were filthy with dried mud, dirt, urine, and excrement. Some of the boys ... their eyes were vacant, just staring at something the rest of us couldn't see. Some with high fevers moaned and thrashed on their litters. Every one of those Marines had malaria. They had all the classic symptoms: shivering with chills one moment and burning fever the next. They were parched, and their skin was hot to the touch. Sweat poured off them as they complained of back pain and headaches. It was obvious they hadn't been eating—they were all malnourished and underweight.

Sick Marines kept coming, and they all needed immediate attention.

As patients were unloaded from the trucks, we filled the beds in the hospital then laid men on the ground under the trees. We started IVs on everyone. For the men under the trees, we hung the IV bags on branches, and waited for supplies and more staff to come out from Brisbane.

We worked 72 hours straight. The mess tent provided us with food, so we didn't have to take breaks. We just walked around with a ham sandwich in one hand and a cup of coffee in the other as we treated our patients. When we got too dirty, we went home and put on clean uniforms and came back.

We admitted 120 Marines a day for over three weeks—so many that the Army moved the remaining elements of the 32nd Infantry Division out of the camp to make way for the First Marine Division. In spite of how sick they were, we lost only two patients—a private with the 32nd Infantry Division, too sick to move, who died of an abdominal stab wound complicated by pneumonia, and a private with the 5th Marines, of malaria and malnutrition.

By New Year's Eve, we'd admitted over 2,100 Marines near as I can tell, and it was the most miserable holiday season I ever spent—I had no Christmas spirit—and if you'd seen what I did, you wouldn't either.

Given the way 1942 ended—our hospital wards overflowing with sick Marines and my dreams of marriage and family dashed—I dreaded 1943. The year started slowly, with the Marines pulling out at the end of the first week of January in preparation for the return of the 32nd Infantry Division. I hadn't heard any more about E. B., so I was pretty low.

I was so depressed that I stopped paying attention to my hair and nails. But I got a lift from a Christmas gift of lavender body lotion. That small luxury and the compliments I got about the delicate scent helped me see outside myself. I tried a new hair style and some new nail polish when I wasn't at work. I even started to date although I was just going through the motions—there was no one special.

In mid-January, we heard that the New Guinea campaign was over and that we had won. Everyone was excited because that meant we would soon be seeing "our" soldiers—the 32nd Infantry Division. We all wondered what kind of shape they'd be in. We got our answer in mid-February when the troops began returning—their condition was appalling, and it wasn't just due to the fighting. It was also the environment endemic to New Guinea.

New Guinea is a tropical island, the second largest in the world and just north of Australia. Our patients described it as the most horrific place in the universe, and one that Satan had gladly abandoned for the relative comforts of Hell.

The troops had been fighting on the Papuan Peninsula— the eastern half of the island—a mixture of atrocious conditions. Mountains ran down the middle of the entire island from east to west, some as high as 13,000 feet. The island was covered with jungle and rain forest, and had a flat, swampy, malaria-infested coast. Temperatures in the lowlands averaged about 80° F while the humidity usually hovered

CHAPTER TWENTY-NINE

between 70 and 90%. Uniforms rotted in a matter of days, leaving our troops with little protective clothing. And the whole island was covered with sharp-edged grass, which cut like a knife.

Because of the extreme heat, humidity, and wartime conditions New Guinea acted as a petri dish for diseases such as dengue fever, malaria, scrub typhus, dysentery, cholera, and jungle rot which our doctors called New Guinea crud. Almost every patient had the crud — horrific skin ulcers, sometimes so deep that we could see the tendons or bones. In addition to the hideous sight of decomposing flesh, we were assaulted with the horrible smell—a cloying, sweet sickening odor. In the worst cases our doctors had to perform amputations to stop the spread of gangrene in the infected tissue. I tell you, once I got that stench in my nose, I smelled it everywhere—in the chow line, walking to the showers, even in bed as I was trying to fall asleep.

I was tired, overworked, homesick, heartsick, reeling from the day-to-day drudgery of working under wartime conditions. I didn't think things could get much worse, but I was wrong. I got a letter from E. B. I was stunned—he was back at work and wanted me to meet him. I didn't know what to think but was afraid if we got together it would be the same old thing—him telling me what to do and how to act so as not to embarrass him or his mother. I decided not to answer his letter.

The next few weeks were especially tough for me. Every time I turned around another troubling incident occurred. Mother wrote telling me that Grandpa Newt had died. "His heart," they said. "In a matter of days ... unexpectedly ...went in his sleep ... thought he was getting better." The most surprising comment was that my dad was taking the death real hard—even though he and Grandpa had never gotten along. Just goes to show that we never really know how we're going to act and feel when someone dies.

Malaria was rampant at Camp Cable—not among the medical

staff, thank God, but among the returning troops. Many of our patients suffered from their fourth or fifth bout of malaria, because if a sick man at an aid station near the front could recover enough to carry his rifle, he was sent back to the battle line to fight. By the end of March, the 155th was overrun with malaria patients. And we had an outbreak of German Measles to boot. Dysentery, with its array of debilitating symptoms like bloody bowel movements—sometimes 30 or more a day—weight loss, high fever, and dehydration, hit many of the troops hard, too.

It might surprise you to know that we treated far more sick troops than ones with battle injuries. But we saw our share of injured men with battle wounds—abdominal injuries from rifle shells, stab wounds from swords or bayonets, broken bones, head injuries—we saw and treated them all.

Workdays were long and tiring—cleaning wounds, changing bandages, encouraging patients to eat and drink, hooking up new IV bags, providing a compassionate ear whenever a patient wanted to talk—and all the time reassuring the men that they would get better and return to their buddies. As patients got better, we put them to work helping with the sicker ones.

As sick as the returning men of the 32nd Infantry Division were, we heard scuttlebutt that General Douglas McArthur was demanding they return to New Guinea for more fighting. We all felt the stress of nursing the men back to health, knowing that once they were well and returned to the battlefield, some would die and there'd be nothing we could do to prevent it.

The final straw—the one that sent me into a downward spiral—was another letter from home and this time it was about Jim Wilson, Metta's husband. He was gravely ill with a recurrence of rheumatic fever like he'd had as a child, and now he'd developed a serious heart

CHAPTER TWENTY-NINE

complication, endocarditis. It's a bacterial infection of the lining of the heart, and Jim wasn't responding to the sulfa medication. Endocarditis was always fatal, but I didn't know how much the doctors back home had told Metta and the folks, and I didn't know how much to tell them either.

THIRTY

It started out the way all my previous hospitalizations had—a night of chills, a day of stuffiness, headache, sore throat, sinus pain, coughing, lots of mucus. If I'd been home, my dad would have treated me with his time-honored home remedy for coughs. We called it 'Daddy's Cough Syrup.' You dissolve two and a half ounces of rock candy in a half pint of whiskey, which takes about ten days. Then you mix in two ounces of glycerin and shake well. The dosage, prescribed by Daddy, depended on how sick you were. Amazingly, Daddy always needed more than anyone else.

However, I wasn't at home, so they admitted me to the hospital—the 155th—with the tentative diagnosis of nasopharyngitis, acute, catarrhal—the military's official wording for the common cold. Let me tell you a cold is nothing to sneeze at in the Army because it means time off duty, spent in quarters or in the hospital and the possibility of contagion to others. And you can't have a bunch of sick people, all down with colds, when you're trying to win a war.

But there was something about this time that was different. "I'm just so darn tired all the time. I don't understand it because that's just not like me. I usually have a lot of energy but these last few weeks…" Major Becker, my doctor, interrupted me.

"How many weeks, Lieutenant Armsbury?"

CHAPTER THIRTY

"Well, three or four, I guess. This last month."

"I see you've been hospitalized a few times before with the same complaint, nasopharyngitis."

"Yes, I never had this problem at home but over here, I seem to be real susceptible to colds."

"Let's take a look at you," Major Becker said as he put the ends of the stethoscope in his ears and prepared to listen to my heart. He gave me a physical exam while a nurse, one of my friends, assisted. After listening to my heart and taking my pulse, Major Becker told me to get on the scales.

"Well, this is odd. Lt. Armsbury, do you know how much you weigh?"

"I think about 130. Why?"

"Your weight is down to 120. That's low. I'm going to order some bloodwork."

You can imagine my surprise when a day later Major Becker came back to talk with me again. "Lt. Armsbury, in addition to the nasopharyngitis, you have moderate malnutrition. That's why you're so tired and listless. You haven't been getting enough to eat. Why is that?"

I was shocked. "Are you sure?" I asked. "I just thought I was losing some weight—my clothes have been a little lose on me lately, but I didn't think it was anything serious."

"Why haven't you been eating, Lieutenant?"

"I thought I was. I mean, I do eat at every meal."

"Lieutenant, I asked you a question."

"Yes, sir." I hesitated for a minute not sure what to say or how to say it. Finally, I blurted out. "My aah, my boyfriend and I—well we were planning to get married after the war, but we had a big fight and broke up. Plus, you know how busy we've been? And we had two deaths in my family…"

"I get the picture, Lieutenant. Bear in mind that all of us have problems, here and at home. You can't let them get to you or you won't be any good to yourself or anybody else. Now, how are you sleeping at night?"

"Some nights I go right to sleep. Others..."

"What time do you wake up?"

"Sometimes I can sleep 'til 6:00 a.m. or so. Other times I wake up at two or three in the morning and can't get back to sleep."

"What do you do?"

I gave a rueful laugh. "I guess I just toss and turn 'til it's time to get up. Aah, sometimes I lay in bed and pray that this damn war will end soon so we can all go home."

"I've said a prayer like that a time or two myself," Major Becker chuckled. "So, in addition to not getting enough to eat, you're not getting the sleep you need. That can make you more susceptible to colds you know."

I nodded in reply. "So, what do you want me to do?"

"I want you to eat more and regain some of the weight you've lost. I'm going to prescribe three meals a day plus snacks including an eight-ounce glass of milk mixed with cream twice a day. That'll put some weight back on you. And get some rest. I'm prescribing nembutal."

I wasn't thrilled. Nembutal was habit-forming, but I was so damn tired, I needed sleep and was willing to try just about anything. I drank quarts of rich milk and cream, ate as much as I could at each meal, took nembutal at night, and after about a week started to feel human again.

THIRTY-ONE

After my hospitalization and treatment for exhaustion and malnutrition, the Army sent me to a fabulous nurses' convalescent home in Brisbane. It was like heaven on earth. I had my own room, beautifully decorated in white wallpaper with tiny pink roses and yellow lace. The sheets were of the finest, pure white cotton I'd ever felt. The room had two tall windows, one on each wall, draped with sheer, white Priscilla curtains that let in cheerful sun in the mornings and gentle light in the afternoons. Antique walnut furniture, a dressing table and matching chair, dresser, and bedside table complimented the sturdy iron bed in which I spent my nights in blissful sleep.

I had been in the midst of a wonderful dream, sitting at the kitchen table back home eating Sunday dinner with the folks when I was interrupted by a knock on my bedroom door. Mother's fabulous fried chicken was my favorite, and I had just asked for another thigh when a sound—knuckles rapping on a door—disturbed my dream dinner. The knocking was so far away that at first, I thought I hadn't heard correctly. But after a moment's quiet—and another bite of chicken—that damn rapping started up again, this time closer and more insistent.

"Ila? Ila are you awake?" Pause. "May I come in?" The voice was familiar but being more asleep than awake, I couldn't place it. I mumbled something as I reached for the mashed potatoes.

More knocking. My dream receded into the mist of my sleep, my eyes fluttered open, I rolled onto my back and stretched.

I sat up in bed, pushed my hair back off my face and fingered the curls so I wouldn't look completely disheveled, fluffed my pillow, straightened the blankets, and laid back down again. "Come in." I thought it was Mary Francis.

I know my eyebrows went up to my hairline when the door opened and E. B. walked into my room, carrying a bouquet of old-fashioned flowers, like the ones Mother grew back home—carnations, snapdragons, daisies, zinnias, and bachelor buttons. I was speechless and just stared.

"How-aa. .. how are you feeling, Ila?" E. B. asked as though we hadn't broken up, hadn't had a fight that felt like a bloodletting in which I was stabbed and left to die, hadn't seen or spoken to each other in almost six months. The fact that I'd survived had nothing to do with E. B. I remained quiet.

"You look good, Honey. Have you lost weight?"

"If you will recall, I am not your 'Honey.' What do you want?"

"Ila..." that's all he got out before his eyes welled up and he began to weep. I tried to maintain my stern appearance, but it pained me to see tears streaming down his face.

"Ila, I've been miserable without you. You're all I've thought about. What I said—what you said—how we could fix this. Please, Ila, please help me fix this." His voice grew softer and wavered at his pleading words.

Lord knows I wanted to fix it, too. Over the past few months, I'd spent hours trying to figure out where we went wrong. Was it my fault, his fault, his mother's fault? I didn't know what to say or do, so I just sat there like a dummy, watching him as my own eyes filled.

"Oh, Honey, don't cry," E. B. whispered as he moved to my bedside, laid the bouquet on top of my covers, and put his arms around me.

CHAPTER THIRTY-ONE

"I'm sorry. I'm so sorry. I was wrong to tell you what to do and I was wrong to not listen to your worries about your folks. I was only thinking about myself and what other people would think, when I shoulda been thinking about you and your feelings." His words poured out as he pulled me to him and rested his chin on the top of my head. That's when I began to sob, and sob, and—you get the idea—while all the time E. B. whispered softly "shh" and rubbed my back. Finally, I stopped crying but neither of us moved. It was so comforting to have his arms wrapped around me, rocking both of us as though we were in a boat, gently moving with the waves.

"Ila, may I sit down so we can talk?"

I mumbled yes but I'm sure all he heard was a muffled "yaaa" into his chest. E. B. slowly withdrew his arms and stepped away from me, but the smile of adoration and commitment never left his face. I watched his every move.

E. B. reached for the room's lone chair, pulled it as close to the bed as it would go, and sat down. He took my right hand, held it to his lips for a soft kiss and laid my hand—with his on top of it—on the bedspread.

"Honey, I'm sorry I couldn't get here sooner. I learned that you were here about a week ago, but it took me that long to get a 24-hour pass. Why are you here? What's wrong?"

It took me some time to compose myself. I'd given up hoping that I'd ever see him again. Now here he was in the flesh *and* asking me how we could undo our hurtful past. I didn't have an answer for that, but at least I could tell him about my health.

"Oh, E. B., I'm all right, really. I got run down. I wasn't eating enough and just got weak. I got one of those sinus things like I always do, but I just couldn't seem to shake it so finally they admitted me. They've been fattening me up like you wouldn't believe. Why they bring me a glass of heavy cream and I lap it up like a kitten with her bowl of milk. They've spoiled me so much I don't think I'll be worth a darn once I'm out of here. I'll expect to be waited on for every meal, have someone fetch my books and magazines, it's awful how selfish I'll be." I laughed as I told him about how I'd spent my days. But E. B.'s face looked somber.

"Have they done blood work and ruled out tropical diseases or parasites?"

"Yes, E. B., of course. I don't have dengue fever, malaria, or hookworm. Just exhaustion and malnutrition but I'm almost as good as new and will be out of here in a day or two. I promise."

He looked skeptical but after repeatedly reassuring him of my vast improvement in appetite, strength, and sleep, he finally seemed to accept the reality that I wasn't dying. It was my turn to question him.

"Why were *you* in the hospital in November? I heard pneumonia. I heard oxygen tent. Somebody said you were getting better, but your mind was worse. I was terrified and I wanted to see you but didn't know if you wanted to see me. What happened?"

E. B. bowed his head and looked at his lap for several seconds before crossing his arms over his chest in a way that looked like he was trying to ward off blows. He looked up at me, his face blushing, and said, "Ila, when we broke up, I went on a binge. I drank more than I ever have in my life. It was stupid, I know."

I was shocked. I knew he drank. So did I. So did almost everybody I knew. But the only person I'd ever known who drank and was sickened by it was my dad and his buddies. And we all knew what had happened to them. This seemed different, and I was still confused. I'd seen soldiers in the hospital after they'd gone on a toot, but usually their injuries were broken bones or severe internal injuries from a traffic accident.

"E. B., I don't understand. What happened?"

CHAPTER THIRTY-ONE

He looked up from his lap, met my eyes and said, somewhat defiantly, "I told you. I drank too much."

"E. B., why were you in an oxygen tent? What did they mean 'his mind is worse'? I've been honest with you, now you need to be honest with me." I gave him my most penetrating stare hoping that would encourage him to be more forthcoming.

He wiggled in his seat and re-crossed his arms over his chest. "I was um ... I was a ... I was at the Oasis Hotel in Townsville, by the swimming pool, with some friends. We were drinking ... well, I was drinking more than anybody else, I guess, and I probably shouldn't of been in the pool. I went under."

"Went under? How do you just 'go under' water?" I demanded to know.

"Well, not exactly 'went under,' I don't think. If you want to know the truth... "

"I do," I interrupted.

"I don't actually remember what happened. I only know what I've been told. I went under at least twice. Somebody said I was unconscious for about a half hour. They gave me artificial respiration for another half hour and pumped about a gallon of water and blood out of me. An ambulance took me to the hospital where they admitted me, and I developed pneumonia, so they put me in an oxygen tent. But now I'm better."

I was speechless. I'd imagined a serious illness, maybe even a heart attack or stroke. Maybe some horrible tropical disease. But this? Getting drunk and almost drowning? Not at all what I'd expected to hear. I felt faint stirrings of fear in my heart as I thought back to my childhood and the times I'd seen my dad drunk.

"E. B.," I whispered, my hands trembling, "You know my dad drank a lot." I paused trying to figure out how to say what I felt. How do you put into a few words an entire childhood and adolescence of seeing your father hung over and your mother crying and raging because of his drinking? Or the heartache and chaos of adultery?

Divorce? Thankfully, I didn't have to worry about that with E. B. All I could think of to say was, "I don't want to marry a man like my dad."

"I know, Ila, I know. I'm not like him. I don't drink all the time. You've never seen me hung over, have you?" I had to admit I hadn't. "That proves it, doesn't it? Look, Honey. I'm not an alcoholic and I know what I did was stupid. I was upset about our breakup. I just thought 'To Hell with it.' I went out and got drunk. It'll never happen again, I swear. I love you, Ila. Take me back; we can work this out. Honest, Honey, I've learned my lesson."

"E. B., I want to believe you and maybe I do. But how will we work out our disagreement? You know I want to work. I *need* to work. Have you changed your mind?" He was quiet for a moment and I feared that we were going to pick up where we left off. But I underestimated him—and his love.

"No, I haven't changed my mind—I don't want you to work. I want you at home where I can see you any time I want and be with you any time I want. But I've thought about this. I'll send your folks money every month. I can afford to do it. You won't have to work but your folks will be okay."

"My dad will never agree to accept a penny from you, E. B. He's a proud man."

"But," he whispered, "not too proud to take money from his daughter?"

That comment caught me off-guard. I had to think a minute before I answered. "Emmett…"

"I know this is serious because you never call me Emmett," he said ruefully as he gave me a fleeting smile.

CHAPTER THIRTY-ONE

I tried again. "Emmett, it's different when Daddy and Mother take money from me. I owe them that and more. They raised me, they helped me with school, they did the best they could, and now they need help. That's what family does—we help each other. Daddy would never take money from a stranger, he's not like that. He'll go out of his way to help someone, but it's hard for him to accept help. And besides, you aren't family."

"But, Ila," E. B. said softly, "Once we're married, I will be." He had a point—once we were married, he would be family. Still, not all our disagreements had been resolved. We still had to decide where to live and if we would have servants. He knew how I felt about that.

"What about the big house and the servants? You know I don't want any servants. I want to do my own cooking and cleaning and laundry."

"I've thought of that, too. We'll live in the country house. It's about ten miles outside of Rockport. It used to belong to my aunt. Mother inherited it when her sister died. It's smaller, cozier than the one in town. You'll like it ... high ceilings, tall windows, wood floors, fireplaces in every room. You don't have to have help, but if you get tired of cooking and cleaning and all that, you can have as many servants as you want. Whatever will make you happy, that's all I care about."

And with that—his compromises and mine—we were back together again.

THIRTY-TWO

E. B. got a ten-day pass and was waiting in the comfortable and welcoming living room of the Nurses' Convalescent Home to greet me the morning I got discharged. We had a leisurely lunch at a little cafe in Brisbane before he drove me back to Camp Cable. I returned to work the next day but spent each evening with him, usually sitting on our wooden tree-sofa down by the river, talking about our future, the number of children we wanted—I wanted five boys but would settle for four—and names for them. It was heaven to be back in his arms and know that our love was stronger than ever and our future secure if we could just survive the war.

The last day of E. B.'s leave, I got a four-hour pass—not enough time to go anywhere—so with help from the kitchen, I packed a picnic supper for us to share at our tree. I borrowed one of the indestructible gray woolen blankets the Australian government issued to its troops. E. B. lay on his back on the blanket, his head resting on his crossed arms, his eyes closed. Sunlight showed through the leaves of the eucalypti trees towering above us. Their heady scent put me in a romantic mood. I had just finished laying out the food on our blanket when E. B. opened his eyes, sat up and stared at me, frowning. "E. B., what is it?"

He didn't answer right away, just stared at me a moment before closing his eyes and sighing. "Ila, this isn't working. I don't think I can take

CHAPTER THIRTY-TWO

much more of this."

I thought my heart would stop and a ball of fear began rolling around my stomach like pool balls ricocheting off the sides of a billiard table. "What do you mean 'you can't take much more of this?' Are you breaking up with me?"

"No. God, no. It's this … this tree … the lack of privacy. We have no place we can call our own. I want someplace where we can be without worrying if we'll be interrupted, someplace private, a place for just you and me."

He'd taken me by surprise, not that I hadn't thought the same thing, too, but that he'd voiced it. I hadn't said anything because I was afraid of where it might lead.

"Ila, I know what you're thinking: if we're alone, something might happen. Well, what of it? I'm not going to deny it: I want to make love to you. I don't want to just kiss you or hug you. I want more than that, don't you?"

How is it possible to dread hearing the thing that you've been longing to do? I could see the trap that had been constructed by my mother's religious edicts about the depravity of sex, the vileness of intercourse, and the sin of fornication, and my own feelings of desire for the sexual pleasure and release I knew were possible but hadn't yet experienced. I had decided that while I loved my Mother very much her religious views were harmful both to her and to me, and I could no longer accept them as a guide for my conscience and my behavior.

Finally, he broke the silence.

"Ila, I'm going to rent a small apartment in Brisbane. It might be just an efficiency; I don't know yet what I can find or when or what's available. But I'm going to get something. Probably not for a few months 'cause I'll be gone for a while and there's no point in doing something now."

"When I find one, I'll let you know. It'll be up to you to decide whether you can visit or not. And if you do, I won't pressure you to do anything you don't want to."

* * *

Life returned to normal—or what passed for normal in a war zone.

E. B. was back in New Guinea working with the U. S. Typhus Commission, which was trying to find ways to diagnose, treat and prevent typhus, one of the worst scourges of war throughout the centuries. He was doing some sterling work for the commission, but he was in the danger zone as one of his letters demonstrated. He wrote:

> "Ila, you should have been here last night! Big doings! My first real raid! It didn't amount to anything though as far as size and damage goes, but it really scared HELL outa me! I thought all hell had broken loose. Tojo dropped a few bombs and the ack-ack was going to beat the band and the sky looked like a fourth of July celebration. On their last run the lights caught them perfectly and the ack-ack boys threw everything but the kitchen sink at them. Quite exciting, everybody yelling and cheering and jumping up and down, that is everybody but me and I was down in the bottom of my slit trench with my tin hat on and my fingers in my ears."

In spite of the danger he was in, he still found time to write about details of our life together once we were married. He told me he'd already purchased a grass skirt and several pairs of native beads to decorate the family room of our first home and sent a big box of keepsakes back to his folks to store 'til we got married. He asked me to start buying

CHAPTER THIRTY-TWO

Wedgwood and Spode china and sterling silver tableware whenever I went into Brisbane. And the biggest surprise of all—he gave me his folks' address and asked for my folks' address suggesting we begin exchanging letters as a way to get to know each other. I was delighted by the idea.

Of course, I worried about E. B. all the time and it didn't help that in October work slowed down at the 155th as the Red Arrow Men began pulling out and returning to New Guinea for more fighting. I kept my morale up by thinking about Christmas—E. B. and I were going to ask for ten-day leaves, and we planned to spend every minute together.

THIRTY-THREE

I couldn't recall being this excited about Christmas since I was a kid. E. B. had found an apartment for us and we were going to be together, although I was undecided about spending the night with him. I thought perhaps we could spend the days and early evenings together: I could fix him some home-cooked meals, and I'd spend the nights with friends.

While E. B. got a ten day leave, I could only get three days off—December 23, 24, and 25. I decided to wait 'til I saw him to tell him so that I'd be there to calm him down after he heard the news. I knew from experience that he could get really riled up when things didn't go his way.

* * *

We met at our favorite restaurant in Brisbane for dinner at six before walking the short distance to the apartment. Although he was disappointed that my leave was so brief, he handled it well, much to my relief. After a lot of soul-searching—mostly me battling the voice of my mother—I decided I would spend one night with E. B. in the apartment, although I had yet to tell him. I reasoned that either or both of us could be killed before this damn war was over, and I wanted to have at least one night

CHAPTER THIRTY-THREE

with E. B.—one night that I could replay in my mind and cherish if anything happened to him.

"Sweetheart," holding my hand in both of his, E. B.'s voice quivered when he called me that. "Please stay all night." He looked beseechingly into my eyes—I could almost hear his silent prayer, "Say yes. Please say yes."

Before I could answer he went on. "I promise. We won't do anything you don't want to do. I want to hold you all night long and wake up to you first thing in the morning. *Please, Ila.*"

I couldn't hold out anymore and I didn't want to. "E. B., I've given this a lot of thought. I'll stay, but no sex." He nodded immediately. "And, I need something to wear. I'm not getting naked with you, and besides that, you know I'm always cold."

He grinned. "I've got just the thing: it's ugly and it's Army, but it will keep you warm." He got up from the sofa and walked into the bedroom of his cozy apartment. He returned quickly, holding out a long-sleeved, khaki cotton shirt.

"You're right. It *is* ugly, but it's warm. I ought to know because I've got several of my own, just didn't bring any with me." I grinned as I took the shirt from him.

"I know it's not real late, only a little after ten, but are you ready to go to bed?" E. B. asked.

I nodded. "I am, but I'm scared, too."

"I know, Honey, but I won't do anything to hurt you, I love you so." E. B. spoke with such gentleness and love I felt immediately more at ease.

"I realize that this is probably not what you had in mind, but would you keep your clothes on, please? It would make me feel safer."

E. B.'s eyebrows shot up with a look of surprise. "If that's what you want, yes."

His words were a soothing balm calming my anxious mind.

I picked up the khaki shirt, walked into the other room and took off all my clothes except my drawers. I could tell the moment I put on E. B.'s shirt, which was way too big, that he had worn it earlier. It smelled like him—that spicy, musky smell that always made my heart beat a little faster. Wearing that shirt was almost like having his arms around me. I buttoned the front to the neck and rolled up the sleeves to my wrists. Then I carried my folded clothes into the living room where E. B. was still sitting on the sofa.

"My God, Ila! I've never considered an Army shirt sexy until now." E. B.'s voice was barely above a whisper and suddenly I felt self-conscious and exposed.

"E. B.," I said more sharply than I intended, "Please don't look at me like that. You're making me nervous."

"I'm sorry, Honey. It's just that ... well, I guess I hadn't thought about how you'd look. I mean, I've fantasized. You know all guys do, " I nodded, "but this is so much better than my fantasies."

I stood there feeling confused and flattered at the same time.

All these conflicting emotions are going to be the death of me, I thought. "How about you go on and get into bed and I'll be there in a minute," E. B. suggested. I nodded, turned and walked into the bedroom.

And that's all I have to say about that night.

THIRTY-FOUR

The workload at the hospital continued to decline as the 32nd Infantry Division pulled out of Camp Cable going north to New Guinea and beyond, fighting and chasing the Japanese across the ocean and back to their homeland. It was just a matter of time before we followed our troops. At the end of January 1944, the 155th Station Hospital was moved from Camp Cable to Ekibin Heights, about three miles southeast of Brisbane, into a brand-new building on a hill overlooking the city. Our first patients, Army troops assigned to a medical laboratory working in New Guinea, didn't arrive until after the first of February. About half had malaria and the other half received surgery or were treated for gonorrhea with the new drug, penicillin.

I wasn't real busy, which is never good because I tend to worry.

E. B. had malaria and was recovering. Even so, I knew we were in for months, if not years, of illness because malaria can reoccur at any time. I got another cold and was hospitalized for six days in April. But this time, after I was discharged to my quarters on April 13, I didn't get better, and they stuck me back in the hospital again three days later. Then came one of the biggest surprises of my life.

"Lt. Armsbury, I'm Doctor Armstrong. How are you?"

"I'm fine. Just tired of this cold and this damn headache, pardon my French." I laughed.

"Don't worry. I've heard much worse than that. Do you know why I'm here, Lt.?"

"Patient Rounds?"

"Well, yes and no, Lt. You may not know this, but while you were hospitalized last week there was a general meeting with all the nurses of the 155th to talk with them about going home."

I sat up in bed and almost shouted, "Going home? I'd love to go home but the war isn't over. Why were they talking about going home?"

"Orders are coming down that will send the 155th to the Netherlands East Indies. I was asked to review the records of all the nurses to see if there are any who shouldn't make the trip due to health concerns. I have to tell you; it was surely a surprise to me to see that 40 of the nurses including yourself have been here over two years with no time off."

I nodded. He didn't seem to want a comment and I couldn't figure out where this was going so I thought it better to wait and see what he'd say next.

"The thing is, Lt. the only way someone can go home right now is on sick leave. Every one of those 40 nurses has something in their medical record that qualifies them to go home. My job is to make the offer and see if anyone wants to take me up on it."

I was shocked. This was what I'd dreamed about … going home … seeing Mother and Daddy again … sleeping as long as I wanted … wearing civilian clothes and not Army uniforms that made me look all straight up and down.

"Yes. That's what I say. Yes, I want to go home." The very next day I was transferred to the 42nd General Hospital but I'd barely gotten settled into my room when my presence was requested in another part of the hospital, a meeting room with two Lt. Colonels, a full Colonel, and

CHAPTER THIRTY-FOUR

a major, none of whom I knew.

"Have a seat, Lt.," directed Lt. Colonel Lewis Gundry whom I learned later was the president of the Disposition Board.

"Lt. Armsbury, this board is here to determine whether you are fit to remain in the military service of the United States."

I was absolutely shocked. No one had told me there was any concern about my fitness, nor had I known that a Board of Disposition was meeting to determine my future.

"I don't understand. What's this about, sir?"

"Lt., your medical record shows that you have been hospitalized numerous times since your arrival in Australia. I have here an abbreviated clinical record of your medical history. I'm going to read it into the record. When I'm done you may comment. Do you understand?"

"Yes, sir."

(Name) Ila L. Armsbury

(Grade) 2nd Lt.

(Organization) 155th Station Hospital

(Date and time admitted) 14, April, 1944 @1430

Pertinent History, Chief Complaint and Condition on Admission.

Repeated attacks upper respiratory infection since July 1942.

Had an attack of Influenza at Fort Leavenworth, Kansas in hospital one week in January 1941. Then was free from any upper respiratory infection until July 1942 at Melbourne, Australia when patient had an acute upper respiratory infection with congestion of nose, swelling of face and severe headache. In 4th General Hospital about ten days.

Transferred to near Brisbane, Australia in August 1942. Was free from upper respiratory infection during summer months until April 1943 while at Tamborine, [the Australian name for Camp Cable] Queensland, Australia. Then had recurrence of symptoms which first developed at Melbourne, Victoria, consisting of congestion of nose, swelling of face and severe headache. Was hospitalized at 155th Station Hospital for about ten days.

During the eight cold months of the past two years, patient has spent 106 days in the hospital plus many more days in quarters. She has had numerous hospital admissions and all forms of therapy have been tried without relief. Then was relatively free from upper respiratory infections during the Australian summer months until the reappearance of colder weather in April of this year.

Lost about 12 pounds during winter of 1943 — regained during last summer. Appetite now fair. No nausea or vomiting. No diarrhea. Has feeling of pressure behind eye, with each acute attack of upper respiratory infection.

Diagnosis: Acute upper respiratory infection, recurrent attacks.

Treatment: No effective treatment successful the last two winters.

It is thought that because of her frequent disabling attacks and

CHAPTER THIRTY-FOUR

because of the onset of the cold weather it would be inadvisable to keep this patient on foreign duty.

"Lt., after a review of your records it is the opinion of this board that you are unfit for military service in this theater of operations. You are to be sent back to the States for further observation, treatment, and disposition."

I was shocked. Unfit? I couldn't even say the word, let alone think it.

"Lt., do you have anything to say?"

"Yes, sir. None of my work evaluations have ever referred to me as 'unfit.' I'm a good nurse and I do good work. I don't want to leave the Army, sir."

"No one is disputing the quality of your work or your nursing skills, Lt. But we are concerned about the frequency and severity of your respiratory illnesses here. So, the Army is going to send you back to the States to the VA hospital closest to your home."

"That's wonderful, sir. But what will happen when I get there, sir?"

"That's for them to determine, Lt. Pack your things, you'll be shipping out shortly.

* * *

Once the determination was made that I would be sent back to the States, I couldn't wait to go. But you know the Army—hurry up and wait and wait and…you get the picture. It was a month before we—a small group of nurses and I—finally set sail for home on the *Doña Nati*, a little Philippine freighter with only nine staterooms.

We—the Allies—were putting everything we had into attacking the enemy and sending them back to Japan, so no naval escorts were available to protect us as we sailed for the states. Instead, the *Doña Nati* followed a zigzag course which meant that our ship didn't travel in a straight line—we constantly changed direction from left to right sailing from Brisbane to the shore of South America. Our ship was also blacked out at night to make it harder for anyone to see us.

One evening after we'd been at sea about a week, I had an unusual experience with one of the passengers, another nurse going home. We were standing at the railing, enjoying a beautiful night, and watching the moon on the water. I noticed she was eating something but because it was dark, I couldn't make it out.

"What is that you're eating? It looks good."

"They are. Here," she said pushing a small paper bag towards me. "Have a couple."

I ate two but still couldn't identify them. "What are these? They taste different, and they're crunchy."

"Chocolate-covered grasshoppers."

I'm sorry to say I lost my dinner and was unable to eat for a couple of days afterwards.

A few nights later, we were jolted awake by the ship's siren because a crewman thought he spotted a Japanese sub. We dressed and spent the rest of the night sitting in our pre-assigned lifeboats, suspended between inky black sky and shimmering black water as the lifeboats hung over the sides of the little freighter.

Some of the lifeboat passengers talked and drank coffee, but one guy had a fifth of scotch that he drank straight. I wondered how they could be so nonchalant?

Me? I was so scared I couldn't drink a thing. The worst part was that because of my anxiety, I started smoking again. I'd quit a year before and was so proud of myself—smoking and respiratory infections don't

CHAPTER THIRTY-FOUR

go together well—but that night I backslid. Given a choice between eating chocolate covered grasshoppers or being hunted by the enemy, I preferred chowing down on bugs.

After hours of sitting in the cold dark, they called, "All clear," and we were allowed to go back to bed. I was exhausted but so keyed up that I couldn't sleep until hours later when it was dark again.

After three long weeks at sea, we arrived at San Francisco, where we were hospitalized for a week at the Presidio—it's closed now—before being sent to VA hospitals closest to our hometowns. Finally, I was going home.

THIRTY-FIVE

"*H*ome! *Home on the Range! Where the Deer and the Antelope play, Where seldom is heard a discouraging word, And the sky is not cloudy all day.*"

I just couldn't help it—I sang those comforting words to myself as I stepped off the train at the station in Topeka. If other passengers nearby heard me, they had the good grace to ignore my off-key singing. God, it was wonderful to be back in Kansas. Now, if I could only get to feeling better. In a letter home, I'd told the folks that the Army was hospitalizing me at Winter General, the VA hospital in Topeka, to treat my ongoing sinus problems, and that was true. What I didn't tell them was that I was depressed and exhausted, and just didn't feel like myself.

Winter General was a 1,000-bed hospital with 900 of the beds reserved for psychiatric patients. I knew I was in the right place because I needed to see a psychiatrist and got right to the point when we met for our appointment.

"I think I have combat fatigue, Doctor. I'm jumpy all the time. I just can't seem to relax." I paused trying to figure out what to say next.

"And there's this smell—sometimes I get a whiff of something— it's horrible—and it reminds me of burned flesh, and I get nauseous and can't eat. And sounds bother me, every little noise—like something hitting the floor, or a door slamming— and I jump ten feet. And crying.

CHAPTER THIRTY-FIVE

Sometimes I cry but I don't know why. And I have nightmares."

"Tell me about your nightmares, Lieutenant. What happens in them?"

I had to think for a moment about how to explain the nightmares to him. Finally, I replied, "The one that bothers me the most is about my dad. I'm standing at my folks' bedroom door, looking in but not sure whether I should enter. I see my dad laying on his back, the blankets pulled up under his chin. His face is pale, and his voice is so soft I can barely hear him. In the dream my dad says, 'Come in, Honey. It's okay. It looks like we've got some trouble here, doesn't it?'

"And this is what's really strange, Doctor, because this first part of the dream is like real life. My dad was sick when I was a kid and became crippled, so part of this really happened." The doctor nodded.

"So, you experienced something traumatic with your father when you were a child?"

"That's right. Anyway, in the dream I say, 'Yes, Daddy, you're sick' and I walk towards the bed and say, 'Daddy what's wrong? Why can't you walk?' and I start to cry. My dad looks at me for a second before saying, 'Don't you remember, honey? My legs were blown off in the war.' Then he pulls back the covers and I see these two hideous stumps where his legs used to be, each blown off below the knee. Bones protruding, muscle and tissue torn and shredded, bright red with blood on the sheets and on him. It's horrible and I wake up gasping for air."

The psychiatrist was quiet for a moment before responding, "So in real life he couldn't walk because of some crippling condition, and in your dream, he can't walk but it's because he was injured in the war?" I just nodded.

"Lieutenant, what you're experiencing is not uncommon. You've been in a war zone. You've seen terrible injuries. In your waking hours, you know that your father can't walk, but it isn't due to a war injury. But in your sleep, the war intrudes. You can't get away from what you've seen and experienced. The two realities—your life with your dad and the war—have become intertwined in your mind. It may be a while before your war memories recede, but they will. I wouldn't worry if I were you. You won't have any lasting effects. And you don't have combat fatigue. You just need some of your mother's good home cooking and some rest. So, I'm going to give you a thirty-day pass to go home." And that's what he did.

It was during my second home visit that I received a notice saying that the Board of Disposition at Winter General was preparing to hold a hearing on August 8 to determine my fate and whether I would have a future with the Army.

THIRTY-SIX

A small meeting room, which could hold about twenty folks, was set aside for my hearing at Winter General. The room was nondescript—white walls, gray floor tile, the U.S. and Kansas flags, a long table and chairs for the hearing officers, a stenography machine and chair, and chairs for the witnesses. Two small windows with wood blinds brightened the room with morning sun but my mood was dark. I was apprehensive, my stomach hurt, and my skin felt clammy. The two cups of coffee I'd drunk instead of eating a good breakfast probably didn't help my nerves, but I just couldn't get any food down. What if they decided that I was unfit for service? I wanted to stay in the Army until E. B. was back and we could make our plans to resign and get married.

The Disposition Board was composed of just three officers, the chiefs of the medical, surgery and neuropsychiatry services. They looked at my medical records, asked me a few questions and concluded that I had two problems, an allergy to aspirin as well as an allergy to something, probably mold, in Australia. Their finding that I was allergic to aspirin surprised me—I'd taken aspirin for pain all my life and never connected it with my reoccurring but intermittent problem of angioneurotic edema— that's medical talk for swelling in my face and hands. But the good news was that they thought I was capable of performing my duties "within the continental limits of the United States." While I was thrilled with their conclusions, there was one more hurdle—a hearing before the Nurses Retiring Board—and that's the hearing I dreaded most.

The board, composed of two majors, two captains, and a recorder, met on September first in a meeting room at Winter General.

"Lt. Armsbury, do you wish to be represented by counsel?"

"No, sir, I do not."

The reporter read the orders convening the board.

"Lt. Armsbury, do you have any objection to offer to any member sitting upon the board?"

"No, sir, I do not."

Then I was sworn in as the first witness.

> "Will you please inform the board of the nature and cause of any disability you may have and when it was first manifested?"
>
> "The first symptoms that I noticed were in the latter part of July 1942, while stationed at Melbourne. I couldn't breathe through my nose, and there was a feeling of pressure behind and around my eyes. I had severe headaches and my nose, eyelids, and upper lip swelled up. That was the first attack. The second was in September 1942 and was very slight. During the summer months over there—from the first of October to the first of April—I didn't have any symptoms. But the symptoms returned when the weather got cold, and from April to the latter part of August I was in the hospital two weeks and out of the hospital two weeks. My symptoms were the same as before. I never noticed these symptoms before I went to Australia nor since then, with the exception of one time when I opened a footlocker when I had the same feeling of stuffiness in the nose and stinging in the nose and eyes. I immediately closed the footlocker and had my folks take everything out of it and air them."

CHAPTER THIRTY-SIX

The next witness was an Army doctor, Major Howard J. Lee, one of two docs appointed as medical witnesses to review my medical records.

"Major Lee, will you please read the joint record of the medical witnesses in this case?"

> *"...This officer has had four attacks of angioneurotic edema, in other words a serious allergic reaction, which causes swelling of the face or throat, since 1937. In July 1942, in Australia, she developed nasal block, sinus pain with swelling of the lids. This recurred in April 1943, lasting until September 1943. There was a return of symptoms in April 1944, which resulted in her evacuation. There was a recurrence of angioneurotic edema in this country after aspirin ingestion as a test and a recurrence of the nasal symptoms when unpacking a footlocker, which had been packed in Australia. It is felt that the nasal symptoms are due to some exogenous substance, probably mold contacted in Australia, and that the angioneurotic edema is probably an aspirin sensitivity. A diagnosis of allergic state, mild, characterized by recurrent attacks of angioneurotic edema, due to aspirin sensitivity, and attacks of allergic rhinitis—inflammation of the nasal passages—due to sensitivity to unknown substances contacted in Australia, is made."*

I was surprised to learn that they had tested me for an allergy to aspirin. No one had asked my permission. Then again, when you're in the Army they don't ask your permission to do anything to you. You're at their mercy ... if they have any.

> *"I see. Major Anderson, do you concur in this report?"*
> *"Yes sir."*

> "Lt. Armsbury, have you been furnished with a copy of the report which has just been read?"
>
> "No, Sir."
>
> "You will receive one with the proceedings of this board. Lt. Major Lee, will you please state whether or not Lt. Armsbury is incapacitated for full active service?"
>
> "She is."
>
> "Is the incapacity or condition permanent, sir?"
>
> "It is."
>
> "Is it progressive?"
>
> "Not necessarily so."

I was writing furiously, taking notes so that I could speak to their concerns when it was my turn. How did they know this was a permanent condition or that it wasn't progressive?

> "Would this officer be able to do limited service?"
>
> "Yes."

I was pleased with this answer. They were agreeing with the Disposition Board and I could live with that. And they weren't recommending that I be discharged, at least not yet.

> "Please state the date of origin of this condition or incapacity."
>
> "It first manifested itself in 1937."

This was news to me. I wrote myself a note '1937???' How did they conclude that?

CHAPTER THIRTY-SIX

"Please state whether or not this incapacity is an incident of the service."

"No."

"Please state whether or not this condition has been aggravated by the military service."

"Not permanently."

"Major Anderson, do you concur in these answers?"

"Yes sir."

"Lt. Armsbury, you are now afforded an opportunity to cross-examine the medical witnesses, if you so desire. Do you desire to cross-examine them?"

"No, only I didn't understand that the angioneurotic edema was considered a part of this allergic condition. That is why I didn't say anything about it when I stated my case in the beginning. I have nothing else to say."

One of the board members, picking up on my confusion about when the allergic reaction started, asked for an explanation.

"Major Lee, you state that this first began in 1937. There is nothing in the record about 1937. She said she did not recognize that those symptoms were a counterpart of the same condition which was manifested upon taking aspirin.

"No, she had some angioneurotic edema in 1937." So, he turned to me.

"Lt. what kind of trouble did you have in 1937? Similar to what you had in Australia?"

"No, Sir, it wasn't. The thing that happened in 1937 was that I had a severe cold over a period of approximately six weeks. I was taking a post graduate course at that time, and rather than

drop it, I kept working during the winter months. I was outside constantly. The weather was severe and as I had this bad cold, I kept taking aspirin. At the end of about a month of this kind of treatment, working and taking aspirin, one time I noticed swelling in my hands, which started with an itching of my palms. There was swelling of the fingers and of the lips and a very slight rash. I didn't report it or do anything, just went to bed and after a period of a few hours, it disappeared. There wasn't any swelling of the face or throat.

"About two weeks later—it never dawned on me that the aspirin was causing it—I still had the cold and I was working outside in the slums—the houses were not heated—well, the cold continued and I kept taking aspirin and about two weeks later I had a very severe attack. I was out on a case and as we finished the delivery, I noticed that my hands itched again. By the time I got back to the emergency room, I noticed that my lips were swollen, my face was red, and there was a rash over my body. While trying to get my clothes off and get a gown on in the exam room, I felt like I was going under the room, I cannot explain it, but I did just that. I don't know whether I fainted, but when I woke up, they had given me ten cubic centimeters of calcium gluconate intravenously. The intern in the ER said they were unable to get my blood pressure at that time. That is the most severe attack I ever had and while I didn't connect it with aspirin, I never had it again until I went into the Army in 1940, and in January I sold an oil painting that I had done, which thrilled me, and when I received the check for it, I broke out again just as I had before. I hadn't had any aspirin then.

"The trouble in Australia was not like that. Coming back on the train, there it was again—the excitement, I was going

CHAPTER THIRTY-SIX

home—and on the train from San Francisco, I had the same symptoms. I had a headache, took ten grains of aspirin and had an attack, but I didn't connect it with what I had in Australia nor with any allergy, and on the physical exam, I said I wasn't allergic to anything because I didn't know I was."

"Is there any other evidence you wish to offer, Lt. Armsbury?"

"No sir."

And that was it. They ended the hearing, asked me to leave the room so they could deliberate, and I walked out into the hall to pace and worry. I was concerned they might think that I knew aspirin caused an allergic reaction and that I took it deliberately just to get out of work. I was also concerned that they might decide I was more trouble than I was worth and just retire me in spite of my desire to stay in the Army. Did I make it clear to them that I didn't know that aspirin was causing me to get sick? Did they understand that I wanted to work, was a hard worker, and that I wanted to serve my country?

It seemed like I waited for hours but it was actually only about 45 minutes before they reconvened, called me back into the room and announced their decision.

> "The board finds that Second Lt. Ila L. Armsbury, Army Nurse Corps, is incapacitated for active service; that said incapacity is not the result of an incident of service; that the cause of said incapacity is not an incident of service; that the cause of said incapacity is a mild allergic reaction, characterized by recurrent attacks of angioneurotic edema, caused by sensitivity to aspirin, and attacks of allergic rhinitis—hay fever—caused by sensitivity to certain allergens, probably mold, contacted [sic] in Australia; "that said incapacity originated on or about 1937, and that said incapacity

is permanent."

"However, this board recommends that this officer be returned to a permanent limited duty status in a fixed installation within the continental limits of the United States."

* * *

It's been 55 years since that hearing. I have my Army medical records in front of me now and can look at them with a clearer understanding of what happened. Here's the facts.

When I was a kid, ten years old, I cut my hand and had to have stitches which the doctor did *without any anesthetic*. It hurt like hell and afterwards I took aspirin for the pain and had no allergic reaction. Same thing when I was 15 and had my appendix removed. And in late 1935, when I had three teeth pulled and one of them had to be broken, chiseled, and pulled out by the dentist while his assistant held my head down. Lots of pain, I tell you, and I took aspirin with no ill effects. I had that episode in 1937, and yes, I had been taking aspirin. I can see the connection now between the aspirin and the angioneurotic edema.

But here's the kicker. I didn't have an allergy to mold prior to going to Australia. My Army medical records show that it was only after I arrived and was exposed to some type of mold that I became ill. Each episode was accompanied by a hospitalization, and with each hospitalization my coughing, wheezing, and breathing problems got worse. And during each of five hospitalizations over the two years I was there, the Army prescribed aspirin to me with never a note that aspirin was causing any allergic reaction. Then in April 1945, after the retirement hearing, the Army diagnosed me with acute bronchial asthma, moderately severe.

Know what I think? I think that I developed an allergy to mold in

CHAPTER THIRTY-SIX

Australia and the continual exposure to that mold led to me developing bronchial asthma but the Army didn't want to acknowledge that, so they wouldn't have to pay me for any service-related disability. Instead, they focused on my allergic reaction to aspirin. And I think they intentionally waited until after the hearing to make the official diagnosis of bronchial asthma and their determination.

I need to say one more thing. I loved the Army and I love my country. I was proud to serve and I'd do it again if I could. But I'll always wonder if my breathing problems, which got progressively worse over the years—even though I quit smoking after the war—were the result of my Army service.

THIRTY-SEVEN

The hearing was over. The sense of *"darkness there and nothing more"* as my favorite author, Edgar Allan Poe, wrote in *The Raven*, had finally left me. I remained a patient at Winter General with a couple more trips back home to Lincoln until October 2, when I was released to go back to work on permanent limited duty. My new orders? Working right there at Winter General.

The work was intense and stressful, and we were short of help with nurses from our unit being sent overseas. With my assigned two wards, three more when the nurse down the hall was off duty, plus one more up the hall, I had six wards every other afternoon and every other morning. Each ward had 33 patients—198 total. They were proof, if ever any was needed, of the horrors of war—arms, legs, eyes, fingers, noses, feet, hands, hair, and muscle missing: broken bones—backs, arms, legs. These were American troops who'd served in England, France, and Italy with another convoy from Australia expected any day. They were at the beginning of their recovery and, I prayed, eventual return to their families.

Some of these returning troops had been identified as neuropsychiatric patients. So, in addition to overseeing two to six wards of injured patients, I took classes taught by Dr. Karl Menninger.

Dr. Karl's idea about caring for the returning troops who needed psychiatric help was opposite the Army's idea at that time. Back in Australia,

CHAPTER THIRTY-SEVEN

if we had someone who was identified as a neuropsychiatric patient, it was common to sedate him and tie him in bed. Dr. Karl would have fainted if he'd known that. His idea was you didn't sedate the patient, you didn't tie him to the bed. You made sure he was in a safe room where he couldn't hurt himself, and if he couldn't sleep at night, it was your job to sit and listen to him while he talked. I loved Dr. Karl and his teachings served me well over the years as I worked more with psych patients.

The only wrinkle in the fabric of my life was that I hadn't heard from E. B. in weeks, and I was getting worried. Just as I was beginning to panic, I got a letter from him. A week later, much to my surprise and delight, I got a note at work from E. B. telling me he had been admitted as a patient in the general medical ward at Winter General. As soon as my shift was over, I hurried over to see him. I knew the admitting nurse slightly and we chatted.

"Ila," she said, "what can I do for you?" I told her.

She looked at her clipboard. "He's requested no visitors. Hmmm. Let me walk down there and see if he's awake and I'll tell him you're here."

She returned shortly. "Go on in. He's excited to see you."

My heart was in my throat as I entered E. B.'s room. I hadn't seen him in months, and we'd both been ill. I was looking pretty good now—I was rested and had gained weight—and my spirits were good because I'd been home a few times to see the family. But E. B.? He looked like a broken, old man, not the active, enthusiastic man I knew and loved. He was so pale I could see blood vessels under his skin and dark circles around his eyes. But the most startling change was how much weight he'd lost. The pajama top hung off his shoulders almost as though he had shrunk.

"Oh, E. B.," was all I could get out before I started sobbing as he put his arms around me. "What's happened to you? Why are you here?"

He rocked me and rubbed my back as he explained. "It's been rough, Honey. Lots of bleeding of the bowel—so much that they couldn't fly me home ... The altitude would have just made me bleed more. There wasn't time to sail back home because I needed surgery, so they moved me to a general hospital and did it over there. That's why you didn't hear from me for so long."

"But what was wrong? Are you okay now?" I blubbered.

"At first they thought I had colon cancer and they ran all kinds of tests. They finally decided it's ulcerative colitis and they're treating it. The surgery helped. I just felt so damn bad I didn't want to eat, and when I did eat, I had a lot of pain. But don't worry, honey. They're making headway and I really am feeling much better even though I look like hell."

He continued holding me as I cried, from fear and relief, knowing he was going to be all right. As he gently pushed me away so he could see my face he said, "I've missed you so ... God, you look good, Honey."

In that moment I knew that our future together was assured and that nothing would come between us. We could tackle any problem, and if we were together, we'd always prevail.

"E. B., I've been so worried I was going out of my mind. When I got that letter, what ... eight weeks ago? ...and then nothing else One night at work, I spent more time in the linen closet crying than I did caring for patients. I'm so relieved." We hugged for a few minutes, no words—just caresses and kisses. Let me tell you there's no salve like the caress and kiss of the one you love.

I looked forward to the end of each shift, because it meant I could see E. B. When I worked the first shift, E. B. and I ate supper together. If I worked second shift, we ate lunch together. For third shift I'd pop in just before lights out and kiss him good night. Life was good—neither

CHAPTER THIRTY-SEVEN

of us was in harm's way, and we had all the time in the world as we waited for E. B.'s discharge from the hospital. Then we'd both put in for retirement and get married. I could hardly contain my happiness. Every dream I'd ever had was coming true.

For the first time in the almost three years that we'd known each other, E. B. and I got to eat Thanksgiving dinner together, on November 23rd, 1944. Winter General, like all the U. S. military commands worked hard to prepare a traditional Thanksgiving meal with all the trimmings. They printed and distributed a menu card decorated on the front with a pilgrim and his musket with a present-day soldier behind the pilgrim in shadow, holding a rifle. The menu was extensive: chilled tomato cocktail; roast young turkey with dressing, cranberry sauce, and giblet gravy; Virginia baked ham; glazed sweet potatoes and snowflake (mashed) potatoes; relishes; rolls and butter; pumpkin and mince pie; fresh fruit; candies and mixed nuts; *and* cigars and cigarettes. What a feast!

In the days following Thanksgiving, I began to notice little changes in E. B. He wasn't as talkative as he had been. He smiled less, and he seemed more tense. The change in demeanor worried me and I couldn't see a reason for it.

One day towards the end of November, I finally broke down and asked him what was going on.

"I got a letter from home. They want me to come home for Christmas, and I'm not looking forward to that visit."

"Why?"

"Well, you know Mother, how bossy she can be. I haven't felt ready to see her. That's why I told the doctor I didn't want visitors except for you. But I guess I can't avoid her forever. I've got a 30-day leave to go home. Do you mind?"

"Of course not. I understand how your mother feels if she's

anything like mine. Besides my folks have already written that they want me home for the holidays, too, and it would be my first time home for Christmas since 1940—four years ago. Just think of all the things we'll have to tell each other when we get back. When are you leaving?" I asked as I hugged him.

"November 29, but I'll be back for New Year's Eve."

THIRTY-EIGHT

E. B. got back from his home visit before I got back from mine. Once I returned to Winter General, I was assigned a couple of double shifts and couldn't see him except briefly to make our New Year's Eve plans—to have a quiet supper in his hospital room. I was so looking forward to it. I didn't have to work New Year's Eve or New Year's Day, so I got my hair fixed before our date, got a new forest green, long-sleeved wool dress—very elegant—and ordered a special meal from the hospital kitchen. I arrived at E. B.'s room at 6:30 p.m. and found him dressed in an elegant tuxedo with an orchid boutonnière and a huge orchid corsage for me. I felt like Mrs. Vanderbilt's pet pup!

E. B. had made arrangements with a hospital orderly who'd somehow obtained a small table, two chairs, a white linen tablecloth, and two napkins. The table was set with the heavy silver service that the Army provided in the officers' mess as well as china and crystal goblets. A bottle of red wine was open and breathing on the table, ready for our first toast. A small radio on E. B.'s bedside table was tuned to a station playing soft music. It was the most intimate, romantic setting I have ever seen in a hospital room.

"Darling, sit down. Let me pour you a glass of wine, and let's drink to our future," E. B. said softly as he pulled a chair out for me to sit.

"I can hardly wait to hear how your visit home went," I said. "How are your folks?"

E. B.'s smile, which had lit up the room, disappeared. "Did you and your mother have an argument?"

E. B. didn't answer. He put down his glass, lowered his hands, and looked down for a moment, as though the answer was in his lap. Then he looked me squarely in the eyes and said, "Ila, we need to talk." The atmosphere in the room changed in a heartbeat, but I didn't know why. However, in just a few moments everything became clear.

"Ila, I'm married, and I have been since 1937."

That's all I heard even though he continued talking. Time stopped. There was no sound not even my heartbeat. In fact, I'm pretty sure my heart stopped. I just sat there—perfectly still. Later I realized that my breathing had become really shallow, like I didn't want to make a sound and allow the threatening predator to hear me. I wanted to be invisible, but stillness was all I could accomplish.

I realized that I was squinting and that my field of vision had shrunk so that I could only see E. B.'s face—like I was trying to see into his soul to understand what was happening. Was this some type of unbelievably sick joke? Was he angry and punishing me for something I'd done or not done? Even though he was saying something—I knew he was speaking English—I couldn't understand the words. I interrupted.

"What do you mean you're married? How can you be married?" He started to answer me, but I wasn't done yet.

"You asked *me* to marry you. You asked *me* to write your parents. You asked *me* to buy china and silver and crystal for our future home. What do you mean, you're married?" I paused for a moment to catch my breath and then growled, "Why in God's name did you ask me to write your folks?"

Nothing...no response. I could feel my throat tightening. When

CHAPTER THIRTY-EIGHT

he finally answered it wasn't to the question I had asked. "I thought if my mother got to know you through your letters, she'd see what a wonderful girl you are, and she'd agree to help me get a divorce."

After a long pause he continued. "Ila, I got married in 1937 to someone I knew my mother wouldn't approve of. I wanted to show her that she could no longer tell me what to do. And it worked for a while. Mother said that Laura wasn't good enough for me. That she had no social standing and was a nobody. And Mother was the queen bee of society in Rockport. Social standing was everything to her. For a while Mother was stumped—she didn't know what to do. But eventually she got her bearings, sort of regrouped, and started up again. She, Mother I mean, hated Laura. Wouldn't invite her to any of her social gatherings. Told her friends they couldn't invite her to anything either. And everyone was afraid of Mother so what Mother said was the law."

E. B. paused, wouldn't catch my eye.

"Mother demanded that I get a divorce. When I refused, she tried unsuccessfully, to have the marriage annulled."

"Did you love your wife?" I asked, barely above a whisper.

The pause that followed seemed to go on forever before E. B. finally answered me.

"Maybe ... Um ... I doubt it. She was a nice girl, a nurse like you. I knew Mother would never approve if I brought Laura home to meet the folks first. That was part of the plan. I didn't take her home. We eloped, got married, and I just showed up with my new wife."

That poor girl, I thought. She was just a pawn in a battle between an overbearing mother and her spoiled brat son.

"So, what was I in this scheme? A way to make both your mother and your wife mad?"

"No, Ila. God, no. I love you. Almost from the moment we first met, I thought you were amazing. Funny, smart, feisty. You wouldn't let me tell you what to do, but you didn't try to tell me what to do either. And you're beautiful, Ila. You. are. beautiful. How could I not fall in love with you?"

"You couldn't because you were already married to someone else," I growled. I stopped for a moment to get my raging feelings under control then continued. "I'm leaving," I said as I pushed my chair back and stood up.

"Ila, wait. Everything will be okay, I promise. Please, please sit down and listen."

God knows I wanted everything to be okay so like a fool I sat down to see what he had to say.

"Has she, your wife, agreed to give you a divorce?"

He searched my face for some sign of encouragement—there was none—before continuing.

"No. She says she loves me. And it's way too late now, several years too late, for an annulment. Mother's not interested in a divorce anymore. If Laura and I got divorced, Mother'd have to pay her a lot of money."

"Why? Why would your Mother have to pay your wife—your ex-wife—a lot of money?"

"Because I don't have any. Mother's got it all. She always has. Money and land and houses. She came into the marriage with all that. My father only has what he's earned from his medical practice. So, you see, a divorce is out of the question."

I started to get up again, but E. B. put out his hand and grabbed my arm, pushing me back into my chair.

"I can get money to set you up in an apartment, a really nice apartment in Kansas City. We can see each other on the weekends, and maybe one or two nights a week. You can work and send money to your folks like you wanted, and we'll just go on like nothing ever happened. It will be like in Australia only better. We might not see each other every

CHAPTER THIRTY-EIGHT

day but we won't have to worry about the threat of war ... that one or the other of us could be killed. Don't you see?"

I saw alright. E. B. was just like my dad—a philanderer—only better dressed in military garb and fancied up with his medical education and his mother's money. "I need to leave," I said between gritted teeth. "I'm going to throw up." I shoved my chair back as E. B. reached out for me again but this time, I dropped my shoulder and whirled away from him so he couldn't touch me.

"Don't," I said. "And don't call me. Now, get out of my way, or I'll knock you down," I growled. He stood there looking shocked for a second, then moved to one side.

I stood up straight, threw my shoulders back, held my head high, and stalked out of that room while tears flooded my face.

THIRTY-NINE

On January 1, 1945—New Year's Day—while others were recovering from a night of too much food and drink, too much laughter and dance, I was numb, except for intermittent waves of nausea or emotional pain. I kept asking myself what kind of person does this?

Someone with no conscience? No morals? Someone who lacks humanity? All that may sound melodramatic to you, but you have to remember that I had lost *everything* that was most precious to me—my future.

I spent the entire day in bed except when I got up to vomit or pee. But the next morning I went to work.

Thank God for work. It became my salvation—a place where I was wanted and needed, where I could make a contribution, where I was respected and valued for myself and my skills.

He—I'm not repeating his name again—made several efforts to see me. Sent cards and letters, flowers, and candy, called. I threw everything away, didn't even open the cards or letters. Gave the flowers and candy to patients. Had a couple of my friends run interference for me when he showed up unexpectedly at my desk, so I didn't see him or even hear his voice.

It took months of grieving and rage, despair, and brief moments of hope—the ups and downs that accompany healing. But finally, I found myself again—the strong, intelligent woman who had wanted a career

CHAPTER THIRTY-NINE

and to travel the world. Who didn't want the restrictive life of her mother, trapped in a loveless marriage and stuck in drudge work in a little family-owned restaurant in a backwater town.

I had lots of time for reflection, and I thought back many years before, when Miss Miller, the chief nurse at Fort Leavenworth, had given me her sales pitch about joining the regular Army and making the Army my career. She emphasized travel, education, free health care and housing, the opportunity to make life-long friends within the service. After all, I had wonderful nieces and a darling nephew who brought me great joy. I wouldn't miss out on anything and I could avoid the aggravation of marriage. I decided I'd make the Army my family.

Over the next several months I saw the benefits of my decision. My work evaluations were "excellent" and "superior." I was promoted from 2nd Lt. to 1st Lt.

V-J Day was the most wonderful day of my entire Army career. We had all waited so long, and lost so many friends and loved ones, but finally the end had come, and we had won the war. I don't know how they handled it at other military installations, but at Winter General, we were all restricted to our respective hospital wards to await further notices. The military police went out and picked up all the service people who were in downtown Topeka and brought them straight back to the hospital. No one could leave for 72 hours.

That didn't keep civilians from celebrating though. You could hear whistles blowing and guns or fireworks going off, horns honking, radios blaring all over the city. Folks grinned and laughed, and many cried with relief, joy, and thankfulness. I thought about the kids still overseas and how happy they must be. They would finally be able to come home.

The Disposition Board changed my status from permanent limited duty to full time. They announced that Winter General was closing before the end of the year and we would all get new assignments.

My future was bright—different from what I'd envisioned a year before but still bright and full of excitement. Looking back, I realized I'd survived my childhood and my dad's selfish desires and craziness, my mother's soul-crushing religious fanaticism, the hatred and intolerance of the Ku Klux Klan, and poverty. I'd survived the lies and duplicity of a second selfish man—one who wrought destruction in his wake, and I'd survived the war. I was ready for my next challenge and whatever it was, I'd not only survive, I'd excel. Nothing and nobody was going to keep me down.

And they didn't.

AFTERWORD

ILA

After Ila broke up with E. B., she struggled with depression for months. She confided to only a few friends, her folks, Wava and Metta the circumstances of the breakup. Everyone who knew, even Florence, was understanding, sympathetic, and encouraging. As in the past, Ila's work became therapy and a refuge.

Ila had remained friends with the family of a young man, Blaine Herman, whom she had dated in high school, exchanging cards, letters, and visits. Blaine, like E. B., wore wire-rimmed glasses but the resemblance stopped there. Blaine was thin and tall, six feet, and had an oval face. He reminded me of David Niven, a receding hair line, pencil-thin mustache, and a kind smile. Sometime in mid-spring 1945 Ila got a letter from Blaine suggesting that they get together for a drink to reconnect. He had already received his honorable discharge from the Army and was working at Kansas City Power and Light.

They agreed to meet for a drink one night after work, while she was still at Winter General. Ila later said it was like they picked up where they had left off. They exchanged letters and phone calls and had numerous dates. Within a few months Blaine proposed. But before they could finalize any wedding plans, Winter General was closed, and Ila was transferred to Jefferson Barracks in Lemay, Missouri, south of St. Louis. She arrived there on November 29, 1945.

AFTERWORD

The wedding occurred in Lincoln, Kansas, at the home of Wava and Nolan Farrington on February 14, 1946. Ila was still in the Army and after a brief honeymoon she returned to Jefferson Barracks. Her military records contain a copy of a memo to the Adjutant General, dated March 7, 1946, reporting the "marriage of 1st Lt. Ila L. Armsbury ... to Mr. Dora Blaine Herman, Jr." and Ila's resignation from the Army Nurse Corps dated March 8, 1946.

Ila and Blaine moved to Topeka, Kansas, where Ila worked full time first as a supervisor in an outpatient clinic, and then as a clinical instructor for obstetrics students at St. Francis Hospital. Blaine went to school full time at the University of Kansas, graduating from K.U. with a degree in civil engineering in 1953. After graduation, he went to work for the Topeka Police Department as a detective.

Their first son, John, was born in 1953, and their second son, Richard, was born in 1956. Ila stayed home with the children during the first few years but returned to work at the new Veterans Administration Hospital in Topeka as a charge nurse for the general medical and neuropsychiatric wards in 1957.

Topeka was an ideal location for the Hermans, because Blaine's folks lived in Kansas City and Ila's family remained in Lincoln. But Blaine wanted to work in his chosen field. In January 1961 he was offered a job with the U. S. Air Force as a civilian statistician, and the family moved to San Bernardino, California. Ila worked as a private duty nurse for neuropsych patients and Blaine continued working for the Air Force, but in 1968, at the age of 51, Blaine was diagnosed with early onset Alzheimer's Disease.

Blaine had been a drinker before his diagnosis of Alzheimer's, but his drinking had not interfered with his job performance. However, as the Alzheimer's Disease progressed, Blaine's work performance suffered. He could no longer do the complex calculations that the Air Force needed, and as he became more frustrated at his inability to perform his job, his drinking increased until he developed alcoholism. In 1971 at the age of 54 Blaine was forced to retire.

Ila continued working until she retired, and she took care of Blaine in their home until 1977 when he was moved to a nursing facility where he died in 1978 at the age of 61.

Ila lived out the remainder of her life in San Bernardino. She traveled back to Lincoln at intervals for class and family reunions as well as traveling to Colorado to visit Metta. Ila died February 29, 2003, after a brief illness. She was 83.

DECORATIONS

Army Meritorious Unit Commendation
American Defense Service Medal
American Campaign Medal
Asiatic-Pacific Campaign Medal
World War II Victory Medal
Honorable Service Lapel Button

E.B.

I'll never know with certainty what E. B.'s life was like, but I believe, based on interviews and old newspaper accounts, it was, as Dr. Wallace Carpenter said, "a life of grief." In order to understand more, I had to learn about E. B.'s parents.

Family heritage was all-important to E. B.'s mother, Agnes Bird Settle. Agnes was the oldest of three girls born to Robert Emmett and Mary Bird. Robert was a third-generation physician in the Bird family and Agnes took great pride in that—so much so that she married a physician, Charles Thomas Settle. Their wedding announcement appeared on the front page of the *Atchison County Mail* on May 6, 1904 and spoke volumes about Agnes' social status in tiny Rock Port, Missouri.

> *Dr. C. T. Settle, of Langdon [Missouri], m. Agnes H. Bird of Rock Port and one of Rock Port's most accomplished and popular young ladies. Dr. Settle is the coroner of Atchison County, very popular and enjoys a large practice at Langdon.*

Charles and Agnes had one child, a son, born July 29, 1906. They named him Emmett Bird Settle after Agnes' father, Dr. Robert Emmett Bird.

Agnes was the one with money and property as became clear from copies of Charles and Agnes' wills. Charles' will, only one page, was signed and dated May 26, 1928 and was never updated. At the time the will was signed, E. B. was 21, turning 22 in two months, and had just graduated from the University of Nebraska with a BA in sociology.

The will specified that E. B. was to receive $1,000.00 with the rest of the estate going to Agnes. But a clause in Charles' will, specifying how assets were to be distributed if Agnes predeceased him, suggested that E. B. already had problems.

In the event that first Agnes then Charles died, E. B. was to receive $3,000.00 in lieu of the $1,000.00, plus all household goods, automobiles, books, medical instruments and equipment and all other property, both personal and real. But Charles also specified that all the remaining assets were to be turned over to the the First National Bank of Kansas City, Missouri, to be held in trust and administered by them for E. B.'s benefit, and to pay him an annual net income from the trust until E. B. turned 35, at which time "or within a reasonable time thereafter" the bank would pay E. B. the principal.

I knew from reading E. B.'s military records that he was already an alcoholic by the time he entered the Army. I began to suspect that something else was wrong, and that suspicion was confirmed when a family member indicated that E. B. had untreated manic depression, the old term for what we now call bipolar disorder, and self-medicated with booze.

After the University of Nebraska, E. B. went to Harvard Medical School where he graduated in 1932 with his medical degree.

Immediately after graduation, he was hired as a pathologist and director of the bacteriology lab at Swedish American Hospital in Rockford, Illinois. He applied to the Army Reserves as a First Lieutenant in November 1933 and received his appointment and commission two years later. He remained in Rockford until 1936.

AFTERWORD

A one-year gap in E. B.'s resume hints at the problems to come, and a divorce petition filed by E. B. in September 1960, explains what happened. The petition reads in part:

> ...in the month of April 1937 plaintiff [E. B.] was mentally and physically ill and suffering from the disease of alcoholism at which time he was hospitalized in a hospital in Omaha, Nebraska: that at said time the defendant [Laura Settle] herein was a registered nurse and was called to special duty as a special nurse to care for plaintiff while so hospitalized.

E. B.'s excessive drinking may have started as early as high school but by the time he'd graduated from Harvard he was an alcoholic.

A common practice among small town newspapers is for readers to submit local news items including wedding announcements which the papers print with few editorial changes. The following announcement appeared on the front page of the April 23, 1937 issue of the *Atchison County Journal*:

> ### Dr. Emmett Settle Weds
>
> One of the real surprise marriages of the spring season became known last weekend when Dr. Emmett Settle arrived home from Omaha accompanied by a wife, who was formerly Miss Elizabeth Coye of Omaha. Their marriage took place on Tuesday, April 13th.
>
> Dr. Settle and Miss Coye became acquainted while the doctor was connected with a hospital at Rockford, Ill., where the latter was employed as a surgical nurse.
>
> The groom, who had been in Omaha some days, taking treatment for infected teeth, had given no intimation that he was

about to become a benedict, and word of his marriage was doubtless as great a surprise to his parents, Dr. and Mrs. C. T. Settle, as it was to his acquaintances.

For the time being, the newlyweds are at the Settle home in Bischof's addition [in a small house owned by Agnes], *where a vociferous chavivari was tendered them about midnight Saturday.*

I suspect that Agnes wrote the wedding announcement. Note the emphasis on "surprise" in the first and third paragraphs. Agnes probably had plans for E. B.'s eventual wedding—a huge social occasion with Agnes as the queen and the bride cast as the princess to be carefully guided and introduced to Agnes' social circle. But E. B.'s quick and quiet marriage to Elizabeth, who was called Laura by her friends and family, robbed Agnes of one of the biggest and best roles of her life. And naturally, Agnes couldn't report how E. B. and Laura had really met so she lied to prevent anyone from learning the real reason E. B. was in an Omaha hospital.

The description of Agnes' treatment of Laura is based on interviews I conducted. Agnes was furious when E. B. brought Laura home as his wife. From the moment they met, Agnes believed that Laura wasn't good enough to be a Settle, and Agnes tried her darnedest to end the marriage with no success. Marrying Laura was probably one of the few times E. B. stood up to his mother, but he used an innocent woman as a pawn, and she suffered for it.

It didn't take long before E. B. was looking for a way out of his marriage and away from his domineering mother. The Army was his escape—he applied for active duty in April 1938, beginning three years of brief excursions from Rock Port to other communities for tours of active duty, usually about 14 days in length. Pearl Harbor was E. B.'s ticket

AFTERWORD

away from everything he hated—the responsibilities and restrictions that accompany marriage, and in E. B.'s particular case, the snobbish and arrogant social demands of his mother.

The Army did, however, provide E. B. with the opportunity to pursue his real passion—medical research. As a result of his work with the United States Typhus Commission in New Guinea he wrote a scholarly article, "A Pathologic Study of Tsutsugamushi [Typhus] Disease" which was published in the August, 1945, issue of *The Journal of Laboratory and Clinical Medicine*, with E. B. as the first author. A second professional article, this one about syphilis with E. B. as the third author, was published in 1947 in the *Archives of Dermatology and Syphilogy*, based on work done at Battey General Hospital. According to his military records, E. B. was awarded a Bronze Star Medal on September 18, 1944, I suspect for his work with the Typhus Commission. No other records were located or appear to exist to explain the circumstances for this medal.

The description of Ila and E. B.'s courtship and what happened in Australia and at Winter General, with the exception of the instances already mentioned in the preface, are accurate and are taken directly from Ila's letters and tape recording. But Ila didn't know what happened with E. B., Laura, and Agnes after E. B. left Winter General. I had to tease out the story by reviewing E. B.'s military records, interviewing family and friends, and examining old court documents and newspaper accounts.

After leaving Winter General, E. B. was sent to Rome, Georgia in early February 1945, where he worked as the Chief of the Laboratory Service at Battey General Hospital (BGH). Laura joined him in July 1945.

Over the next six months, E. B. was hospitalized three times, once for colitis and twice for heart problems. In January 1946, the Army

Retiring Board decided that E. B. was "permanently incapacitated for active service." He was diagnosed with "arteriosclerosis, coronary arteries, moderate, manifested by severe attacks of coronary insufficiency and angina pectoris, and paroxysmal tachycardia, moderate, type undetermined."

E. B. arrived back home in Rock Port on January 30, 1946, without Laura, who stayed behind in Georgia to oversee the packing and move. Her absence allowed E. B. to tell his friends and family an amazing story, one his friends believed.

According to three different sources, E. B. told everyone that he had met and fallen in love with an Army nurse in Australia; that they had planned to get married after the war, but she died. I believe he was talking about Ila. When I asked how he could speak of love, romance, and a wedding when he was already married, all three were genuinely surprised and said they thought the wedding between E. B. and Laura didn't happen until after the war, perhaps sometime in 1945 or '46.

The only explanation I have for this apparent contradiction is that after E. B. left for active duty in early January of 1942, and considering how shabbily Agnes treated Laura, I believe Laura must have returned to Omaha and her family for the duration of the war. Unfortunately, I could find no census records, and all the voting records before 1956 were destroyed, so I was unable to test my theory, nor was I able to find any of Laura's descendants who knew her or her story.

Laura returned to Rock Port probably in the early summer of 1946 where she and E. B. resumed living in the little house owned by Agnes. If their marriage was bad before the war it became much worse afterwards. Several people reported that E. B. abused Laura verbally and emotionally and carried on numerous affairs until his death.

Once home, E. B. joined his father's medical practice until Dr. Charles' health began to decline and he developed dementia and retired. In 1952 E. B. took on a new partner, Dr. Wallace Carpenter. Dr.

AFTERWORD

Carpenter described E. B. as "a difficult partner because of the drinking" and as "a brilliant doctor" whose ability was impaired by alcohol.

Dr. Carpenter also knew Agnes, whom he described as "a ringtailed snorter," a term I had not heard before. When pressed for an explanation, Dr. Carpenter described Agnes as "more than just a determined woman; she dominated E. B."

E. B.'s father died in 1953, and Dr. Carpenter left the practice to go out on his own in 1954. E. B.'s drinking got worse as he slowly destroyed his medical practice. Even one of his closest friends and admirers admitted that she didn't allow him to deliver her baby because he was drunk that day. Several people described E. B. as a gifted physician "when he wasn't drinking." Unfortunately, those moments of sobriety became less and less frequent.

E. B. remained in his one-person medical practice and also worked as the pathologist for St. Francis Hospital in Maryville, 41 miles east of Rock Port. According to multiple sources E. B. had a girlfriend in the Kansas City–St. Joseph area whom he visited every weekend. Finally, E. B. separated from Laura, rented a small apartment in Maryville and on October 8, 1960, filed for an annulment or "in the alternative that if the court determine that there was and is a valid and lawful marriage between plaintiff and defendant that plaintiff be divorced..."

Laura retained an attorney, and on November 2, 1960, answered E. B.'s petition, laying out proof of their marriage. Two hearings on the petitions were scheduled for November 14, 1960, and February 20, 1961, the first continued at E. B.'s request, and the second a no-show. I suspect that during the interim Agnes put the screws to E. B.—I can almost hear her now: "The publicity. Think what people will say. Emmett, if you do this, I'll cut you off without a dime. You made your bed, now sleep in it."

Something like that must have happened because on April 23, 1961,

E. B. killed himself. He left no will, no estate and numerous debts. His obituary, which must have been written by Agnes, appeared on the front page of the *Atchison County Mail* on April 27, 1961.

Dr. E. B. Settle, Prominent Local Physician, Dies

Dr. Emmett B. Settle, 54, prominent Rock Port physician, died Sunday evening at the Maryville hospital. Services were held at 2:30 pm Wednesday at the Rock Port Methodist church, conducted by Rev. Carl Hackman.

By a proclamation of Mayor Wayne S. Peck business places were closed the hour of the funeral.

Dr. Settle was born in Rock Port July 29, 1906, the son of Dr. and Mrs. Charles Thomas Settle. He was a graduate of Rock Port High School, Nebraska University and Harvard Medical school. He was a member of Sigma Chi fraternity.

He was a veteran of World War II and served with the armed forces for three years in New Guinea and Australia with the rank of Major.

He married Elizabeth Coye Apr. 13, 1937.

Dr. Settle practiced medicine in Rock Port for over 20 years and worked with the Fairfax and Maryville hospitals and the St. Joseph clinic. He was a noted surgeon and pathologist and delivered many lectures on his profession. He was radiologist and pathologist at the Fairfax hospital at the time of his death.

Dr. Settle could have commanded top posts in many metropolitan hospitals but preferred to attend the people he knew and loved in the town where he grew to manhood.

He was a past commander of Ralph Greer Post 49 American Legion and a member of Legion 40 and 8.

AFTERWORD

Dr. Settle was preceded in death by his father. Survivors are his wife and mother, Mrs. Agnes Settle, Rock Port.

Note the Freudian slip: "his wife and mother, Mrs. Agnes Settle."

DECORATIONS

Bronze Star Medal
American Campaign Medal
World War II Victory Medal
Asiatic-Pacific Campaign Ribbon
World War II Honorable Service Lapel Button

PHOTO GALLERY

Inside Ira's Lunch, photo circa 1929. Florence and Ira Armsbury behind the counter. Ila, age 14 sitting at a table; Ila's aunt, Mayetta Armsbury, age 19, standing by the counter. Florence and Ira changed the name of the restaurant several times over the years. By 1929, it was called Ira's Lunch.

PHOTO GALLERY

Ila in nursing school at the University of Kansas. Date of photo is sometime between 1934 when she started school and 1937 when she graduated.

2nd Lt. Armsbury in Lincoln, Kansas, standing in front of her parents' restaurant, Ira's Lunch. Photo circa spring 1941 or 42.

PHOTO GALLERY

Ila had these two photos taken at Fort Leavenworth just after she got her orders. The glamorous one on the left was for E.B. The photo on the right was for her grandparents. The notation on the back reads: Mr. and Mrs. I.N. Armsbury.

ILA'S WAR

All three of these photos were taken in Melbourne, Australia, where the 155th Station Hospital was assigned to Travancore Hospital, a hospital the size of approximately one square city block, composed of five buildings. Travancore was a school for "mentally deficient children" prior to the war. The top two photos are dated on the back, August 22, 1942.

Ila showing off the latest in U.S. Army Nurse Corps accessories.

PHOTO GALLERY

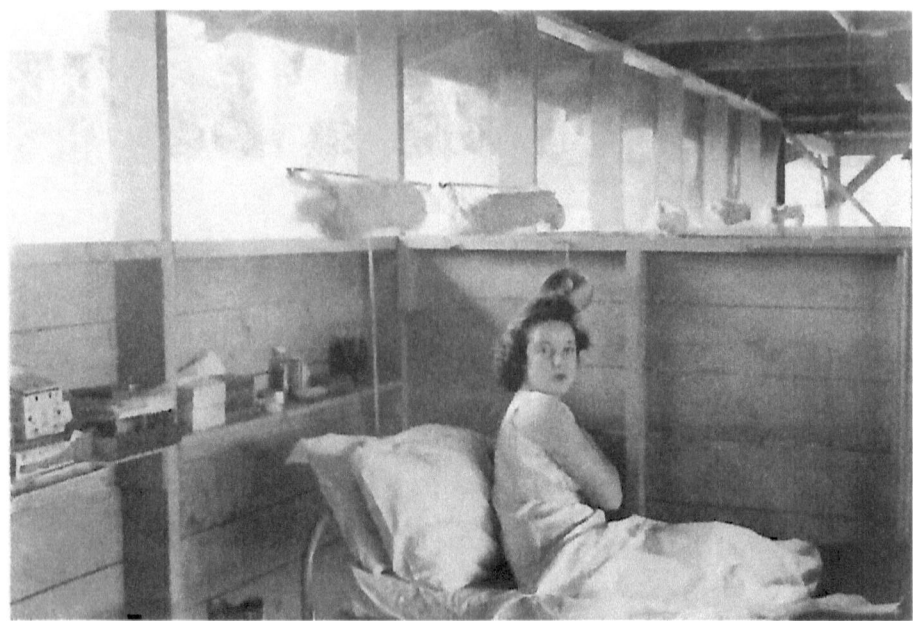

The nurses' barracks at Camp Cable, Queensland, Australia, where the 155th was located from October 6, 1942 - January 28, 1944 when they moved to Ekibin Heights in Brisbane. The nurses' barracks slept 12-24 nurses to a building. Note the rolled-up mosquito netting above each bed. Malaria wasn't indigenous to Australia, but Dengue Fever was.

After a few months Ila and a friend of hers moved from the barracks to a two-woman hut where they had more privacy. They worked hard to make it look and feel homey.

PHOTO GALLERY

Ila, in front of the hut she shared with another nurse.

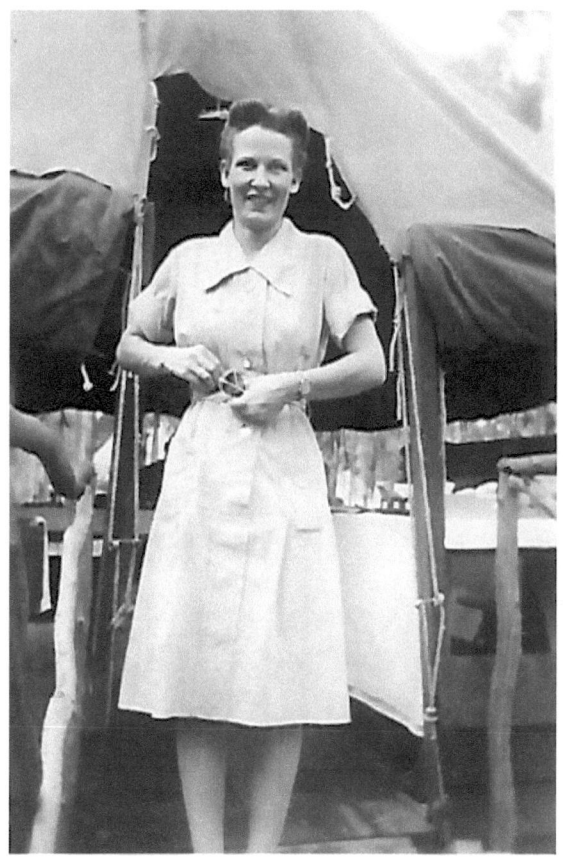

Ila preparing for a shift at the 155th Station Hospital at Camp Cable.

PHOTO GALLERY

Due to multiple hospitalizations in Australia for sinus infections, Ila was sent back to the states in mid-1944. She left Australia on May 23, 1944 and arrived in San Francisco June 11, 1944. Once in the states, Ila was sent to Winter General Hospital in Topeka, Kansas, the closest veterans' hospital to Lincoln, Kansas. Ila was a patient there from June 24, 1944, until September 12, 1944.

Ila wrote on the back of the photo above, "My girlfriend, Ellen Hurt. I met her as a patient in Topeka at Winter General. Her mother died and she is all alone, so I took her home with me for a week. We were in the Memorial Day parade. She was in New Hebride Islands when I was in Australia.

After her discharge as a patient, Ila was assigned to work at Winter General as a nurse.

PHOTO GALLERY

This photo was taken by my grandmother, Wava Farrington, of my family and me at the Memorial Day celebration, May 1951, at Delhi country church and cemetery, near Lucas, Kansas. Top step: Ira and Florence Armbsury, my great grandparents. Bottom step foreground: Rosena Armsbury, my great great-grandmother. Behind Rosena, barely visible is my grandfather, Nolan Farrington. Behind him is my mom, LaDonna Burke. I'm the baby sitting in front of her—all you can see of me is the bonnet. And the large man is my father, Lloyd Burke, Jr.

Delhi has a prominent role in the story because that's where I'm guessing that Florence learned of Ira's three-year-long affair with Mary E. Wilkerson. His affair set the stage for all the future travails in the family.

ENDNOTES

Chapter 3

(p. 58) Mother and Daddy decided that more drastic measures were needed because of Mrs. Wilkerson's persistence... According to Metta, Ira left home several times, traveling to different towns in central Kansas, trying to escape Mrs. Wilkerson, but she followed him every time. Finally, Florence and Ira decided that the only way Ira could escape Mrs. Wilkerson was to move to Colorado.

Chapter 4

(p. 60) "But I don't want to move," In the summer of 1994 I drove Grandma Wava and other family members to Waldo, Kansas, because Grandma wanted to see the house. According to her it hadn't changed much although it now had gray asphalt shingles in place of the wood siding. Grandma walked around the front and back yard of the house, smiling broadly as she pointed the location of Florence's garden and the privy. As we got ready to leave, she turned to me and said, "I loved living here. This was my favorite house."

(p. 68) *"My parents told me not to smoke;"* When Grandma Wava gave me her three copies of Captain Billy's Whiz Bang she smiled and said, "Now Cindy, I had to hide these, you know, because Mother said they were evil."

Chapter 8

ENDNOTES

(p. 101) "Mother, he walked into my classroom and just sat down. As big as day." Sadly, this is true. Metta never could figure out how Mrs. Wilkerson found them, but she did not believe Ira told Mrs. Wilkerson where they had moved. I'm not so sure, but another possibility was that Wava might have told a classmate where the family was moving to, and the classmate might have mentioned it to Earl.

(p. 105) ...got in his car, and he drove us to the train station. Both Metta and Ila talked about sleeping on rags on the floor of the house in Rocky Ford. Ila said, "It was the worst night of my life." According to Metta, Florence sent a telegram to Rosena and Rosena sent money back for Florence to return to Lucas from Rocky Ford.

Chapter 9

(p. 111) "Heard that she's filed for divorce... or her husband has ... don't know which." According to the Bumbery Genealogy Research Project, Mary E. Wilkerson and Gideon A. Wilkerson were divorced in Waldo, Kansas, sometime in 1921. And, according to court documents filed with the Russell County, Kansas, District Court, Mary Wilkerson returned to Waldo, KS. Ira went to Dodge City.

(p. 114) With the help of Grandpa Newt, Mother found a job at a small restaurant... An old black and white photo shows Florence wearing a white apron, her hands behind her back, standing in front of the plate glass window of the cafe in Lucas. Painted across the top of the window are the words "Chicken Dinner."

Chapter 10

(p. 116) As she unpacked her valise, Aunt Lottie, her face grim, said, "Florence, divorce him." I didn't make this up. According to Metta, it was Lottie who encouraged Florence to get a divorce.

(p. 119) It was filed on May 9, 1921 on the grounds of adultery and gross neglect of duty. This is all true and I have a copy of the divorce filing to prove it. But what's even more interesting and something that none of the girls ever knew, not even Metta, was that on March 15, 1921, two months prior to filing for divorce, Florence's attorney sued Mary Wilkerson for $10,000.00 because of her "machinations, arts, artifices, designs and attentions" which she used to "[induce] the plaintiff's (Florence) husband to neglect his wife and neglect her, and alienated his affections from plaintiff and to transfer the same to the defendant (Mary Wilkerson) ..." (Armsbury vs. Wilkerson, March 15, 1921) The law suit was dismissed without prejudice two weeks later.

Chapter 11

(p. 120) It was the tiniest house I've ever lived in ... During an interview, Metta mentioned that Florence rented a tiny house in Lucas for herself and the girls right after Eloise was born and that all the relatives helped furnish it.

(p. 121) Mother's divorce hearing was held on October 3, 1921. The October 4, 1921, journal entry of the divorce proceeding reads in part, "That the defendant has been guilty of repeated acts of extreme cruelty against the said plaintiff. That the defendant has been guilty of GROSS NEGLECT of DUTY, and of the acts charged against him in the plaintiff's petition and that the plaintiff is entitled to a divorce."

(p. 125) "It's your father. He's been arrested. He's in jail." Ira was charged under the 1913 Kansas law known as The White Slave Law, rather than the federally enacted Mann Act or The White Slave Law. I could find no records of the trial in Russell county. According to staff in the office of the Clerk of the District Court of Russell County, it was not uncommon for documents pertaining to salacious trials to be destroyed if the defendant was found not guilty.

I was initially shocked when Metta told me that it was Florence's testimony that kept Ira from going to prison. Florence's testimony at trial was probably similar to information contained in her petition against Mary Wilkerson seeking $10,000.00 in "vindictive, and punitive and actual damages." The petition read in part:

> She [Florence] is the wife of Ira Armsbury and that she was married to him on November 6th 1907 and ever since they have been husband and wife and that they lived lovingly happily together until the year 1920, that is this year they lived at their home at Waldo, and during this year and frequently during this year at Waldo and

other points in RUSSELL County and Osborne and other points in the State, also at Colorado and at Colorado Springs, and Rocky Ford, in Colorado, also at Natoma, Kansas, [illegible] husband was frequently in the company and society of one Mary E. Wilkerson and [illegible] her marked and noticeable [sic] attention, and that the defendant would have the plaintiff's husband meet her at the home of the defendant and elsewhere, and that he would remain at her home in the absence of her husband at unusual hours and at late hours, also would take her out riding in his automobile, also go riding in the auto of the defendant's or her husband, and that they would take long drives at late hours, and that the defendant formed an attachment for the plaintiff's husband, and plaintiff's husband would visit the said defendant at her home at Waldo, as she lived there until the latter part of the year 1920 when she removed to Colorado Springs, Colorado, and that while at Colorado Springs, the plaintiff's husband would leave this plaintiff at home and go to the residence of the defendant and remain away from home all night and neglect this plaintiff. (Armsbury vs. Wilkerson, March 15, 1921).

Chapter 13

(p. 135) **I don't know how long we could have gone on like this if Grandma Rosenie hadn't stepped in to help.** Rosena believed it was her fault that Ira was an alcoholic because when he was teething as a baby, she rubbed whiskey on his aching gums. To make amends she insisted that Newt provide money to Ira for every business venture.

Chapter 15

(p. 147) **Donley, the son of a local farmer ...** John (Jack) William Donley was born August 19, 1906. He graduated from Lincoln High School around 1925 and enlisted in the U. S. Navy. He served on the USS *Lexington* and was discharged in early 1930. After discharge he purchased a Model A Ford Roadster. On September 25, 1930, while returning to Lincoln from the Kansas State Fair in Hutchinson, Kansas, he was killed in a rollover accident. He was single at the time of his death. He is buried in the Lincoln Cemetery.

Chapter 16

(p. 154) "Don't worry, Ira. Won't be no more fighting. The Klan's gone. We run 'em out of town and there won't be no more trouble from them." "...the Kansas supreme court rendered [a] decision ... ousting the Klan from 'doing business' in Kansas on the basis that it was a foreign corporation not approved to do business in the state by the then state charter board." (Hope, p. 54)

(p. 159) Dr. Malcolm Newlon was a physician and surgeon in Lincoln. Malcolm Newlon was born and raised in Lincoln. He graduated from the University Medical College of Kansas City in 1910 and was a member of the Kansas Medical Society. Dr. Newlon served in the U. S. Army during WWI and was "slightly wounded." (Journal of the American Medical Association) After the war, Dr. Newlon returned to Lincoln where he built the first city hospital. He died at the age of 50 on November 18, 1936 and is buried at the Lincoln Cemetery.

Chapter 19

(p. 174) The day that Grandpa arrived to help us is the day Mother first heard that there were other men in Lincoln just like Daddy. The April 30, 1930 issue of the Lincoln Sentinel-Republican printed an announcement that Ira was home sick and that Mrs. I. N. (Rosena) Armsbury had traveled to Lincoln to help care for him. The story was wrong because while Rosena did drive down to Lincoln with Newt, Newt stayed to care for Ira and Rosena took Eloise back to Lucas.

(p. 176) "Jamaica Ginger! You drank poisoned Jamaica Ginger and that's why you're crippled!" A common belief held by the general public, including my family members, was that Jamaica Ginger was bad boot-leg hooch made in a lead-lined boiler or radiator during prohibition, and that lead poisoning was the cause of Ira's becoming crippled.

But they were wrong.

Jamaica Ginger, also called Jake, was an over-the-counter patent

ENDNOTES

medicine, legal during prohibition even though it was 70 to 90% alcohol. It was available before 1930, (Parascandola, p. 124) but in 1930, newspapers began publishing accounts of drinkers, mostly men, who developed mysterious symptoms of numbness in the legs which developed into a paralysis with a dropped foot. (Ibid, p. 123) Jake could be purchased without a prescription in one- or two-ounce bottles from grocery stores, pharmacies, and dime stores. (Baum, p. 51).

Ira and his cronies bought theirs out of the back door of the Lincoln, Kansas, Rexall Drug Store. The directions on the label read: "Dose - For an adult, from 15 to 30 drops in sweetened water. Children in proportion to age." Ira mixed his with Coca Cola.

Back then there was no federal Food and Drug Administration like there is today, so manufacturers could and did put just about anything in the over-the-counter medications of the time. But federal officials decided that too many people were imbibing in alcohol during prohibition, so they ordered the manufacturers of Jamaica Ginger to make it taste worse. The generally accepted recipe was grated ginger and alcohol, so most manufacturers just added more ginger which made the stuff taste even more fiery. But a couple of manufacturers back east used a neurotoxin - tri-ortho cresyl phosphate or TOCP – cheaper than grated ginger. (Baum, p. 55) The result became all too clear within two weeks of ingesting the stuff. (Parascandola, p. 123) By the time it was over, 50,000 men and women across the U.S. were permanently crippled. (The Jake Walk Effect) Some, like Ira, were paralyzed from the chest down. That meant they were crippled and impotent. Others lost muscle control in their hands and arms, and a few experienced paralyses of both arms and legs. The new disease was named Jake Leg, and Ira was one of the more severely crippled users because he drank more than most.

I was 13 when Ira (Grandpa Armsbury to me) died, so I remember his distinctive walk. He had to swing his long, floppy legs from the hip around to the front and his toe hit the floor first - making a slapping sound - followed by the heel.

ILA'S WAR

Chapter 20

(p. 186) Sometime after the first of the year, January of 1934, a rumor ... I think Florence is the one who started the rumor based on some comments Ila wrote in a letter to me dated March 1, 2000.

> *Mother asked me if I was going to do anything about going to nurses training, and I said "No - not if I can't go to K. C. [Kansas City]." She said, "Well you send in your application, and if you are accepted, I think he'll let you go!"*
>
> *Well, what had happened was he heard they got 700 applications a year and took only 40 - So he didn't think I had a chance!*

Chapter 21

(p. 191) "But Miss Lewick, I'm only a probie ... A probie was a student who had completed six months of training.

(p. 197) My next stop—home to tell my folks. In her tape, Ila talked about borrowing money from Judge Joslin for a train ticket to Lincoln to borrow money from the bank to finish school.

Chapter 22

(p. 200) ...I was an assistant supervisor at the Kansas University Hospital Maternity Center. Ila talked at length about working in the slums.

> *My job was to go out into the... slums in Kansas City ... to teach the medical students the sterile set up. And once we got into the home and called the resident and told him that the woman was in labor, then we had to stay 'til she delivered ... sometimes two days ... I had to help ... cook and feed the family, you know, the woman was in bed and in the Black family I had to learn how to do the kids' hair ... I had to help get the kids ready for school.*

(p. 202) response. A couple of weeks later we heard back. On

ENDNOTES

November 1, 1940 ... According to World War II Selective Service Records, a total of 21 women from Lincoln County, including Ila, joined the military and served their country during WWII. (World War II Selective Service Records)

Chapter 23

(p. 208) NBC Red ... In 1926 the National Broadcasting Company launched two radio networks - NBC Red and NBC Blue. NBC Red had a "stronger line-up of affiliated stations [and] often carried the more popular, 'big budget' sponsored programs. [NBC Blue] ...carried a somewhat smaller line-up of often lower-powered stations and sold airtime to advertisers at a lower cost." (NBC Red Network)

(p. 210) *Several Lincoln County boys are in the danger zone. Mary Bird's brother is on the ship Oklahoma...* Rumors, not all of them true, were rampant around Lincoln in the hours and days after the bombing.

The fact was that Mary Bird's brother, Oscar, was not on the USS *Oklahoma*, not even in Hawaii on the morning of December 7th. According to a newspaper account published in the April 9, 1942, issue of the *Lincoln Sentinel-Republican*, Oscar was on the aircraft tender USS *Langley* in Manila on December 6, 1941, but his parents didn't know Oscar's location because of the slowness of mail from ship to shore. And his earlier letters talked about his stints in Hawaii, the Philippines and Guam so Lincoln residents believed Oscar was dead.

Sadly, Oscar Bird did not survive the war. Oscar and several of his crew mates were rescued from the sinking USS *Langley* by the naval tanker USS *Pecos*. However, the *Pecos* was sunk south of Java after being attacked by Japanese aircraft. (*Lincoln Sentinel-Republican*, 1942.) Although Oscar's body was never recovered there is a grave marker honoring his memory in the Lincoln, Kansas cemetery.

(http://www.navsource.org/archives/09/02/09020311.jpg. Accession date unknown)

However, the story about Daniel Dyer was true... he died in the bombing. Dyer was a Technical Sergeant with the U. S. Army Air

ILA'S WAR

Corps, stationed at Hickam Field near Honolulu. (Lincoln Sentinel-Republican, December 11, 1941)

Lincoln County also had one Medal of Honor Recipient from WWII. Warrant Officer Machinist Donald K. Ross, a Lincoln County resident from Beverly, Kansas, became the first person awarded the Medal of Honor following the attack on Pearl Harbor. Admiral Chester Nimitz presented the award to Ross on April 18, 1942. Ross' Medal of Honor Citation read in part:

> *"For distinguished conduct in the line of his profession, extraordinary courage, and disregard of his own life during the attack on the Fleet in Pearl Harbor, Territory of Hawaii, by Japanese Forces on 7 December 1941. When his station in the forward dynamo room of the U.S.S. Nevada became almost untenable due to smoke, steam and heat, Lieutenant Commander Ross forced his men to leave that station and performed all the duties himself until blinded and unconscious. Upon being rescued and resuscitated, he returned and secured the forward dynamo room and proceeded to the after-dynamo room where he was later again rendered unconscious by exhaustion. Again recovering consciousness, he returned to his station where he remained until directed to abandon it." (Vachon)*

In 2011, a portion of Kansas highway 18, "From the US-81 interchange to the Lincoln/Russell County line" was renamed the Donald K. Ross Memorial Highway to honor his bravery during the bombing of Pearl Harbor. (Picking)

Chapter 24

(p. 211) "Thank you all for being here this cold January morning," The entire scene about how Ila and Dr. Settle met is entirely made up because Ila did not explain in her letters or tape how they met. Records do show that they were both assigned to Fort Leavenworth at the same time, and her letter of March 20, 1942 introduces him to Ira and Florence. My research also showed that Dr. Settle did give lectures about pathology, so the elements of the scene are plausible. In her letter of introduction, Ila wrote:

> *I don't get very tired, not for long, - I mean well, you see my man*

ENDNOTES

has come - He's a doctor in the Medical Corps - a captain - age 36 - name Emmett B. Settle - I call him Eeby - Do you remember that I was waiting and waiting for him Valentine's night? - Well, it's the same one. He's ugly as sin, so I won't have to worry about anyone making eyes at him, but he's so nice and sweet. So, when the war's over, and I'm glad to wait, I guess I'll be settling down.

Only in her letter of introduction to her folks did Ila write that she called her boyfriend "Eeby." In all her following letters, she spelled it EB.

(p. 213) Finally, I got my orders. I was to report to the 166th Station Hospital... The U. S. Army developed a variety of hospitals during WWII. Each type served a different function, depending on its proximity to the front lines. A Station Hospital was a fixed hospital (meaning it was not mobile) in or near a military camp or post. Medical and dental care were provided by the hospital staff to troops assigned to the post.

(p. 213) Francisco, where I departed on the USS *West Point* for parts unknown. The USS *West Point* was originally named *America* and was launched on August 31, 1939. It was built as a luxury ocean liner but was converted to a troop transport ship in 1941. (West Point II AP-23)

Chapter 25

(p. 214) Australia and they drive on the wrong side of the road." Based on Ila's correspondence, it's unlikely that her family knew that Australia came under attack from both Japan and Germany. Japan conducted a total of 114 separate air raids on Australian cities from February 2, 1942 until November 12, 1943. Fourteen of those raids were in the state of Queensland where Camp Cable was located. (Dunn, 1999) Throughout the war, Japanese submarines and German "armed merchant cruisers or surface raiders" operated in Australian waters laying mines, sinking allied ships, and disrupting shipping routes. ("Enemy Action...")

(p. 214) "Good afternoon, ladies." You could hear the murmur of women's voices as Miss Harper... Margaret Harper joined the Army Nurse Corps in 1941 shortly before the start of WWII. Her first overseas assignment was as the chief nurse of the 155th Station

ILA'S WAR

Hospital. "Harper's resolute leadership style featured an intriguing blend of humor and candor. One co-worker described her as having 'a real down-to-earth philosophy.'" Harper retired from the Army in 1963 and died on December 13, 2000. Her rank was Colonel at the time of her death. (Sarnecky, September 19, 2018)

Chapter 26

(p. 219) "I thought we'd go see a movie at the Athenaeum Theater..." The Athenaeum Theatre was established in 1839 and is still in use today. (Athenaeum Theatre)

In a letter dated August 2, 1942, Ila wrote about her date.

> *EB and I went to dinner, and then a movie and my heart is so full I had to write. . . . Everyone has heard about it by now and every time we're together someone comes up and makes some crack about 'some people have all the luck' or something to that effect. We just sit and grin like two skunks. Do you realize how marvelous it is to have two people (lovers) go half-way around the world and accidentally meet? I never will get over it. He won't either!*

Chapter 27

(p. 221) Camp Cable Camp Cable was originally named Camp Tamborine because of its proximity to Mount Tamborine and the village of Tamborine. It was located in Queensland, on the Albert River, with Logan Village to the north and Tamborine Village to the south. Camp Tamborine was renamed Camp Cable on September 16, 1942, following the death of Gerald O. Cable, a member of the 32nd Infantry Division, who was killed when the division moved from Camp Adelaide, in the Australian state of South Australia, to Camp Tamborine. (Dunn, 2000)

(p. 224) The sloping banks of the river were covered with a dense forest of exotic trees and shrubs... To see photos of some of the exotic and endangered plants near Camp Cable go to

ENDNOTES

logan.qld.gov.au/environment-water-and-waste/plants-and-trees/threatened-plants and go to "View Threatened Plants of Logan (PDF 6752 KB)"

Chapter 28

(p. 228) **"My mother is related to the Bird of EBT.** Although EB's mother, Agnes Settle, told others that she was related to the Bird of the Emery, Bird, Thayer Department Store, I could find no evidence to support her assertion.

Chapter 29

(p. 231) **"What's coming in, sergeant?" I asked.** Ila took to heart the saying, "Loose Lips Sink Ships" and did not write about troops from Guadalcanal. But she spoke at length about them in her tape recording.

(p. 232) **shivering with chills one moment and burning fever the next.** Information about the influx of Marines from Guadalcanal comes from Ila's tape recording and from the Annual Report for the 155th Station Hospital. (United States Army)

(p. 233) **In mid-January, we heard that the New Guinea campaign was over and that we had won.** The 32nd Division losses included 602 killed in action; 88 dead from wounds; 17 dead from other causes; 62 men missing in action; 1,680 wounded in action; 211 diagnosed with concussion and shell shock; and 287 with battlefield injuries that needed medical attention. (Milner, pp. 370-371)

(p. 234) **I was tired, overworked...** The unit reports for the 155th SH indicate that Colonel Steinhoff, the CO of the 155th SH, under-reported and omitted information about a malaria epidemic at the camp as well as an outbreak of German measles. And the 155th was so overwhelmed by patients from March to May 1943, that the 107th Medical Battalion, attached to the 32nd Infantry Division, set up a temporary SH with 609 beds for sick troops from the 32nd Infantry Division.

(p. 234) **Malaria was rampant at Camp Cable...**

There were 5,358 cases of malaria among the almost 11,000 troops of the 32nd Division who served in New Guinea—4,000 first attacks, and the rest recurrences. In addition, the medical record showed 17 deaths from scrub typhus, and 2,147 cases of "miscellaneous disease," including dysentery and dengue fever ... A total of 2,334 officers and men were dropped from the division in September 1943, because of their continuing malaria relapses. (Ibid, p. 372)

(p. 236) responding to the sulfa medication. Penicillin might have worked, however, the War Production Board (WPB), which oversaw the manufacture and distribution of penicillin had as its goal an adequate supply of penicillin for every wounded soldier on D-Day in Europe. Because penicillin supplies were limited, Dr. Chester Keefer, chairman of the National Research Council's Committee on Chemotherapy, was charged with rationing supplies to civilians. When a private citizen needed penicillin, his or her physician of record had to submit a complete record of medical treatment to Dr. Keefer for his approval. Metta did not know about the Committee on Chemotherapy, but she did inquire about the use of penicillin and was told that even if it were available to civilians it would cost at least $40,000.00.

Chapter 31

(p. 243) "Why were *you* in the hospital in November? I heard pneumonia. All of the information about EB's hospitalization including why he was hospitalized came from his military records which also included notations about three separate incidents when he left the hospital without permission and returned drunk. As far as I can tell, Ila never learned of those episodes.

(p. 246) "I've thought of that, too. We'll live in the country house." In a letter dated May 22, 1943 Ila described the reconciliation between herself and EB and EB's concession for them to live in the smaller country house without servants.

Chapter 32

(p. 248) "Ila, I'm going to rent a small apartment in Brisbane. Ila

ENDNOTES

made only one reference to EB's apartment in a letter dated November 15, 1943, to Florence and Ira. She wrote, "He mentions finding a flat for us - Don't get excited - I'll have to stay at a government billet, and he will, too, but we want someplace where I can cook our meals and we can be alone a little."

(p. 249) working with the U. S. Typhus Commission... Typhus, a potentially deadly bacterial disease that has plagued humanity since ancient times, was of immense concern to the Allied forces during WWII. The disease is spread by infected lice, mites, or ticks, which suck blood from their victims while also depositing feces which contains the typhus-causing microorganisms near the site of the bite. Allied forces knew from their experiences during WWI that typhus outbreaks would be devastating not only to civilian populations but to fighting units. In December 1942, President Roosevelt signed an executive order creating the United States of America Typhus Commission. Research groups worked in the European, African and Southwest Pacific areas to develop delousing methods. (Snyder, 1946)

Chapter 33

(p. 251) I couldn't recall being this excited about Christmas... Ila and EB did spend Christmas of 1943 together but not in EB's apartment. They spent Christmas with Vic and Nan Birkbeck, a Brisbane family with whom Ila formed a close and lasting friendship.

In a letter dated September 12, 2008, Mike Birkbeck, grandson of Vic and Nan, wrote me about his grandparents and Camp Cable.

> *The little I remember about her [Nan] - she was an extremely kind generous woman. Pillar of the Church of England, etc. The alter at the church is in memory of her. There is a memorial at the Southport Bowling Club.*
>
> *"Nan" came from a reasonably well-off family. They owned the timber mills and hardware businesses in the area. With her husband, Vic, founded Birkbecks Jewelers in 1912. My daughter, Julia, is the fourth generation in the business.*
>
> *The hospital at Camp Cable was moved to the Southport School*

ILA'S WAR

many years ago and is now the music room (I think). The Southport School was also used as an American hospital during the war.

Chapter 34

(p. 254) gonorrhea with the new drug, penicillin. The first shipment of penicillin to the Southwest Pacific area was in October of 1943. A soldier at the 118th General Hospital was the first to be treated and he was cured of sulfa-resistant gonorrhea. From then on, the military began using penicillin widely - even before D-Day. (Cowdrey, p. 187)

(p. 259) *Doña Nati* followed a zigzag course... Zig-zagging was a defensive maneuver developed by the Allies in WWII for Allied ships which had to sail through enemy waters without a protective escort.

> *Ships were completely darkened at night; radio communication was prohibited; merchant ships were armed; convoy destinations were kept secret; and in especially dangerous areas, convoys didn't travel in straight lines. Zig-zagging - the practice of frequently altering direction to port or starboard - was designed to disguise a convoy's true course and confuse the enemy. All ships followed the same pattern, one of several top-secret zig-zag diagrams, created by Admiralty anti-submarine experts. Before leaving port, the convoy commodore issued each ship's master with the zig-zag diagrams and signals to be used enroute. At sea, communication between ships was limited. To coordinate the convoy's movements, zig-zag clocks were synchronized by a signal from the commodore's flagship. At predetermined times, the clock sounded an alarm, indicating when to change course.* (Zig-zagging: how to confuse the enemy at sea)

(p. 260) a week at the Presidio—it's closed now... The Presidio, formerly a U. S. Army base, is located on the Pacific Ocean side of the San Francisco Peninsula. During WWII, thousands of war casualties were treated at Letterman Hospital in the Presidio. Ila passed through there on her way to Winter General Hospital in Topeka, Kansas. In 1994, the Presidio became part of the national park service. (Presidio of San Francisco)

Chapter 35

(p. 262) And I have nightmares." One of the topics that Ila and I discussed during her 2000 visit was the movie "Saving Private Ryan." I warned her that it was extremely graphic and that I thought she might not want to see it. She replied, "Don't worry, Honey. I never watch war movies or even the news when it's about a war. I still have nightmares and if I watched a movie like that, I'd have nightmares for a month." However, the description of Ila's nightmare to the psychiatrist is from my imagination because she and I did not discuss the content of her nightmares.

Chapter 36

(p. 267) "Lt. Armsbury, have you been furnished with a copy of the report which has just been read?" The lack of counsel coupled with not receiving a copy of the report prior to the hearing meant that Ila did not have an opportunity to read and consider the Army's findings. She did not realize that the Army examiners ignored or overlooked the information about her allergic response to mold and instead focused on her allergy to aspirin. Had Ila received legal counsel who would have thoroughly examined the records, she might have been awarded military disability benefits.

Chapter 38

(p. 279) "Ila, I'm married, and I have been since 1937..." In a letter dated January 4, 1945, written to Florence and Ira, Ila wrote:

> EB leaves for Washington Saturday or is supposed to, and then I'll start getting in shape... I have so much to tell you, Mother - but I want to talk to you, instead of writing. It's about EB - and I'm taking it on the chin! But it's all kinda funny, too, you'll get a bang out of it—I'll be glad when he leaves.

(p. 279) "What do you mean you're married? How can you be married?" Ila didn't disclose in her letters what EB said to her about his marriage. But my interviews with people who knew both EB and his mother, Agnes, described in detail how Agnes ruled his life. EB really did encourage correspondence between his mother and Ila. I found EB's parents' address in Ila's address book and Ila mentioned in her letters that she corresponded with his folks.

(p. 281) "No. She says she loves me. And it's way too late now, several years too late, for an annulment. EB filed for an annulment in 1960 but he died before the case was heard in court.

Sources

Almonsees. "North America's Inland Sea." -hubpages-. May 28, 2012. Accessed December 11, 2018. https://hubpages.com/education/NorthAmericaInlandSea

Armsbury vs. Armsbury. District Court, Russell County, Kansas. 9 May 1921.

Armsbury vs. Armsbury. District Court, Russell County, Kansas. 4 October 1921.

Armsbury vs. Wilkerson. District Court, Russell County, Kansas. 15 March 1921.

Armsbury vs. Wilkerson, District Court, Russell County, Kansas. 5 August 1921.

Atchison County Mail. "Settle/Bird," May 6, 1904.

Atchison County Mail. "Dr. E. B. Settle, Prominent Local Physician, Dies," April 27, 1961.

Atchison County Journal. "Dr. Emmett Settle Weds," April 23, 1937.

"Athenaeum Theatre." -eastend-. Publication date unknown. Accessed December 8, 2018. http://eastend.melbourne/venues-history/athenaeum-theatre

Atlas of Atchison County, Missouri. Des Moines, Iowa: The Anderson Publishing Company, 1921.

"Auto Trail." -wikipedia-. Publication date unknown. Accessed December 12, 2018. https://en.wikipedia.org/wiki/Auto_trail

SOURCES

"Back to Australia—Rest, Rehabilitation and Training." -32nd-division-. March 15, 1999. Accessed December 11, 2018. http://www.32nd-division.org/history/ww2/32ww2-1.html

Baum, Dan. *The New Yorker.* "Jake Leg." September 15, 2003, 50—57.

Bellafaire, Judith A. "The Army Nurse Corps."-history.army-. April 14, 2011. Accession date unknown. https://www.history.army.mil/books/wwii/72-14/72-14.htm

Blakeley, Major General H. W. *The 32nd Infantry Division In World War II.* Nashville: The Battery Press, 2000.

Britton, Peg. "History of the Baker Hotel." -kansasprairie- Publication date unknown. Accessed January 29, 2015. WayBack Machine. http://kansasprairie.net/from_our_past.htm

Campbell, James. *The Ghost Mountain Boys: Their Epic March and the Terrifying Battle for New Guinea—The Forgotten War of the South Pacific.* New York: Three Rivers Press, 2007.

Captain Billy's Whiz Bang. Robbinsdale, Minn.: W. H. Fawcett, date unknown.

Case, Mary E. (Mollie). Accessed May 23, 2020. www.bumbery.com

Childers, Thomas. *Soldier From the War Returning.* New York: Mariner Books, 2009.

Coker, Jesse M., Ed.D. *My Unforgettable Memories of World War II.* self-published, 1994.

"Colorado: Communicable Diseases. Notification of Cases. Quarantine. Embalming. Diseases of Animals. (Reg. Bd. of H., February 7)." -jstor-. Public Health Reports (1896-1970) 31, no. 39 (1916): 2730-734. Publication date unknown. Accessed December 12, 2018. http://www.jstor.org/stable/4574156

Condon-Rall, Mary Ellen and Albert E. Cowdrey. *The Medical Department: Medical Services in the War Against Japan.* United States Army in World War II, The Technical Services. Washington, D. C.: Center of Military History, 1998.

Cowdrey, Albert E. *Fighting For Life: American Military Medicine in*

World War II. New York: The Free Press, 1994.

"Discovery and Development of Penicillin." -acs-. Publication date unknown. Accessed December 8, 2018. https://www.acs.org/content/acs/en/education/whatischemistry/landmarks/flemingpenicillin.html#wwii-penicillin-commercial-production

Dubin, Al and Warren, Harry. "Boulevard of Broken Dreams." -revolvy-. Publication date unknown. Accessed November 20, 2018. https://www.revolvy.com/page/Boulevard-of-Broken-Dreams-(Al-Dubin-song)

Dunn, Peter. "Japanese Air Raids in Australia During WW2."-ozatwar-. January 2, 1999. Accessed December 12, 2018. https://ozatwar.com/bomboz.htm

Dunn. Peter. "Camp Cable." -ozatwar-. August 7, 2000. Accessed December 11, 2018. https://www.ozatwar.com/usarmy/155thstationhospital.htm

Dunn, Peter. "1st Marine Division 'The Old Breed' United States Marine Corps (USMC) in Australia During WW2." -ozatwar-. June 4, 2003. Accessed December 11, 2018. www.ozatwar.com/usmc/1stmarinedivision.htm

Ehernberger, James L. and Francis G. Gschwind. *Smoke Above the Plains*. Callaway, Nebraska: E. & G Publications, 1965.

Emporia Weekly Gazette. Thursday, May 15, 1930.

Emporia Weekly Gazette. Thursday, May 22, 1930.

"Enemy Action on the Australian Station 1939—45." -clik-. Publication date unknown. Accessed November 2, 2018. http://clik.dva.gov.au

"File:Kansaspacificgrants.jpg." -commons- November 10, 2016. Accessed December 11, 2018. https://commons.wikimedia.org/wiki/File:Kansaspacificgrants.jpg

"Final Experts. Highways to the Sky: A Context and History of Colorado's Highway System." -codot-. April 24, 2002. Accessed December 12, 2018. http://codot.gov/programs/environmental/archaeology-and-history/highways-to-the-sky/highwaystothesky.pdf

1 Cor. 7: 8-9. (Revised Standard Version).

SOURCES

"Gideon Ashbrook 'Giddy' Wilkerson." -bumbery-. Publication date unknown. Accessed December 8, 2018. http://www. bumbery.com

"Got the Jake Leg Too." -fresnostate- Publication date unknown. Accessed September 25, 2012. http://www.fresnostate.edu/folklore/ballads/RcGtJLT.html

Greenwood, John T. "The Fight against Malaria in the Papua and New Guinea Campaigns." -history-. Publication date unknown. Accessed December 9, 2018. https://history.army.mil/armyhistory/AH59newOCR.pdf

Handy Railroad Atlas of the United States. Milwaukee: Kalmbach Publishing, 1923.

Homan, Dorothe Tarrence. *Lincoln — that County in Kansas.* Lindsborg, Kansas: Barbos' Printing, 1979.

Hope, Clifford R., Jr. *Kansas History A Journal of the Central Plains."* Strident Voices in Kansas Between the Wars." Spring, Vol. 2, no. 1, Spring 1979, pp. 54—64.

"Howard Springs in World War 2." -museum- Publication date unknown. Accessed December 11, 2018. https://museum.mil.idaho.gov/australia.htm

Hutchinson News, Tuesday, May 27, 1930.

Journal of the American Medical Association. "Medical Mobilization and the War," vol. 72, no. 14, April—June, 1919, p. 1622.

Jungwirth, Clarence. *Diary of a National Guardsman In World War II: 1940-1945.* Oshkosh, Wisconsin: Poeschl Printing Co., Inc., 1991.

"Kansas Limestone History". -bluestemstoneworks-. 2007. Accessed December 12, 2018. http://bluestemstoneworks.com/History.htm

"Kansas." -naturalkansas-. Publication date unknown. Accessed December 10, 2018. http://www.naturalkansas.org/images/PDF/ PRByway.pdf

ksrose. "Oscar Huron Bird." -findagrave-. July 1, 2010. Accessed December 12, 2018. https://findagrave.com/memorial/54344117/Oscar-huron-bird.

"Lincoln Center, Kansas." -en.wikipedia-. Publication date unknown. Accessed December 12, 2018. http://en.wikipedia.org/wiki/Lincoln_Center,_Kansas.

Lincoln Sentinel-Republican. "Mrs. I. N. Armsbury, Lucas," April 17, 1930.

Lincoln Sentinel-Republican. "I. N. Armsbury who has been," May 1, 1930.

Lincoln Sentinel-Republican. "Emporia, the abode of William," May 15, 1930.

Lincoln Sentinel-Republican. "That old saying about the ill," May 22, 1930.

Lincoln Sentinel-Republican. "Mr. and Mrs. I. N. Armsbury," July 10, 1930.

Lincoln Sentinel-Republican. "Mr. and Mrs. Nolan Farrington," July 31, 1930.

Lincoln Sentinel-Republican. "Announcement is made," January 9, 1941.

Lincoln Sentinel-Republican. "Report Oscar Bird Missing in Naval Action." April 9, 1942.

Lincoln Sentinel-Republican. "War Strikes Home, Beverly Young Man Among First Killed," December 11, 1941.

Lincoln Sentinel-Republican. "History from the pages of the Lincoln Sentinel." vol. 125, no. 27, p. 3. July 5, 2012.

Lucas 125th Centennial Committee. *Lucas Looking Back—Moving Forward in the wonderful town of Lucas, Kansas.* Lucas, Kansas: Lucas Publishing Company, 2012.

Marriage Records Book No. 19, Page 98, October 1936—April 1939, Mills County, Iowa.

"Melbourne Athenaeum." -wikipedia-. November 4, 2018. Accessed December 8, 2018. https://en.wikipedia.org/wiki/Melbourne_Athenaeum

Military, Compiled Service Records, World War II. National Personnel Records Center, St. Louis, Missouri.

Milner, Samuel. *The War in the Pacific: Victory in Papua.* Washington, D. C.: Center of Military History, United States Army, 2003.

SOURCES

"Mobilization, Training and Deployment to Australia." -32nd-division-. March 15, 1999. Accessed December 11, 2018. http://www.32nd-division.org/history/ww2/32ww2-1.html

Morgan, John P. "The Jamaica Ginger Paralysis." JAMA, October 15, 1982 - vol. 248, No. 15, 1864 - 1867.

Munsey, Cecil. "Paralysis in a Bottle." Bottles and Extras. Winter 2006. 7-12. Vol. 17, No. 4.

"NBC." -centuryoldsounds-. December 2, 2018. Accessed September 17, 2018. http://www.centuryoldsounds.com/PHNBCRed.html

"NBC Red Network." -ipfs-. November 14, 2016. Accessed December 6, 2018. https://ipfs.io/ipfs/QmXoypizjW3WknFiJnKLwHCnL72vedxjQkDDP1mXWo6uco/wiki/NBC_Red_ Network.html

"New Guinea." -history.army-. October 3, 2003. Accessed December 12, 2018. https://history.army.mil/brochures/new-guinea/ng.htm

Norman, Michael, and Norman, Elizabeth M. *Tears in the Darkness: The Story of the Bataan Death March and its Aftermath*. New York: Picador, 2009.

Office of the Chief Engineer, General Headquarters Army Forces, Pacific. Airfield and Base Development. vol. 6, Engineers of the Southwest Pacific 1941-1945. Washington, D. C.: U. S. Government Printing Office, 1951.

"Organization History 632nd Tank Destroyer Battalion. -tankdestroyer-. Publication date unknown. Accessed December 11, 2018. https://www.tankdestroyer.net/images/stories/ArticlePDFs/632nd_Org._History_1941-1942-4_pages.pdf

Parascandola, John. *Pharmacy in History*. "Pharmacology and Public Health: The Jamaica Ginger Paralysis Episode of the 1930s." vol. 36 (1994) No. 3, 123—131.

Poe, Edgar A. "The Raven." Accessed July 3, 2020. https://www.poetryfoundation.org/poems/48860/the-raven

"Presidio of San Francisco." -nps-. Publication date unknown. Accessed

December 11, 2018. https://www.nps.gov/nr/travel/wwiibayarea/pre.htm

Public Relations Office 32nd Infantry. *13,000 Hours: Combat History Of The 32nd Infantry Division, World War II*. Whitefish, Montana: Kessinger Publishing, LLC, date unknown.

Rand McNally and Company. *Rand McNally Commercial Atlas of America*. 55th ed. Chicago: Rand McNally & Company, 1924.

Sarnecky, Mary T. *A History of the U. S. Army Nurse Corps*. Philadelphia: University of Pennsylvania Press, 1999.

Sarnecky, Mary T. "Colonel Margaret Harper 11th Chief, Army Nurse Corps." -e-anca-. Publication date unknown. Accessed September 19, 2018. https://e-anca.org/history/superintendents-chiefs-of-the-anc/colonel-Margaret-Harper

Settle vs. Settle, Circuit Court of Atchison County, Missouri, October 8, 1960, Box 23, File 6.

Settle vs. Settle, Circuit Court of Atchison County, Missouri, November 2, 1960, Box 23, File 6.

Skelly News. "Slush Pond As 'Jakefoot Health Shrine.'" Skelly Oil Company. vol. IV, no. V, May, 1930.

Snyder, J. C. "Typhus Fever in the Second World War." europepmc-. Publication date unknown. Accessed December 11, 2018. https://europepmc.org/backend/ptpmcrender.fcgi?accid=PMC1643864&blobtype=pdf

"Summary of the 155th Station Hospital Daily Diary from October 1st to December 31, 1942." National Archives and Records Administration, Washington, D. C.

The Daily Oklahoman. "Poison Liquor Feared Cause of Odd Illness," March 7, 1930.

The Daily Oklahoman. "Poisoning May be From Lead in 'Jake' Drink," March 9, 1930.

The Daily Oklahoman. "'Jake Victims Are Improved,'" March 12, 1930.

The Daily Oklahoman. "New Theory in Ginger Poison," March 13, 1930.

SOURCES

The Daily Oklahoman. "Dry Agents to Get Samples of 'Jake,'" March 18, 1930.

The Daily Oklahoman. "'Jake Wobblies' Hit Shawnee; 50 Cases," March 20, 1930.

The Daily Oklahoman. "Jake Paralysis," March 21, 1930.

"The Jake Walk Effect." -ibibilio-. Publication date unknown. Accessed December 11, 2018. http://www.ibiblio.org/moonshine/ drink/jake.html

The Kansas City Star. "Moving to New Hospital Clinic," September 30, 1940.

"The Medical History of the 107th Medical Battalion From 1 April, 1943 to 30 June, 1943." National Archives and Records Administration. Washington, D. C.

"32nd US (Red Arrow) Infantry Division (Overview text)." Accessed December 11, 2018. http://ajrp.awm.gov.au/ajrp/remember.nsf/Web-Printer/7F5B2C27DFA D0B60CA256CCD000E16A3?OpenDocument

Thurston, Hester I., Eisenbise, Mary A., Clifford, Rita. "University of Kansas School of Nursing 1906—1990." Paper submitted to the Kansas State Board of Nursing, Topeka, Kansas, November 1, 1990.

Tomblin, Barbara Brooks. *G.I. Nightingales The Army Nurse Corps in World War II.* Lexington, Kentucky: The University Press of Kentucky, 1996.

University of Kansas, Lawrence, Kansas. Thirty-Seventh Biennial Report Including the Medical School at Kansas City, October 15, 1938, 106.

United States Army. "155th Station Hospital, Base Section 3, Report for History of Medical Activities, 155th Station Hospital, up to December 31, 1942. National Archives and Record Administration, Washington, D. C., 1943.

Vachon. Duane. "Pearl Harbor's First Medal of Honor—Captain Donald Kirby Ross, U. S. Navy (1910—1992)." -hawaiireporter-. March 28, 2011. Accessed December 9, 2018. http://www.hawaiireporter.com/pearl-harbors-first-medal-of-honor-captain-donald-kirby-ross-u-s-navy-1910-1992/

van der Tuuk, Alex. "Re-Dating the New York Recording Laboratories'

L-Series Matrixes (Grafton, 1929—1932): An Update." Accessed 5/23/2020. www.tapatalk.com/groups/blindmanfr/annals-of-epidemiology-jake-leg-t44717.html

Wallerstein, Robert S. *American Imago*. "Karl A. Menninger, M.D.: A Personal Perspective." vol. 64, no. 2(2007) 213-228.

Weingroff, Richard F. "From Names to Numbers: The Origins of the U. S. Numbered Highway System." -fhwa- . June 27, 2017. Accessed December 11, 2018. https://www.fhwa.dot.gov/infrastructure/numbers.cfm

"West Point II AP-23." -historycentral- Publication date unknown. Accessed December 11, 2018. https://www.historycentral.com/navy/ap/West%20Point%20II.html

Williams, Mary H. *Chronology 1941—1945*. Washington, D. C.: Center of Military History, United States Army, 1994.

Woolf, Alan D. *Veterinary and Human Toxicology*. "Ginger Jake and the Blues: A Tragic Song of Poisoning." vol. 37 (3), 252—254.

World War II Selective Service Records - Kansas Historical Society. Accessed September 3, 2020. https://www.kshs.org/kmi/kmi_wwiiselectives/search/surname:/fname:/branch:/county:LC/servicenumber:/year:/submit:SEARCH

"Zig-zagging: how to confuse the enemy at sea." -rmg-. Published December 9, 2014. Accessed December 11, 2018. https://www.rmg.co.uk/discover/behind-the-scenes/blog/zig-zagging-how-confuse-enemy-sea

Index

1st Marine 17
5th Marines 232
32nd Infantry Division 20, 221, 232-233, 235, 254, 321-325
42nd General Hospital 255
155th Station Hospital 17, 20, 25, 213, 215, 221, 231, 235, 237, 250, 254-258, 303-304, 307, 320, 322
166th Station Hospital 221

A

adultery 113, 119, 245, 312
Agnes (*see* **Settle, Agnes Bird**)
alcoholic 245, 291-292, 314
alcoholism 289, 292
angioneurotic edema 264, 266, 268, 270-271
Armsbury, Ila
Armsbury, Dwight 44, 203
Armsbury, Florence 8, 21, 31, 35, 39-40, 53-54, 65, 67, 112, 116-117, 121, 136-137, 155, 172-173, 176, 287, 299, 310, 311-313, 317, 319, 324, 326
Armsbury, Ira 7, 21, 31, 39-40, 42, 45, 47, 49, 51, 53, 60, 65, 89, 96,

INDEX

111-112, 117, 121, 122, 125-129, 136-137, 142, 146, 150, 154-155, 168, 171-174, 176, 193, 235, 244, 256-260, 299, 301, 310, 311-326

Armsbury, Newt 33-34, 42, 61-66, 74, 89, 106-114, 117, 124-125, 131, 135-137, 161, 171-180, 196, 234, 312, 314-316

Armsbury, Rosena (Mason) 310, 312, 314, 315

Army Nurse Corps 203, 270, 288, 303, 320

Atchison County 19, 290, 292, 297

Auntie Ila (*see* **Armsbury, Ila**)

Aunt Lottie (*see* **Lottie**)

Australia 18, 214-220, 233, 247, 256-257, 264-282, 294-298, 303, 304, 308, 320-321

B

Battey General Hospital 294
bipolar disorder 291
Bird, Mary 210, 290, 318
Bird, Oscar 318
Board of Disposition 256, 263
Brisbane 221, 223, 226, 231-232, 240, 247-251, 254, 257-259, 304, 323

C

Camp Cable 18, 20, 221-222, 226, 234, 247, 254, 257, 304, 307, 320-324
Captain Billy's Whiz Bang 67, 311
Catholic Church 147
Catholics 141, 147

Charles (*see* **Settle, Charles**)
Christmas 50, 87, 102, 130, 154, 183, 208, 210, 233, 250-251, 276, 324
Colorado Springs 60, 63, 70-71, 78-82, 129, 314
combat fatigue 261, 263
Craig (*see* **Olsen, Major Craig**)
crippled 19, 174-184, 228, 262, 315-316

D

Daddy (*see* **Armsbury, Ira**)
Decoration Day 43-44, 50, 56, 127
Delhi 43, 47-48, 127, 310
dengue hemorrhagic fever 215, 222, 234, 243, 304
Dinsmoor, S. P. 123-124
Disposition Board 256, 264, 267, 284
divorce 111, 116, 118-119, 121-123, 126-131, 245, 280-281, 292, 296
Nati, Doña 258-259
Donley, Jack 19, 24, 147-149
Dyer boy (*see* **Dyer, Daniel**)
Dyer, Daniel 210
dysentery 234-235

E

E.B. (*see* **Settle, Dr. Emmett B.**)
Eeby (*see* **Settle, Dr. Emmett B.**)
Elizabeth 292-293, 297
Ellsworth, Kansas 70-77, 106-108, 116
Eloise 113, 120-124, 131-133, 139, 145, 153-156, 161, 164-173,

INDEX

182-185, 189, 193, 197-198, 210
Emmett (*see* **Settle, Dr. Emmett B.**)
Endocarditis 243

F

family tree 11
Farrington, Wava 13, 31, 42, 45-51, 54-55, 57, 59-125, 129-157, 172, 194-195, 210, 287-288, 310
Farrington, Nolan 142-151, 157, 194, 288, 310
Fort Leavenworth 202, 204-209, 211, 216, 256, 284, 302

G

Garden of Eden 123-124
German Measles 235
Grammy (*see* **Farrington, Wava**)
Grandma (*for Grandma Rosenie, see* **Armsbury, Rosena (Mason)**). (*For Grandma Minda, see* **Rogers, Minda**)
Grandma Rosenie (*see* **Armsbury, Rosena (Mason)**)
Grandpa (*see* **Armsbury, Newt**)
gross neglect 119
Guadalcanal 17, 231

H

Herman, Blaine 287-288
Hughes, Mrs. 83-87, 100, 120
Hundertmark, Mr. 19, 146-147

I

Ila (*see* **Armsbury, Ila**)
Ira (*see* **Armsbury, Ira**)

J

Jamaica Ginger 15, 19, 176, 178-179
Jefferson Barracks 204, 208, 287-288
Judge Joslin 157, 165, 187, 196

K

Kansas City 184, 187, 190, 198, 200, 208, 212, 219, 228, 281, 287-291, 296
Kansas Territory 7
Karl (*see* **Menninger, Karl**)
KKK (*see* **Ku Klux Klan**)
Kluxers (*see* **Ku Klux Klan**)
Knoch, Herman 141-142, 174, 287-288
K.U. 175, 184-190, 199-203, 288
Ku Klux Klan 15, 19, 141-142, 145-146, 148, 285

L

LaDonna 157, 194, 310
Laura 280-281, 292-296
Lee, Major Howard J. 266-268
Lewick, Miss 191-192
Lincoln County 7, 9, 19, 154, 210

INDEX

Lincoln, Kansas 9, 13, 15, 19, 43, 58, 129, 132, 136-143, 149, 151-156, 159-162, 172, 174, 181-188, 193-198, 202-203, 210, 218, 220, 273, 288-289, 301, 308
Lottie 116-118
Lucas, Kansas 9, 38, 43, 61, 64, 82, 89, 105, 109, 114, 120, 123-124, 130, 138, 141, 143, 149-150, 161, 179, 194, 310

M

malaria 215, 232-236, 243, 254, 304
manic depression (*see* **bipolar disorder**)
Marguerite 200
Mary (*see* **Wilkerson, Mary**)
Mary Francis 214, 217, 241
Max 65-68, 70, 109-110, 114-115, 130
Maxine (*see* **Max**)
Melbourne 214-218, 221, 257, 303
Menninger, Karl 273-274
Metta 17, 31, 42, 45-48, 51-72, 76-88, 93-94, 98-135, 139, 141, 143-146, 150-153, 156-157, 161, 164-165, 174, 182-183, 189, 193-196, 210, 235-236, 287, 289
Miller, Ella M. 205
Minda (*see* **Rogers, Minda**)
Mitchell, James 162-163
Mother (*see* **Armsbury, Florence**)

N

NBC 208
New Guinea 19, 221, 233-235, 249-254, 297

Newlon, Malcolm 159
Newt (*see* **Armsbury, Newt**)
New Year's Eve 232, 277-278
Nolan (*see* **Farrington, Nolan**)
Nurses Retiring Board 265

O

Oat (*see* **Trexler, Oat**)
Olsen, Major Craig 216
Oscar (*see* **Bird, Oscar**)

P

Pearl Harbor 15, 293
penicillin 254
Philippines 195
Phyllis 157, 194
polio 172
Popular Cafe 156
pregnant 119-120

Q

Queensland 221, 257, 304

R

Red Arrow Men 20, 221, 250
Rev. Noah (*see* **Rogers, Reverend Noah**)

INDEX

Rocky Ford, Colorado 24, 88-89, 97-99, 105, 112, 129
Rogers, Minda 35-38
Rogers, Reverend Noah 35-37
Rose, Miss 191-192
Rosenie (*see* **Armsbury, Rosena (Mason)**)

S

scrub typhus 234
Settle, Agnes Bird 290-298
Settle, Charles 290-291, 295-297
Settle, Dr. (*see* **Settle, Dr. Emmett B.**)
Settle, Dr. Emmett B. 17-21, 211-213, 216-234, 241-254, 264, 274-282, 287, 290-298, 302
sex 34, 36, 38, 40, 127, 248, 252-253
slums 200, 269
smallpox 38, 90, 92
Station Hospital (*see* **155th Station Hospital** or **166th Station Hospital**)
St. Patrick's Catholic Church 147

T

Thanksgiving 276
Trexler, Oat 19, 116

U

Uncle Walter 89-91, 112
University of Kansas 184, 288, 300
USS Langley 318

USS Oklahoma 318
USS Pecos 318
U. S. Typhus Commission 324

V

V-J Day 284

W

Waldo, Kansas 8-9, 42-43, 60-63, 84, 110-111, 122, 126-127, 138, 189
Wava (*see* Farrington, Wava)
white slavery 126
Wilkerson, Mary 53, 56-58, 101, 110-113, 126-130, 310
Wilkerson, Mrs. (*see* Wilkerson, Mary)
Wilson, Jim 25, 235
Winter General 261-265, 273-274, 276-278, 284-287, 294, 308, 309
World War I 8, 203
World War II 9, 15, 297

Z

zigzag 325
Zink, Porky 140-141, 147, 171

Cindy Entriken

Cindy Entriken is a person with strong likes and dislikes. She hates cooking, exercise, and hot weather.

She loves being outdoors, gardening, and learning, which explains the two Master's degrees and the 31 hours toward a Ph.D. She adores cats and her two grandsons. And she can't go a day without reading—preferably mysteries, nonfiction, history, novels, almost anything she can get her hands on.

She lives in Wichita, Kansas, with her husband, Jim Hammer, one rescue dog, and two cats. She is the author of *Ila's War*.

www.ingramcontent.com/pod-product-compliance
Lightning Source LLC
Chambersburg PA
CBHW021052080526
44587CB00010B/226